Life Beyond the Mask

Life Beyond the Mask

By Paul Ryder

www.lifeperformancestrategies.co.uk

First Printing, 2015 in the UK

ISBN 978-0-9569335-5-3

www.lifeperformancestrategies.co.uk

Main image design (The Mask) with thanks to
Pete Rems,
www.peterems.com
12503 Lake Buynak Court
Windermere. Florida 34786
USA

To mum with love

For being there for me when
I couldn't be there for myself

Contents

Acknowledgements

There are a great many people in my life that helped with the creation of this book. I realise now that the lessons of life come in the good times and the hard times and it is often in the 'hard' times which we can learn the most profound lessons.

So in essence although I am not grateful for 'how' other people treated during the hard times, I am grateful for the experience and the lessons I learned. It sometimes feels the easiest thing to turn away from what feels uncomfortable, to avoid what needs to be done… to do what is easy! Though the 'easy path' is a poor teacher! So I feel it only right to say thank you to life itself and for the past hardships it brought me so that I could grow. Also for the inner peace I found after learning the lessons.

A huge thank you to my mum who taught me the ability to love and to feel connected. Even though dark times descended through my younger years, the sense of connection to the essence of what the human race is truly about kept me going when I often felt like giving in.

Another huge thank you to all of the people that came along in my times of need. Each and every person who brought their own unique gifts that helped me become who I am today. I feel what makes the world so unique is that everybody is so different and that truly is the spice to life!

Alanis Morissette

"Hand In My Pocket"

"And what it all boils down to

Is that no one's really got it figured out just yet"

Introduction

Hello and welcome. My name is Paul Ryder, and I am pleased to introduce to you over 20 years of my own research, which has been compiled to create the Life Beyond the Mask programme. It is my sincere aim that it serves you as it has served me and the countless others who have shared this style of coaching and self-awareness.

As we all know…life should be abundant! We were not born to 'constantly' struggle with lifestyle or conflicting emotions, nor were we created to continually analyse everything we do in a continual loop of observing life rather than living it!

Although it is true that life should (and can) be abundant, it is also a fact that many people are 'not' living their life in an abundant state!

However, 'surely' it is the truth that we can have all we want if we just want it badly enough? Surely if we just write out our goals and say them over and over then we can reach the pinnacle of success? Surely it is just a case of following the often quoted personal development rule of simply

staying focused for 30 days which will build a new habit and life will then become a dream?
Well, although those actions have their place, let's face the truth…for many people who take these actions…their input doesn't always bring the returns they desire!
They set the goals and have stuck it out, they have read the books and gone on the courses, and they have been as focused as they possibly can! But what happens? For many of those people, as we know all too well…their old habits eventually creep back in!

This happens time and time again in the personal development world.
People give up smoking only to start again…
People set up a business only to struggle with confidence…
People do their very best to overcome low self-esteem and face their fears only to watch their insecurities once again cloud their judgement and obscure their view!

But why?

Is it because they are lazy, cutting corners or just simply not dedicated? No…it is none of those! The reason that most people struggle to reach their aims is not because they are 'cutting corners', but because they are being held back by something within them, something which is stronger than their will power…something hidden! Most people are being held back by a part of their mind which is getting confused between reality and what their mind thinks is reality.

Now when I say something hidden I do not mean the often-quoted 'limiting beliefs' that many people hold, such as a fear of failure or social anxiety. As we know, many people find those limiting beliefs straight away and create the reframes by visualising and telling themselves that they are good enough and that they can achieve what they want. Again, if we take a view of those people who do the reframes and can disprove a reason for their anxiety…for a large percentage of those people…their old habits still return!

But again…why?

Well, the truth that needs to be realised is that there is something much deeper within the mind than many of us have ever been taught. This deeper concern is a loop programme which goes much deeper than social anxiety, low self-esteem or low confidence, and for millions of people who set goals to try to 'overpower' this loop programme, the result is that eventually their motivation or focus wears thin and the old habits return!

So should we just double our efforts? Think even more positively? Stand even taller and say 'I CAN' even louder? With MORE vision boards and positive quotes?

In my opinion (and my experience) if you are taking actions that are not truly effective, doing more of them will not get you where you want to be any quicker!

"If the ladder is not leaning against the right wall, every step we take just gets us to the wrong place faster."
Stephen R. Covey

Walking the road less travelled!
If you are one of those people who have taken lots of action, written your goals and stood tall shouting them out every morning and 'still' not gained the results you wanted, then I can fully empathise!
Whilst going through this book you will not only learn powerful psychological models and strategies, but you will also hear parts of my own journey and the frustration I found whilst taking many of the actions I mentioned above. The reason I include my own experiences is to show you the pitfalls and challenges which I faced, so hopefully you can navigate around them to make your own journey as smooth as possible.

Although 'now' I see taking action as an adventure, when I first started taking action to face my own insecurities many years ago I found that sometimes even doing the smallest task could drain my energy. It was fine for people telling me to 'just do it', but it is not as easy as that when your anxiety takes hold. It can sometimes feel very confusing to look within or to take action when you feel like avoiding it all. So, I have done my best to make this process as easy as possible for you by explaining the metaphorical science behind it.

Through the pages of this book I am going to give you a very 'real' view of how the mind can play games and then how to negotiate your way forward. However, for that to happen it is essential that you not only read and self reflect, but also take patient responsibility!

Jumping into every anxiety with guns blazing will not get anybody anywhere and neither will wrapping things up in pretty ribbons and glitter. To reach the states such as inner peace and abundance requires patience, understanding, strategy and knowledge.

In all honesty, when I first started out on my journey many years ago I found the whole world of personal development very confusing. One coach would tell me one thing and another something completely different. Yet if your mind is stressed or unsure of which way to turn…confliction is the last thing you need to hear!
In my own opinion, although it feels like the field of therapy is changing into a more 'holistic' approach, I still meet many people who can be unsure which 'therapy' to choose. Is hypnotherapy better than NLP? Should I get a life coach and then sort my finances? Or should I go on a 6-month yoga retreat? There are so many options!
If the mind is unsure about the validity of any path it will start to jump from one to the other, dissipating the energy and eventually losing focus.

Therefore, with this book my aim is to bring the entire structure of personal development together in harmony. Just like the human body, all the different therapies actually complement each other very well and adopting this view can make life and progression much simpler. Be prepared to use everything that you can to your advantage! Inner resourcefulness is a great gift!

Before I cover the chapters within this book, I would like to ask you a question…

Introduction

Have you ever wondered why so many people are not living the life they really want?

How many people ask themselves that question each and every day?

It was a question I used to ask myself all the time when I was in the continual loop of believing that I was not good enough or simply just not able to gain traction on where I wanted to be in the various areas of life.

Let me also ask you a few more questions…

Q: Why is it that some highly skilled and talented people can end up in a job they can't stand working 60 - 80 hours a week for a dream which is not their own?

Or

Q: Why is it that some kind-hearted people who are thoughtful, caring and loving either end up in unfulfilling relationships or as 'unhappy singles'?

Or

Q: Why is it that some people who give and give and help other people as often as possible…can end up flat-out broke and miserable?

Let's face the truth…this happens all over the world! True, it is not everybody, but many people struggle and don't know why!

Is it to do with luck? Bad luck? Good luck?

How many people do something each and every day that they do not want to do, or stay in a situation they do not want to be in, but seem unable to escape?

The list of situations that people can become ensnared in is endless, but the most common ones are: staying in a job they don't like, being in a relationship they do not want to be in, unable to get into a relationship, financial poverty, never feeling like they 'fit in', never feeling like they can fully enjoy life or feeling unable to let go and have fun.

As mentioned, though the list is endless, they really all come down to the same result…

A person feeling unable to fully live the life they want!

As you read through this book you will soon realise that it is not one of those books that contains page and pages of 'think positive and all will be well'. Nor is it going to suggest that you make a list of your fears and 'chop them down' by facing them like a platoon leader in battle. The truth is…taking extremes when working with the emotional world will cost you precious time and precious energy.

In the next chapter you can read about parts of my own path and not only how I discovered this information, but also how I became immensely frustrated with the stream of books I read which promised me 'peace of mind in just 30 days'. They promised me that I could stop my depression and anxiety with a 'new' technique which the grand masters had kept hidden, but now it could be mine for only 3 easy instalments of £x…though the result of doing many of these 'new' techniques was very little improvement, if any. I used the 'gold pen' to write my goals, meditated for several hours a day and took action in every way they suggested, but 3 years into my journey and about £5,000 later, I felt crushed. Fortunately though, there were other coaches and trainers out there who did know the way through the confusion of the personal development world, and for their teachings I will be forever grateful!

My hope with sharing my own story in part of the next chapter is that it offers you support to know that I have walked this path myself. I have seen a great many of the pitfalls and challenges that the mind and world can throw. So, with this in mind I want to assure you that this book is not another list of exercises and techniques intended to get you jumping up and down on your chair. Nor is it intended to claim that you are in any way lazy and need motivation. Rather, this book intends to explain to you a psychological structure of how it is possible for your mind to unknowingly become trapped in time and repeat old programmes and behaviours, but from a deeper source than what you can see straight away. These programmes can easily loop over and over without you ever knowing that they are there. This then creates habits, actions and coping strategies to deal with the two different realities that your mind is trying to process (I will cover these 'two' realities in much further detail through this book).

Having old patterns and behaviours in your mind is limiting enough, but what is more important to know (and the core of this book) is that:

Whilst you unknowingly hold on to these hidden limiting beliefs…other people can unknowingly influence or manipulate you! Also, what is more alarming is that if you are caught up in the mask and the con (to be explained soon)…you may unknowingly help others to manipulate you!

Upon hearing the previous statement, many people can sometimes find it a little hard to accept. Surely other people would not do that to them? Surely other people in their life would only be supportive and kind, right? Yes, they may well be, but the opposite is most definitely a possibility too. Just like when you are looking for your keys and they vanish from right in front of you…for millions of people there is a reality happening right in front of them which is holding them back but hiding in plain sight!

Welcome to Life Beyond the Mask!

Throughout the chapters of this book you and I will be going on a journey that many people unknowingly avoid, but because it is so obvious they think it can't be that simple! Like it or not, for millions of people all over the world there is something going on behind the scenes of their mind which is costing them a great deal of their happiness and fulfilment. Without realising it, millions of people each and every day are being tricked into doing things that are actually holding them back.

The journey ahead

I will now cover the journey we are going to take in this book and why it is so essential to read through each part and make notes. Each part of this book is content rich and each chapter is part of a jigsaw puzzle. If you skip chapters you will miss the end picture and when we reach the chapter on the mask and the con, it won't make complete sense. Some chapters may require that you re-read them and make extensive notes, so take the time you need!

The journey ahead…

Chapter 1 – Own Your Story!

The first chapter I will cover is about owning your own story! Each and every one of us will have a different life experiences and it is essential to recognise that. Many may have been shamed into feeling guilty and that we should 'not moan' as there are others worse off, and others will have been taught to gain a huge amount of attention by playing the victim. Yet comparing these two experiences will only lead to an endless loop of confusion.

In this chapter I will be covering how to take a reflective look at your own journey and to work on accepting that it is yours. It is not to compare or to judge, but just to accept!

Here I will also be covering my own journey to give you an insight into how and why the information in this book came to life. Again, this is not to say that my journey was harder or easier than anybody else's, but just to share how it can feel to look within.

Chapter 2 – Preparing for Your Journey!

Failing to plan is planning to fail! So many of us have heard that, yet so many still try to avoid it… why? The reason this happens is not as obvious as it may seem, but either way, avoiding it will still cost you dearly.

In this chapter I will cover how and why the mind (or part of it) will sometimes do its best to avoid preparing for the journey ahead and then how to accommodate for that. This may take time and practice, but once the techniques have been adopted and integrated, preparing for challenges will be much easier. Forewarned is forearmed!

Chapter 3 – Are things as they appear?

Do you ever get the feeling that there is something that is stopping you from reaching for the life that you want, but you are not sure what it is? Have you ever tried many different techniques and strategies that didn't create the results you aimed for? Or what about the millions of people that set New Year's resolutions only to give up in February?

The mind has many powerful abilities and one of them is to restrict parts of your awareness in order to keep you protected. Sometimes though, it can become confused and try to overprotect you and restrict your awareness too much. In this chapter I will cover how and why that happens so you can prepare for what is known as 'the hijack'!

Chapter 4 – Discover Your Mind!

As a coach and trainer over the years I have heard many people say that they have irrational beliefs or irrational behaviours, however this is not true. Believe it or not, the human mind is working perfectly all the time (injury and medical aside). The challenge, though, is that we are rarely ever taught how to understand it. Without an understanding of the mind it can appear as if it is doing its own thing and has limited structure. However, the mind has immense structure and is powerful beyond measure as long as we know how to use it effectively. In this chapter I will cover how to understand all the different functions of your mind to bring you the greatest leverage.

Chapter 5 – Belief Structures

Although we think we see reality, we actually see what 'we think' is reality. Our world is made up of perceptions of situations that we have experienced and then internalised. This is why different people have different points of view and different attitudes in life. In this chapter I will cover how to recognise the traits of those beliefs that are useful and those which are overly protective.

Chapter 6 – Stress, Fear and Anxiety

Stress and anxiety are commonplace in many lives in the modern-day world. Unfortunately, in some parts of the world it is reaching an epidemic, but why? Although stress and anxiety seem to be the most intense, they are in fact a reaction from a deeper cause.

In this chapter I will give a comprehensive review of the intricate details of how stress, fear and anxiety can take so much control over the mind, creating confusion and distortion.

Chapter 7 – The Peer Idolisation Scale

Have you ever noticed how some fully-grown adults can revert back to the attitude of a younger child in some challenging situations? How about why an aggressive manager may reduce a member of staff to tears, or why so many people seem to doubt themselves in social situations?

In this chapter I will be covering how a person can unknowingly become caught in a loop that can trigger a variety of insecurities when confronted with an authority. This can be extremely distressing for many people when in its grasp as it can feel as though all of their confidence and self-esteem vanishes right in front of their eyes when they need it the most.

Chapter 8 – Shame and Guilt

Shame and guilt are by far two of the most destructive emotions that any human can face. The reason this happens in humans and less so in the animal kingdom is simply because of the development of the physical brain. Both shame and guilt are at the core of all other limiting emotions and are the main two emotions that will cause a person to attack their own self-esteem and confidence.

In this chapter I will be covering how we can learn shame and guilt through other people projecting their own insecurities and unrealistic high expectations on to children or young adults. This creates a misaligned self-image which is then projected upon to the world they live in. This can then leave the person feeling that no matter what they do it is never good enough.

Chapter 9 – The Self Esteem Recovery Model

As mentioned earlier, structure is essential if there is to be a solution to any challenge or limiting belief. The self esteem recovery model is my own design to explain how a person can go one of two ways when experiencing a challenging situation in their lives. They can learn and grow which is path 1, or they can shut down through their internal pain which is path 2. Path 2 is the main area of focus in this chapter. Here I will cover all of the different coping strategies that the mind can take whilst it is trying to regulate the internal confusion and anxiety.

Chapter 10 – The Dependency Cycle

Through the course of life we will experience three different stages. The first is dependency, which is a stage where a person needs others as they are unable to support themselves; the second is independence, in which a person will be autonomous; and the third is interdependence, in which people with different abilities work together for the harmony of all concerned.

Through this book I will be covering a lot of detail in regards to the area of social challenges, and this chapter is one of the main ones.

The dependency cycle is a loop habit in which a person can unknowingly give all of their power to another person to reduce a potential or imagined threat. If this happens long enough and with enough emotional intensity, it can spread to all areas of life. This can be seen in many workplace challenges where an employee who is more than capable becomes anxious to (or appears to be anxious to) make their own decisions.

Chapter 11 – Discover the Con

The con will be covered in great detail throughout this book, but here I will give you the insight of how to recognise it if it is happening in your own life. Basically, if you ever feel an anxiety around situations in life and or you feel that you have no choice without feeling a heavy burden of guilt, you will be in the con. The con itself is many levels deep and can result in a person running back and forth in the hope that they can reduce their anxiety towards something that may never happen in the first place. Although this may sound confusing, all will be explained. Do not be tempted to skip ahead to this chapter as it requires the rest of the book to make sense.

Chapter 12 – Ignorance is Bliss?

How many people do you know who will leave their bills until the last minute? Or what about those people who have a challenging situation in their relationship yet will ignore it in hopes that it will just go away? Facing challenging situations can be very uncomfortable and sometimes the most difficult thing to deal with, but ignoring the situation can in many cases make it worse. In this chapter I will cover how to be aware of whether your mind is tricking you into avoiding situations by creating de-motivation.

Chapter 13 – Are You Addicted?

Making any change to a well-practiced habit can be a challenge, as any person setting a New Years Resolution will know. However, as you will find when you go through this book, the emotions that you can become addicted to are more complex than they may first appear. In this chapter you can discover how letting go of anger can sometimes be more painful to the mind than keeping it! Or how a person feels so insecure that the only thing they feel they can depend on is the drug of their choice. Trying to change things in life without taking the adequate precautions can sometimes be a futile action.

Chapter 14 – Create a Cocoon and Build Your Strength

As mentioned in the explanation of the last chapter, making changes without preparation can lead to a loss of energy. In this chapter I will be covering how to strengthen your energy in regards to any insecurities that you may be facing. The mind needs to know that it is safe before steps can be taken to make the changes. Here I will be covering six very essential steps of how to use everything in your life (good or challenging) to build your strength and skills or reduce anxiety, which can then allow true motivation to flow.

Chapter 15 – Break the Cocoon and Fly Free

In this chapter I will be covering the 8 stages of personal development, which cover all aspects of lifestyle success. This will start with stage 1 and how to ground your energy and focus on exactly where you want to go, all the way up to stage 8, which is true fulfilment of abundance and living the life you want. Through the in-person coaching and training programmes each of these stages are covered in great depth, and in this book I will share with you a thorough and comprehensive overview.

Make NOTES!

As with any book it is always recommended to make notes and with this book it is highly recommended. Learning new information can be a challenge in and of itself, however when you are learning new information that is regarding a reflective look within, it can take on a whole new paradigm. As you will discover through this book there is a part of your mind called your protector self and the protector self is there…to protect you. The only thing is though is that if it assumes that change could cause stress, it may think it is helping you by restricting your awareness. Therefore, making notes can almost be likened to a backup drive on a computer. My advice…make close friends with a journal and a pen!

I wish you all the best in your journey through this book.

Paul Ryder

Online supplemental training

Due to this being such a large book, I wanted to offer the greatest support to your learning and as such have provided you with a bonus online training to complement your book.

Each chapter of Life Beyond the Mask will be supported by its own module on the online learning centre. Each module will have a variety of videos, downloads and tips to offer what I aim to be the most effective learning for you whilst you complete this book.

To access the supplemental course please visit:

www.lifeperformancestrategies.co.uk/life-beyond-the-mask-the-book/

Life Beyond the Mask

1

Own your story!

Are you being heard?

Many years ago I remember a friend of mine reiterating a situation about how he was at a party when he suddenly felt a stabbing pain in his two of his toes. However, his pain was different to most other people's pain in the fact that he'd had both of the toes amputated. The pain he was feeling is known as 'ghosting' or feeling the sensation of a part of the body that is no longer there.

As this happened, another person at the party asked my friend what had caused the pain. My friend explained that his ghost pain was starting to weigh heavy on him and it was getting him down. In response to this the person whom my friend was talking to replied, "Well, it could be worse as you may have lost your foot!" This reply did not go down well with my friend who felt angry, ignored and patronised.

How often does this happen? How often has a person tried to share their personal view about a life situation or just how they are feeling in that

moment and felt unheard by having their views contrasted by somebody who 'has it harder' in life?
The truth is that the 'trying to make you feel better by contrast' reply rarely makes the situation better. What a person is really trying to do when they share their view is to connect to something within and then let it out. The reason they are trying to let it out is so that they can understand themselves and what they are feeling. When this self-expression is blocked by a lack of understanding in the other person it usually causes the person to feel disconnected.

So many people are walking around with suppressed emotions from unresolved situations during the course of their lives, but many feel that they just have to bottle them up and keep on going. We have all had experiences that have caused us pain. Feeling pain from traumatic or stressful situations is natural, however holding onto that pain is not natural and is in fact very unhealthy.
Through the years of working in emotional therapy I have seen it time and time again where people will downplay their past challenges as something that is not really an issue. Although this can be seen as 'being strong', it is in fact it is just the opposite and more importantly this 'suppression' will eventually take its toll.

However, most people may suppress their emotions for one or a combination of three main reasons…

Reason 1: The stiff upper lip!
Having lived in the UK all my life I have often heard the British quirk of 'keeping a stiff upper lip'! This phrase basically means…

"A person who doesn't show emotion when they are upset."

Although in 'some' cases it is a useful ability, in most cases it usually causes major internal confusion, leading to a backlash of emotions and stress. The stiff upper lip attitude can be likened to a pressure cooker with no valve. Indeed, allowing the pressure to keep building with no outlet will soon enough start to have a negative effect upon the health.

Reason 2: Feeling guilty!

How many people do you know who keep their emotions trapped within and refuse to ask for help because they do not want to burden others? As you will find further along in this book, guilt is an anxiety of a person believing that they have done something wrong (or will do something wrong). If when a person was younger they were made to feel that they were 'a burden' for being upset or wanting to connect, then this guilt can easily carry on to adulthood (if not resolved). Unfortunately a great many children have been exposed to this attitude and we can see its effect when people become upset or cry and then immediately start to apologise.

Reason 3: No support structure or outlet

We covered this at the start of this chapter, but it is a very important area to cover again. This area can be split into two further subsections.

Area 1: There is nobody to turn to

This area can be a particularly challenging situation for those people who keep themselves socially isolated. As human beings we are social creatures and as such sometimes need other people to turn to. However, if there is nobody there to speak to for support then all the stresses and strains of life can soon build up to breaking point.

Area 2: Are you being heard?

Have you ever been talking to somebody about something which is important to you and it felt like they were either not listening, didn't understand or just didn't want to understand? Sharing a feeling which falls on deaf ears can be a trauma in and of itself.

However, this may not be as easy to determine as sometimes we can meet a person who is really trying to help but just can't understand, then in other situations we may meet others who simply don't care as they are too consumed with other things.

For every cause there is an effect!

As Isaac Newton explained, for every cause there is an effect, and this area is no different. Keeping conflicted emotions or daily stresses trapped within the psyche will be having much more of a detrimental effect on your health than you may realise. Believe it or not, it is holding onto these suppressed emotions which is the number one cause all of the trauma and stress that the human mind can ever face!

However, although it is important to own your story and to understand any trapped emotions around it, it is also essential to do it in the correct way!

"But everybody has faced challenges, so why should I think mine are an issue?"

It is the truth that every human being alive will face stress or trauma at some point in their life and each stress and trauma is different for each individual. Some people may experience physical violence, some emotional abuse and yet others may face loneliness. As mentioned though, each person's journey is different. Although everybody will face different challenges along the way, it is not always the challenge itself that needs to be addressed.

As you will discover through this book, if a person feels unable to cope with a challenge their body will respond and try to protect itself. This reaction, as we will soon discuss, is what is known as stress. If these stress reactions are not vented in a healthy manner they will start to compound and it is the 'compounding stress' that causes the real damage.

By continually allowing the stress reactions to build up, the pressure gains more and more momentum, eventually taking its toll. The toll could be depression, low self-esteem or a whole host of other reactions. Dealing with these pressures alone can sometimes become too overwhelming if the emotional resilience is not available. However, having the option to understand why it is happening or to connect to others can have a profound effect on its release…providing it is worked through in the correct manner!

However, the main area I aim to cover in this chapter is that it is essential to own your story and how it made you feel!

Owning your feelings is the foundation to the process of finding inner peace! It is irrelevant if other people have seemingly experienced more trauma or challenges than you have. What is relevant is that if you have never really connected to your stresses through your life then they will remain suppressed. If they remain suppressed…they WILL take their toll.

In many situations, it is not always 'what' has happened more than 'how' it made you feel after. If you feel uncomfortable about something which you have experienced, then you have a right to feel uncomfortable. If you feel frustrated that you have suppressed your voice many times in the past…then you have a right to feel frustrated! In this chapter it is not about downplaying or over-exaggerating your challenges, but simply to see them as they are. You have a right to your feelings!

Remember… Own your story!

You are not alone

Another reason that I am choosing to share my own journey with you is because sometimes it is easy to feel alone with your challenges. As mentioned earlier, I feel that there are far too many people walking around with the 'stiff upper lip' approach to life. So often it is possible to have the view that everybody else is happily getting on with their lives and it is just you who is feeling challenged or stressed. Yet the truth is that millions of people all over the world are putting on a brave face when really something else is going on behind the scenes.

True strength is about admitting the reality of life. Sometimes when we hear of another who has gone through hardship (or admits that they are struggling) it can give us the strength to look within at our own challenges - a strength to look within without feeling that it is wrong or that we should be ashamed for doing so.

In all honesty, I will admit that when I first started to look within and face my own insecurities my mind was racked with shame - shame that I should have been stronger, shame that I shouldn't be so weak and shame that I needed help.

During the first few months of this journey I felt alone in this view, but soon enough I found other people who said they felt the exact same way. Hearing this from other people changed my view; for the first time I didn't feel so alone.

The truth of life is that everybody will feel stress or emotional pain at some point in their life. That is natural and it is important to acknowledge the inner feelings. As mentioned it is irrelevant if other people have had a harder or easier time than you, as everybody is different. What is relevant though is that you acknowledge what you feel. Own your story!

The path I walked - by Paul Ryder

The good times and bad!

As I share my own journey with you now I just want to add that although there were many challenging times, there were many happy times too. Sometimes it is easy to feel that there is nothing to look forward to or the light has completely vanished, but if you look hard enough there is always something to keep you going.

During the times of emotional struggle, I started to notice the smaller things that I had never really noticed before, such as the kind acts of those with nothing to give, how things can be turned around with the right strategy, and even life itself! For all the things my challenges taught me the greatest one was the feeling of gratitude for the things which are so easy to take for granted.

"The mind is its own place, and in itself can make a heaven of hell or a hell of heaven."

John Milton, 1608-1674: English poet

My first years

Although I faced many challenges through my school years, the first few years of my life were built upon happy memories. To my awareness I had the ideal family and the ideal opportunity to grow. Although I only saw my dad on weekends as he was out working I felt he was a fantastic authority figure to aspire to. My mum and I spent quality time together where I was allowed to grow with true creativity, and my sister would help me learn new things and support me in many areas, such as my fond memory of me learning to ride a bike as I went off wobbling down the gasworks road, excited at the realisation that she was no longer holding the seat. Even the 7-month stay in hospital when I was 3 years old seemed an easy challenge in my mind. It almost seemed strange then that with this great start to life, it could turn so painful so quickly.

My dad's influence

There is no doubt in my mind that my dad loved me in his own way. Although there were very difficult times, I still have many fond memories of his protective energy and the toy fights on a Sunday morning which he often let me win. However, some people say that being a parent can be one of the hardest things and I can imagine it can, as unbeknown to me there was something within my dad that he was struggling with.

Although I only remember the odd smack from my dad's hand for pushing my boundaries too far, it wasn't his hand that I feared the most. As mentioned, although there was a lighter side to my dad…there was also a darker side. This 'darker' side would feel like a wolf ready to attack in anger…waiting in the shadows but never actually emerging. My dad, like millions of people across the world, used to suppress his emotions. However, trying to suppress your emotions is like trying to contain smoke…very difficult!

In many ways it felt like I had two dads; one was the adventurous and protective guy that would tell me exciting stories, and then the other side which felt like he could turn psychotic at any time. Although he never did turn psychotic, to me it felt that the switch could happen if the wrong button was pressed.

Being a child dependent upon my family but living in a sometimes erratic environment I quickly learned to adapt to the environment by adopting the best personality I felt I could at the time…the personality I adopted was submissiveness. Although it felt that adopting this personality did not really do me any favours in upcoming years, it was the best I could do at the time with the resources I had.

The junior school years

Although in many ways I was usually seen as the quiet kid who wouldn't be taken seriously, the rough and tumble of life up to the age of 11 was moderate. I never really felt I had a voice and just got on with life, but the people I spent time around (I would use the term *friends* lightly) were just getting on with their lives too. The most dramatic thing I really ever noticed during these years was that my timid attitude would sometimes cause confusion when I was insinuating to the other pupils that I 'could' do something, only to back away the next moment. Although during this time I was unaware that my low self-esteem was gathering steam, I would soon enough come to realise that this withering self-belief would bring my life to a grinding halt.

High school

Going to the school across the field for me was one that I couldn't quite attribute to any particular emotion at the time. During the first few months I was really just trying to find my feet.

The first year of high school was the levelling-out year. It was that year where nobody really knew each other and we were all in 'assessment mode' of each other. However, something happened in that first year of high school that would change my life forever!

Although at certain times in my home life I felt terrified of overstepping the mark, I also believed that there was a very strong family bond. In this bond, although we had our challenges, I felt part of something and more importantly I felt loved.

So, with the confidence of being part of my family unit, I could never really understand why I was bundled off to school and told that I should learn what I was 'told' to learn. What was the point of me learning French or Chemistry when I was 11? Nobody told me why I should learn this information except for stating that "this is what school is" and I should do as I was told!

The truth was though…I did not like the topics at the time! Soon enough I became bored and disinterested. My report cards began to mount up with the same old statements of 'Paul doesn't listen' and 'Paul daydreams', which I admit was completely true. I didn't listen as I was bored, I didn't know why I had to remember all this information and write it down in an exam to prove to somebody that I could remember it, and why should I call these teachers Sir or Miss just because they told me to? The school system confused me with all its bland rules because when I was at home my mum would allow me to be totally creative, my sister would help me draw and my dad would tell me stories of adventure. In all honesty I felt I grew quicker from my home life than I did sitting in a classroom being taught 'what' to think rather 'how' to think.

So, naturally I became frustrated with school and stopped joining in with the things that I didn't like. However, no matter how hard I tried to explain that I was bored, the dogmatic school system deemed me a 'slow learner' and before the end of my first year I was packed off to remedial class. This was definitely not the best form of support they could have offered (at that school anyway).

Remedial class was noted by some (or many) of the other school kids as the 'thick class', the class for the idiots or the troublemakers. However, for an 11-year-old boy with very low self-esteem I had a deep sense of foreboding.

NB: *Through all my years of learning about other people I have learned that many of the children who are also packed off to the 'slow class' for struggling or being classed as a troublemaker are not as 'slow' as they appear. Yes, it is true that there are some children who struggle in the academic world, but this does not mean that they are slow. Each and every one of us has our own individual way of learning and in my opinion too many children are classed as slow, when in reality it is just that they do not fit into the rules of what that particular school sets as the 'norm'.*

Some of the most creative and skilled people I have ever met, such as artists, musicians and public speakers, shared a path in their school life much the same as mine. For more information on this please look into 'kinaesthetic learning'.

Just because a child may not fit the expected rules of a particular school does not mean that they are slow. However, it is great to see that more schools and teachers are becoming aware of this type of learning.

The bullying begins

I am unsure if bullying happens in all remedial classes, but it did in mine! Take the scene…a room full of aggressive or overly shy children feeling frustrated through major amounts of suppressed emotion…and me…a timid boy with a very slight frame trying to avoid attention.

Although I felt frustrated and patronised by the well-meaning teachers asking me sums such as 10 plus 5, or how to spell a so-called advanced level word like 'house', I actually had a more pressing concern. This concern was lurking silently in the classroom watching my every move with curious eyes…namely…the other pupils. The class that I had to endure for the next four and a half years was a mixed bag full of pupils who were also trying to survive in a difficult time. As the more aggressive pupils sat in their seats it was noticeable that they were watching me, studying me and assessing whether I would be an effective target for their frustration. Each day, as I saw the flickering eyes that were monitoring my movements, I started to feel a cold prediction of the future.
Although the old adage goes 'just stand up for yourself if the bully pushes you around', it is not as easy as that when low self-esteem weighs heavy on you. When your mind is telling you that you will lose no matter what you do, you are beaten before you start…and this was most definitely me at that time!

It is hard to remember how the bullying started. I assume it was a few insulting words to test the water and then grew from there. Although I do not remember how it started, I do remember that as the bullying increased…my self-esteem withered even further.

So with this 'game' in play I'm sure I could be forgiven for becoming distracted from my schoolwork. I'm sure I could be forgiven if the teachers realised what was happening, but the only thing is 'they didn't' (or at least they didn't acknowledge it). In class, writing a word like 'house' or answering a simple maths question became a challenge due to a

lack of focus and stress. To the teachers it would appear that I was a slow learner, yet this was not the truth. The truth was that in reality answering the teachers' questions was the furthest thing from my mind. The more prominent question on my mind was "how do I escape if the teacher leaves the room?", but this was of no interest to my teachers.
In my opinion, it felt more than obvious that they knew what was happening, but then I am sure that they were also perplexed as how to stop it from happening. How can a teacher actually stop bullying? They can't watch all of their pupils continually. Another thing I also realised was that some teachers were in fear of some of the pupils. In essence, the teachers were being bullied by the pupils. For many people school can be a very confusing time.

NB: *In many ways (from personal experience) I realise now that a teacher can make things much worse by intervening in the incorrect way. Many teachers do their best, but troubled children are a hard breed to tame. Hopefully though, things are changing and there seems to be a growing number of truly amazing teachers out there who are changing the system. I now realise that teaching can be an extremely hard job.*

I will condense the next few years at school so as to not take up endless pages of this book, though I can assure you that the situation I feared turned out as predicted. Soon I became the runt of the litter, just trying to survive, but struggling each and every day.
Attacks such as being punched, kicked, stabbed by compasses, a near shattering of my metacarpals by the chop of a plastic ruler on its side became a daily - or if I was lucky, every few days - occurrence.

Yet the physical attacks were of little comparison to the emotional abuse. The comments such as "we are going to get you…after" would play on my mind for hours after the school day had finished (but when was… 'after'?). When I was young I was told 'sticks and stones may break my bones but names will never hurt me', yet I quickly learned that this is a lie! The sniggering, the isolation and the insults were much worse than any punch or kick I ever received.

All of this eventually pulled my self-esteem under even further until I gradually sank into a deeper and deeper anxiety and depression with a crushed self-esteem and self-worth. As mentioned, many people told me to stand up for myself and fight back, but that's easier said than done when you are completely convinced you will lose. The old style of 'punch the bully in the face' is not so easy when your arms turn to jelly and your legs buckle. The mind is the master of your actions and can be either your best friend or worst enemy!

Bunking school

School had become so traumatic for me that I just simply stopped going. It started out with me missing one day, then two, but before I knew it a grand total of six weeks had passed when my parents found out…that was not a pleasant moment!

Much to my surprise though (as I thought of climbing out of the second-story window to escape), they both just sat me down and asked me why. Although very confused, I was also very grateful as I couldn't have taken much more stress in life.

I made up another reason as to why I had not gone to school. I didn't mention the bullying due to the shame I felt about my perceived cowardice. So with that (and my shame buried), I begrudgingly went back to school to face the abuse and degradation once more.

My dad's last drink

However, although I had my own challenges to face, another member of my family was also dealing with his own inner demons, demons that had haunted him before he married my mum and before the birth of my sister and I. My dad's demons were his low self-esteem and low self-worth. Little to my knowledge, the few drinks a week my dad had been having since as long as I can remember had actually been mounting to many per day. During my fourth year of high school these few drinks had spun into full-blown alcoholism. The stress which he had tried to suppress and overpower had eventually overpowered him, and he was losing the battle. It was a strange sight to witness a man who I had seen as such a powerful figure in my life slowly wither into a shell of despair, but when the mind is overwhelmed it will seek an escape. I remember a phrase my dad used to say about himself: 'I bottle up my problems'…it was a phrase which always stood out in my mind, and no other phrase could have been so ironic! The alcohol eventually took his life shortly before I left school.

The big wide world

I assumed that leaving school would be the end of my problems, but I was wrong! I can still remember the hopeful (and free) feeling of that last day of school that would hopefully bring new adventure, but the reality was that I was a 16-year-old boy, with no exam results, a body weight of 6 stone 10 lbs and a broken spirit.

Like many children (or a young man, as people now classed me) I looked for a career. However, back in 1990 the only career advice I received was being told to learn a trade in engineering. I somehow managed to get a job as a welder, but as I soon learned my strengths DO NOT lay in welding. The staff of the company I worked for took great delight in patronising me and telling me how useless I was. Once again I was in the grip of bullying. The result? My self-esteem plummeted even lower. It seemed that no matter where I looked I was doomed.

The light in the dark!

My one huge ray of light in all of this though was my mum! I had moved to live with my mum when my dad's drinking had become too much. Although we had our challenges I realised on many occasions that she was there for me even when I wasn't. It is in times of intense trauma that you notice these things. There would have been many times I would have gone under if it wasn't for her. We may not have had much financially, but we had each other, and that was one of the greatest gifts I have ever been blessed with. She is stronger than she knows and many times she relentlessly put up with my anger outbursts and insults as I projected my own self-hatred. She could have asked me to leave or thrown me out, but even though I vented my anger onto her and her home, she just stuck it out. It is only in these last few years that I am realising how much strength that takes!

There was a lot more darkness in my younger years than I am writing here, darkness such as worthlessness, self-hatred, rage, self-loathing and jealousy. These emotions however are not the best combination to win friends…so let's add loneliness into the mix too! Although there was a lot more than I am writing, my aim here is to give you an overview, something to which you can relate as to the motivation behind this book. After all, this book is about 'you', not 'me'!

The changing wind

It is said that if we blame others we stay a victim, and until I was 17 that was me all over! In my opinion, all the pain which I felt was everybody else's fault! In my eyes the world was cruel and unfair! However, as I took some time out of work life and worked on my stress, something within me started to emerge.

Although I had been labelled a 'slow learner', at school I was anything but slow. By the age of 17 I had read virtually all the books on science and self-help in my local library. Soon enough my mind was filled with the structure of human physiology, psychology, maths and anything else that I could read. Learning took on a whole new meaning to me and I started to feel a newfound confidence in my own abilities.

During this time I also had the fortunate experience of meeting a neighbour (Bill) who was ex-special forces. Unbeknown to me at the time, he offered me the support and kindness of the mentor that I so desperately needed. Even though I was still being bullied at work (and he knew it), he did not offer to fix my problems, but he was slowly showing me how to fix them myself. The one main gift Bill taught me was to train my body hard, to push myself beyond all my limits, to fight when I felt like giving up. Bill was wiser than I realised at the time and it was obvious that he had seen many troubles in his own life. I feel that having walked a hard path himself gave him the ability to truly empathise with me. With Bill, it was almost as if he could see into my mind and knew what to do and what to say. His intuitive gift brought me a strength I had never imagined.

For the first time in my life…I had started to fight back!

The gift of friendship!

After getting sacked from my job in the welding industry, I turned my hand to health and fitness. Although many people in the engineering world told me how useless I was, I seemed to have a gift for teaching. So I went to college to get qualified!

Although I never really gained glowing reports from the academic side of college, I did succeed in teaching and finally found my feet. However, I came out of college with something much more than any qualification, and that was my first true friend (Karl). Although it puzzled me how one of the most popular kids in the class made such an effort to be my friend, I'm grateful he did as he brought my confidence and self-esteem on no end. For the first time I started to realise that I could have value in the social world and that I could have a voice. There were many amazing times in those years and I'm sure more to come as Karl is a friend for life!

After meeting Karl, although I still met my fair share of game players and manipulators I was fortunate to meet two other life friends...Leo and Paul. Both had their own gifts to bring me, but the biggest gift was trust. Over the years I had met many people who betrayed me, so for me trusting others was not easy, but neither Karl, Leo or Paul have ever betrayed my trust and as such I cautiously opened up.

As the phrase goes, "trust can take years to build and seconds to lose", and for me that was the truth. I had built up walls of steel to protect me. So it is with a deep sense of gratitude to Karl, Leo and Paul, who came in to my life in different stages and stood strong to their word.

However, my unease was not always the easiest to connect to. On many occasions I can remember pushing each one of them away and being flaky in an attempt to protect my feelings, but they kept coming back and allowed me to work through my fear of rejection.

A big turning point was Paul's dedication to me as a friend, who I recall would sit there and re-educate me (a 25-year-old man) on how to feel the 'high' of seeing somebody who cares for you. I pushed him away many times, but he kept coming back. A gift that no money could ever buy!

Truth be known, at that time I was like a robot…dead on the inside. Though through their support (that they were not even aware of but which was just their nature), my walls eventually came down and I honestly feel that if it wasn't for their support, I have no idea how long I could have carried on for. It has been a long time since those connections initially formed and it was a struggle, but eventually I gained strength and conviction to realise that I did matter to others and I had worth.

NB: *When times feel hard it is easy to think less of yourself, but having walked that path myself, to you as the reader I am here to tell you that you do matter and you are important! Please do not see that as one of those happy clapper statements as they are just positive thinking, but I mean it! You do matter and you are important! Never give up no matter how hard it gets!*

The confusing climb back out

As mentioned, I had read every book I could possibly find on the mind and confidence within the library and the local bookstore. However, as the years had passed, I had read at least 300 books, had several years of therapy sessions (totalling several thousand pounds), changed my career AND became a successful personal trainer…BUT STILL I still suffered a looming shadow of worthlessness…why? Why after all of that therapy had I only made such little change? Yes I could survive and was 'successful', but I still felt worthless or that I was going to be found out…this completely puzzled me! How could I still feel this way when I had put so much effort in? I had done what the personal development 'gurus' had told me, yet each day was still a battle? Why?

The reason was because the self-development 'gurus' I had listened to at the time had missed something vital, and therefore so had I…

The illusion of mass market personal development

It used to puzzle me that after many years of studying leadership, confidence building, self-esteem and goal setting that although I could appear confident on the outside, on the inside I still felt like I was going to fail at any given moment.

The conundrum used to grate on me as I had been to so many groups and heard so many 'self-developers' who claimed that it was all about the focus! Set big goals and big dreams, but I had done those and still only felt marginally different about my self-image. So I went back to the groups and the courses (that get you to jump up and down on your chair for motivation) and their reply was "BE EVEN MORE FOCUSED!"...but something seemed amiss. Why, after all the years of therapy, reading books and achieving my goals, was I not 'really' improving on the inside? I then had to ask myself the question...

"Was the 'majority' of the personal development and therapy world all it claimed to be?"

The thought of having to meditate every two minutes of the day if I felt self-doubt made me feel heavy. Was this the way it was going to be for the rest of my life? Living like that did not sound much fun and it just takes too much time and headspace.
Yet time and time again I heard the chant of 'look forward not back' and 'make it big and bright in your mind' coming from the weekly meetup groups. The question loomed...is this 'really' all there is?

Although that was all I heard from the people I spoke to, something inside me said that there was something wrong with this very simplistic approach. There must be something amiss if the same people who say these words never really seem to improve. Although they chose to keep on setting their goals and chanting...that path was not for me!

From my point of view, be aware of phrases like:
Look through your front window, not in the rear-view mirror!
Forget about the past and live in the future!
And the worst one...
Mind over matter – if you don't mind it doesn't matter!

The understanding
Burying your past when it still bothers you will not make it go away. I tried doing that for many years and I ended up suicidal! My dad tried ignoring his depression and died an alcoholic! My godfather tried ignoring his depression and died an alcoholic! Anybody that I have ever met who had buried their past without coming to terms with it has suffered with

some form of guilt, shame or anxiety. The expression of suppressing emotions can arise in many ways - whether through weight issues, eating disorders, people pleasing, shame, anger, turning to crime, drugs or the multitude of other avoidance strategies that curse people's lives.

Yet too often many authors, coaches and therapists in the world of personal development still tell us to 'look forward not back' (in essence, to ignore our past). They ask us 'is it real today?' and if it's not real…then just let it go! Stop worrying and only think beautiful thoughts or cut off people who cause us distress…because of course IT IS THAT EASY!!

However…how many of those people who ignore their past demons are really 'truly' happy?

We shall find out further on in this book!

Question reality!

Fortunately I walked AWAY from the beaten track of old school personal development after years of spinning my wheels. I then chose to look at another side of life. I started studying martial arts, philosophy, eastern cultures, and the trauma therapy side (going within). To my surprise I found that many of the same people I had hired as therapists over the years were actually still living in anxiety themselves, though they did a very good job of posing as somebody different.

NB: *I want to make a point that this is not to berate the entire therapy world. The 'lost therapists' I am referring to are the ones who feel it is possible to overpower the mind with simple meditations and reframes. This is not all of them, but as the therapy world is so undefinable it can unfortunately be an open field for anybody to claim that they are…a therapist!*

There is no doubt that self-esteem can sometimes feel elusive. However, the key to your freedom is not just a case of fighting the fear or the demons with a vengeful attitude. Rather, it is about understanding your anxiety and becoming at one with it. There are so many people who talk about a 'war on fear' or 'fighting their demons', but this will only cause internal confusion. To be at war with yourself is to attack who you are. If you attack yourself, then you can never be at peace. To gain complete peace and clarity in your heart, you must become one with all aspects of yourself. We cannot just 'let go and forgive' without understanding why we had anger and resentment in the first place. Any other path will just force the mind into an endless loop of denial.

The peace

During my younger years, although many wrongs had been forced upon me, I openly admit that I was one of those people who blamed everybody else for my circumstances. I lived with pure rage and resentment deep within my heart, played the violin of pity and felt like a victim of bullying. I was one of those people who claimed life was not fair - only to join the ranks of the others who agreed that life was cruel as well. I learned then that misery really does love company, though I also realised that living this way does not get you very far. To truly excel in life you need to accept who you are and be at peace with the past. This is obviously much easier said than done, but strategy and persistence bring great rewards!

Through taking the philosophical AND psychological approach rather than doing the positive thinking, things began to change! Once I accepted the different expressions of my personality, life became much easier. Sometimes it felt like the pace was slow and other times huge leaps would transform my life. However, after lots of patience, inner reflection and uncovering layer after layer of masks, I eventually found the inner peace that I was longing for!

Let me express one more time though, that it is not simply a case of thinking positive and standing tall and saying that you can reach your dreams and then put all your troubles behind you. That is DENIAL!

Having worked with literally thousands of people over the years I have been educated by the best, and the best education is life. As a personal trainer I have seen people who have desperately tried to change their body in the hope that they will feel more valuable and those who overeat to try to shroud their wounded self-image from the world they fear.
In the coaching and emotional development world I have seen just about every type of suppression the human mind can conjure up - alcohol, narcotic drugs, fame, money, power and control. It has been very

sobering to see extremely powerful people as they fall from their self-created pedestal or to see that undeniable look in a person's eyes as they realise that they can no longer suppress their inner anxiety. Although I see it in a different way with clients, the first time I really noticed it was in my dad's eyes, and then a few years later as I looked in the mirror. In my opinion, looking within is sometimes the hardest thing a person can do, but the rewards are great!
For myself I cannot begin to describe the amount of anger I had towards others who wronged me, but because I would never attack them outright…I turned it inward. The hate and frustration I personally felt nearly caused me to take my own life, and there were many touch-and-go experiences.

However, although I do not agree with what the bullies did to me, as wrong is still wrong, I have let the trauma go and I am at peace with my past, the bullies forgiven and the love for my dad restored. I found many years ago that to spare ourselves the pain of really feeling…we may create anger. Anger keeps the mind distracted and therefore there is no headspace to really feel. Though once the anger, sadness, anxiety and sorrow have been resolved, there is only headspace and peace! That headspace can then be filled with whatever you choose, such as connection, abundance, love, joy or many other things.

The teacup story
A long time ago, there was a wise Zen master. Throughout the land many people would seek his counsel and his wisdom. Many would come and ask him to teach them, enlighten them in the way of Zen.

One day a powerful businessman who was used to being in charge came to visit the master. "I have come today to ask you to teach me about Zen." He demanded that the master help him to open his mind to enlightenment. The tone of the powerful man's voice was dominance and control.

The Zen master smiled and offered the man a cup of tea. When the tea was served the master poured the man a cup. He poured the tea continually until it began to spill over the table and finally onto the robes of the powerful and wealthy man. Finally the man went into a rage and shouted for the master to stop pouring the tea, "Enough! You are spilling the tea all over. Can't you see the cup is full?"

The master stopped pouring, smiled at the man and said, "You are like this teacup, so full that nothing more can be added. The mind cannot absorb the knowledge of enlightenment if it is already full of anger. To allow wisdom to flow you must empty your cup of what is already in there."

"The mind is its own place, and in itself can make a heaven of hell or a hell of heaven."
John Milton, 1608-1674: English poet

Chapter summary

We are only human!
Each and every one of us will face some form of challenge in our life. When we have a challenge that we cannot cope with, the body and mind react in stress. It is easy to feel that we should be stronger and able to deal with more, but if the stress builds up too much it will take its toll. Be aware that stress is a natural reaction and is simply the body and mind trying to cope.

Own your story!
Each person in life will face different challenges. Each challenge brings with it different emotions, but these are not to be compared. If you feel a stress reaction today from something which happened many years ago then it is important that you recognise it. Burying your emotions because you have been told that other people have had it worse will not help resolve the suppression. Take a truly reflective look at your life…but through the eyes you had at the time when it happened. To a young child that situation may have been devastating.

Are you suppressing yourself?

In this chapter, we covered three methods of how people may suppress their emotions - the stiff upper lip, feeling guilty and unable to connect to other people. Take a reflective look at if you can relate to doing any of these and if you are, ask what effect this is having on you.

Do you have support?

Do you actually allow yourself to turn to others? Are there people in your current life who will support you and that you can trust? This can be a challenging area for some people and may require careful consideration.

All that glitters is not gold!

In my advice, be very careful before you start investing in personal development. By investing I do not just mean money, but more importantly…your time. As I mentioned, although there are some truly amazing coaches and therapists out there, there are also many who are in it for the fame and money…trust me! Go with your gut! I have also attached a few recommended authors (my own view) at the end of this book.

Keep the end in mind!

Taking the journey to look within and becoming your true self can require lots of patience and dedication. There will be setbacks and there will be challenges, but keep the end in mind. Create a vision of the lifestyle you want to attain, the lifestyle you want to live and revisit it daily. It is surprisingly easy to get caught up in what is known as 'paralysis by analysis'! Paralysis by analysis is a hidden coping mechanism where the mind becomes caught up in thinking rather than doing. The protective part of the mind will do this as it is attempting to distract the awareness from a deeper concern or anxiety. If this happens though…life will be passing you by whilst your mind is looping on the same topics!

2

Preparing for Your Journey

It is said that "By failing to prepare, you are preparing to fail" and when crossing new or unfamiliar territory this quote is definitely the truth! A great deal of time can be taken up by dealing with issues that could have been rectified in minutes if only a preparation plan had been put in place beforehand. Yet how many people find themselves stood by the roadside with an immovable car because they didn't fix that leak or tapping noise in the engine?

In this chapter we will look at essential steps that are highly advisable to work through before you set off on your journey of discovering the mask and the con. Never assume in any area of life that preparation is something that can be overlooked. Remember:

"By failing to prepare, you are preparing to fail."
Benjamin Franklin

In this chapter we will look at the following areas:

1. Your nutrition habits
2. Your sleeping habits
3. Your exercise habits
4. Your emotional well-being
5. Your lifestyle environment
6. Your social lifestyle

To make this more visual and easier to define we can put each area into the diagram below. This diagram is called the wheel of preparation. You may have seen this image before if you are familiar with the various different coaching models. If you have seen it and worked through it already this will be an easier process for you. This is a basic coaching model, but is an essential area to cover as the book will soon progress to cover more advanced coaching methods.

The purpose of this chapter is to take a reflective observation of each of these areas and their subsequent subsections to assess if there are any parts that you need to prepare for. These will be essential as you get ready for the changes you want to make in your life.

As you go through each section please be aware that some of them may feel uncomfortable and sometimes you may feel the temptation to avoid them. If this happens, please remember that it is vital to prepare adequately and it is in the areas that feel the most uncomfortable which are the ones most in need of your attention.

We shall now go through the entire exercise step by step.

The wheel of preparation

Step 1:
Take a piece of paper and draw a circle about two-thirds of the page and divide into 6 equal sections. On each line a marker of 1 to 10. 1 is the centre of the circle and 10 is the outside of the circle.

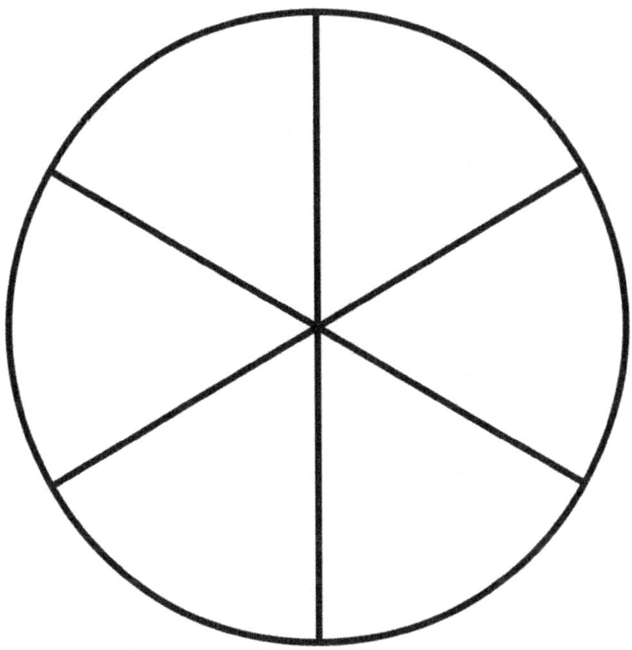

Step 2:

Label each section with the following titles:

1. My nutrition habits
2. My sleeping habits
3. My exercise habits
4. My emotional well-being
5. My lifestyle environment
6. My social environment

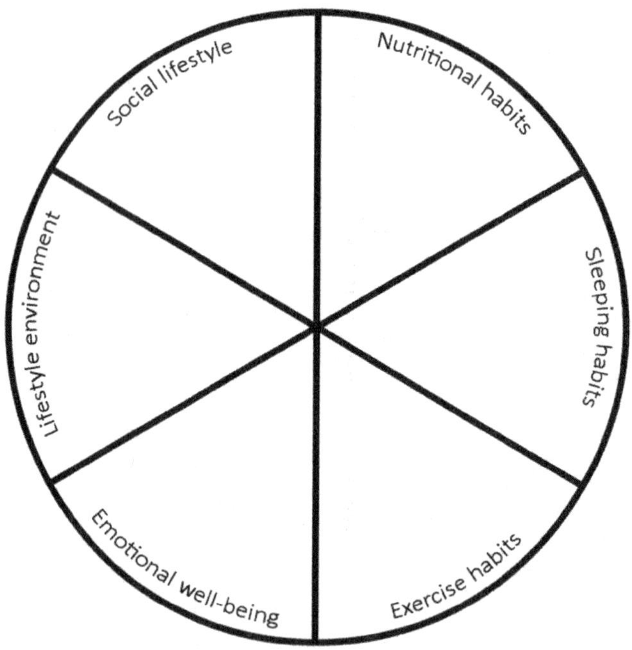

Step 3:

Now mark on the scale an overall view of how happy you are with each section in your life.

1 = Very unhappy (centre of circle)

10 = Very happy (top of section)

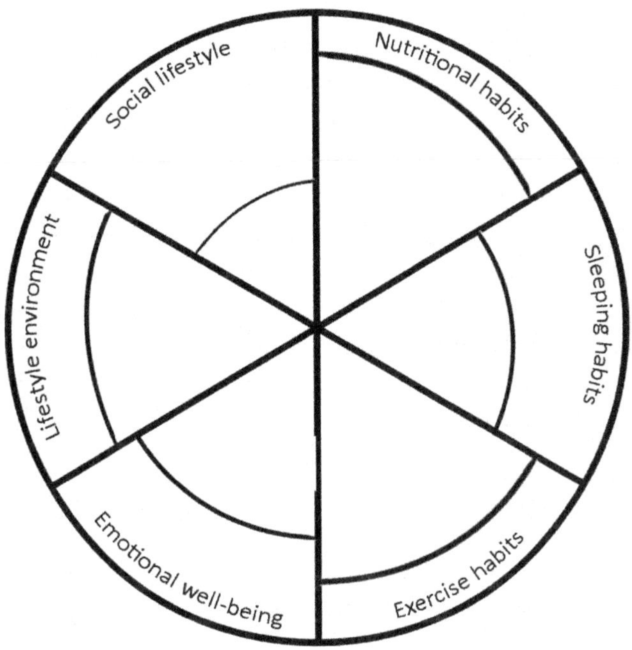

Wheel of preparation.

Step 4:
Take another piece of paper and write your ideal state for each section. Your ideal state is referring to what kind of lifestyle you would have if this section was 10 out of 10 for you (or close to that).

Here is an example statement for section 1:

1. My nutrition habits

"I have full control over my eating habits and my energy is at a high level. I always eat at regular times and the food I eat is healthy, clean and nutritious. This provides me with sustenance to complete the tasks that I have in my daily life. I enjoy my food."

Please write your own statements for each of the six sections. If you feel that there are more specific areas you want to write about, just focus on an overview at this stage as we will split each section in upcoming steps.

With each written statement, please ensure that it feels motivating for you to read. Anything less than 7 out of 10 will not be enough to create desired change.

Step 5:
Now take each of the 6 titles and further divide them into sub-sections of that area which have relevance in your life.

For example:

4. My emotional well-being

- *Confidence*
- *Self-esteem*
- *Anger issues (road rage)*
- *Coping mechanisms*
- *Negative self-talk*
- *Learning ability*
- *And so on…*

Step 6:
Then create an ideal outcome statement for each of the subsection areas.

For example:

Section 4 – Part 3 – Anger issues (road rage)

"I now feel calm when I drive my car and if there is an erratic driver on the road I slow down and let them pass. I know that my life is more important than proving myself to another driver."

Quick review
At this point let's just recheck what you have completed:

1. A full wheel of preparation with each of the six sections marked on how happy you are with that area in your own life.
2. A statement of each of the 6 sections that would reflect how you would feel if you were at 10 out of 10 (or close to that).
3. Subsection lists of each of the six main sections that you feel are relevant to you.
4. A statement on each of the subsection areas that would reflect how you would feel if you were at 10 out of 10 (or close to that).

How do you feel?
It really is important to do this for each area of your life that you have looked at so far as it will give you a chance to focus on what you want to attain or attract. HOWEVER, even though you have written the statements out, how do you honestly feel? Usually people feel one of 3 reactions:

1. **You feel motivated and focused!**
   If this is how you feel then that's great, the exercise has had the desired effect.

2. **You feel indifferent!**
   Doing this exercise may bring a feeling that you have done this before and although it changed your life in some way, you may feel that it is not something that can bring lasting change.

3. **You didn't like doing the exercise at all!**
   If you have done this before and felt that this level of coaching does not create long-term results, then your motivation may be low. You may have done this several times before and feel like you're going down the same path.

It is extremely important to continually assess how you feel at all stages of this exercise and all the other exercises throughout this book as the higher your energy, the more you will learn.

So why do this exercise if it doesn't create permanent results?
Although it is the truth that simply doing this exercise and creating written statements will not revolutionise your world permanently, it is important to give your mind something to focus on that you want to attain. In the preparation stages of the mask it is vital to manage your state. Even if the statement of being the calm happy driver (when really you feel like screaming at other drivers) may seem too far away at this time (or not, depending on how the statements make you feel) it is important to create focus. Focusing on what you want rather than what you do not want means that you can begin to focus on leverage.

Step 7:
In this step please go through each of the subsection areas and list all the potential risk factors associated with that particular area. The reason for doing this is so you can be completely aware of all the potential trip hazards before they occur.

For example…

Section 4 – Part 3 – Anger issues (road rage)

Statement: *"I now feel calm when I drive my car and if there is an erratic driver on the road I slow down and let them pass. I know that my life is more important than proving myself to another driver."*

Subsection area concern:

1. *"I feel that I can't control my emotions when another driver carelessly drives near me."*

2. *"I feel that when a driver is careless that not only is my life in danger, but I also feel an irrational anxiety that they are doing it on purpose and this makes me angry for several hours."*

Once you have listed all of these, then mark them on a level of 1 to 10. This time the numbers are reversed. This time 1 is 'not' a threat and 10 is a serious potential trip hazard.

Step 8:
Asking questions

I remember attending a workshop a few years ago and the speaker asked me to name an outcome I would like to attain. At that time my aim was to stop feeling so shy when meeting new people. So, I made a statement that I was a happy confident person who can talk to anybody and that I take things in my stride. Upon reading it back though, no matter what I wrote I felt like a liar, because underneath I knew that social anxiety consumed me. However, he then put a twist on the exercise…

He asked me to ask myself two questions of how I could reach that outcome, such as:

"How can I feel more confident in social situations?"

"What would I need to do to see things as they are rather that what I assume they are?"

By doing this I noticed a dramatic change in my conscious focus. By asking questions, I forced my mind to create an option of change rather than focusing on the problem. The mind after all is a humble servant.

Go through each of your statements in stage 6 and if your motivation is not above a 7 when you read the statement, create 2 or more questions that you can ask yourself to create options or another way of looking at the situation.

For example, Joe Bloggs may say in his statement:

Section 4 – Part 3 – Anger issues (road rage)

"I now feel calm when I drive my car, and if there is erratic driver on the road I slow down and let them pass. I know that my life is more important than proving myself to another driver."

Honest feeling: The statement does not feel like it is true.

Anxiety: *"I feel that I can't control my anger when another driver carelessly drives near me."*

Question 1: What could you do to keep calm in erratic traffic?

Answer 1: I could record my own children or my friend's children when they are playing and laughing and listen to it as I am driving.

Answer 2: I could leave earlier and miss the heavy traffic.

If you did those, how would you feel about the original statement?

"I now feel calm when I drive my car, and if there is erratic driver on the road I slow down and let them pass. I know that my life is more important than proving myself to another driver."

Answer: I feel it is more attainable and my motivation is now a 7 or above

Note: If it is not above 7 then simply ask more questions until your energy changes.

Prepare, prepare, prepare!

Personal experience: In a martial arts class I attended many years ago, I remember my Sensei (the instructor) made me practice a single punch and block over and over whilst I watched everybody else doing spinning kicks and high jumps and 'cool stuff'. I felt my frustration reach boiling point. So, I stopped doing the punches and asked to join in the class so I could do the 'cool stuff' (not a wise move). My instructor agreed and then said that I should spar with some of the other students who I wanted to join in with (but in my ignorance I failed to realise that they were more advanced than I was). The result…I got physically hurt.
To this I played the 'poor me violin' and claimed that I was the victim, but my instructor knew me better than I knew myself and understood that the best lesson for me to learn was to learn by doing rather than what he said. He then explained that the lesson he taught me was like life as a whole. And then he went on to explain…

"Life will bring us challenging odds (like the other students' fighting skills in comparison to mine as a beginner in that class) and many people will want to join in with things in life whether that is a business, a sport, a relationship or any other area. However, many people who go for the thrill of the chase are simply not prepared to handle the situation in tough times, but they join in anyway, assuming the preparation is not important. The result…they get hurt…then they either feel sorry for themselves, blaming other people for their misfortune, or they go back to the drawing board and learn new skills by practicing the fundamentals! However, if you prepare for what may come beforehand, life may still trip you up, but at least you will be better equipped at getting back up. It is always a choice."

After that lesson I finally understood why it is so important to prepare and to accept the reality of your current abilities. Yes, it's important to stretch beyond our boundaries and it's impossible to prepare for every outcome (although many try to, as we will see further along in this book), but do not to become too overly confident when the outcome is uncertain as overconfidence can lead to blatant errors that can lead to 'unnecessary' pain or loss.

Remember!

1. Take time to get to know your terrain!
2. Do not let an erratic mind control you!
3. Look at all options!
4. Be aware of the things you may not want to see!
5. Develop your sense of discipline!
6. Practice often!

3

Are Things As They Appear?

See things for what they are…rather than what you think they are!

Have you ever been so convinced that something was the truth that you would have gambled everything on it…only to find out later that it was incorrect?

The human mind guides itself around the world by using an internal map made up of perceptions of what it 'thinks' the world is. These perceptions are also known as beliefs. Further along in this book we shall discuss beliefs at great length.

However, the fact that beliefs are made up of 'perceptions' of what the mind 'thinks' the world is does not mean that the beliefs are fact! It simply means that they are what the mind believes is a fact!

Although there are great advantages to the mind interpreting the world in this manner, it can also bring with it a great disadvantage….

You can unknowingly be taught the incorrect map!

Through this chapter I have one main aim that I wish to convey to you, and that is to…QUESTION EVERYTHING!

When we are young we look to the people around us to educate us in the ways of the world, which will set us up for the best advantage in life. As children we are completely dependent upon those around us because we are unable to fend for ourselves. If we are taught correctly then we will have acquired the necessary skills to create our own abundant life, but what if we were not taught correctly? What if the information we have been learning is missing something that we have never realised?

Personally (even at a young age), I always found it curious as to why the school I attended would demand that I learn subjects such as geology and history when what I really needed was to learn how to survive school. What was the point of learning chemistry when I found it nearly impossible to speak to classmates?

Do you feel that the information which you have been taught during the majority of your educational life was as relevant as 'you' needed it to be?

Asking questions such as this is not to insinuate any blame to any particular education system as that would be of no value, but my point is to ask that you reflect on what you have really been taught. Is it a possibility that you may have been taught by people thinking they were teaching you correctly, but in reality the information may not have been as effective as they thought?
Also, if this has happened, please consider these two questions…

1. How would you know?
2. What could this have cost you?

Take the following story…

Meet Joe (story)

Many years ago in a small village just on the outskirts of London, there lived a young man called Joe. However, Joe was no ordinary young man - he had a thirst for knowledge and wanted to expand his mind and grow.

The village in which Joe grew up had very limited opportunities for its residents' education. The limited options frustrated Joe as he always wanted to move to London, a thriving city where he could truly express himself.

Although he had set his heart on living in London, he also knew that his lack of education would stop him from moving forward. To solve this problem Joe begged his father to hire a teacher to educate him and help him get to the big city. As there were no schools in the village, his father agreed to hire a private tutor to help Joe attain his dreams.

Within a week, a gentleman arrived in the village and announced himself as Joe's new tutor. Joe was very excited by this and told the tutor that he would do as instructed and listen patiently. The tutor was happy with Joe's attitude but explained that there was one condition that Joe had to agree to. The condition was that Joe must listen and never question the tutor. Joe agreed.

Joe was a good student and always did as requested. Through the weeks he worked very hard, listened intently and remembered all he had been taught. Joe completely trusted the tutor and the process; why wouldn't he? The tutor was an authority after all!

After three months, the teaching came to an end and Joe was awarded his qualification. Joe felt very confident and immediately packed his bags and headed off to London. Once in London he told all the employers of his high level of education, and being very impressed one employer gave Joe a job that day as a builder's merchant in charge of stock.

Joe arrived on his first day with unstoppable energy and worked hard. When five o'clock came he was very tired, so he said to all his new team that he looked forward to seeing them again tomorrow and went home to enjoy a sound night's sleep.

The next day Joe got into work with his huge smile beaming, but to his shock the owner of the company was not smiling. The owner was furious and began to shout at Joe as soon as he walked in to the office: "All the orders you sent out yesterday were wrong. You have cost us thousands of pounds! You can't add up Joe!"
"Rubbish," Joe protested, "all my adding was correct – I'm highly educated!"
"Okay then," said the manager, "what is two plus two?"
"Five," said Joe proudly.
Poor Joe was sacked immediately.

On his way home Joe came to a cold realisation that the tutor had taught him the wrong information. Joe felt let down and very confused. "How could this happen?" he asked himself, "the tutor was supposed to educate me in the correct way, but he didn't??"
Joe also then felt let down, because not only was the information incorrect, but he had also trusted his tutor and if he couldn't trust his tutor, then who could he trust?
He then asked himself what else he may have learned during the course of his life that was also incorrect!

Question everything!

Quite often when I teach my own courses and workshops I will add into the syllabus one of the most powerful techniques I have ever learned that can help students grow. The technique is to allow the students to question the reality which they think they know.
The technique is as follows…

I will wait until we are over halfway into the course and the students have got to know each other and feel comfortable. Then I will ask them to take all of the notes that they have made and all of the information which I have personally taught them and ask them to find every possible inconsistency, every reason why the information is invalid and even to question my own skills as the coach and trainer.

Usually I will make this into a 20-minute exercise and then ask the groups to present their findings. Although this for me as a trainer may sound like class suicide, it is just the opposite.

True learning happens when a person who is learning information not only has the option to absorb the information, but also to cross-reference it with other things. If any student who attends a course blindly accepts the information without question, then there is a possibility that they have only 'half learned'.

It is always interesting to watch students' reactions when I do this exercise. Some students feel guilty about questioning me as their trainer, while some students feel irritated that I am insinuating that there is a possibility that the information may be flawed, and other students simply feel confused. How often do trainers ask you to 'doubt their information'?

There is much more of a greater lesson with this technique though. The lesson is to train people to learn information and then to cross-reference what they have absorbed rather than just accepting it. When we learn information and then question it, it can bring the creative part of the mind into play and much more knowledge can be absorbed. It is also advised that you do this with this book - question it! Ask yourself, is this information correct? Get into the habit of questioning everything! This is an essential skill!

For me as an author I am not here to say I know everything. I am just here sharing the information which I believe is correct from my research and experience, but unless you can question it you will not have truly grasped the essence of my message.

The school of life!

Although there are some parts of the education system which are flawed, there are also many great advantages to it as well. Some of the greatest minds we have ever known may not have been able to achieve the levels they did if it was not for truly great teachers that helped them focus their skills.

My point here is not to criticize the education system, but just to be aware of what you are learning and its relevance to you. As mentioned, simply accepting the information which is being taught to you without questioning it could cause potential risk.

When many of us think of the education system we may envision schools, colleges and universities, but there is another education system which has much more influence over our belief systems than we will ever know, and that is the school of life!

The place that we will learn most of our beliefs and expectations about the world is in daily life. Each and every day our mind is working away like a computer, storing and analysing our environment and creating belief systems from the information it gathers. So if we can be taught incorrect information from our education system…the same can happen in daily life!
However, in daily life the information we learn is much different. Whereas in the education system we are learning skills based upon a syllabus, in life we are learning so much more!

Take a moment now and ask yourself…

How did you learn to speak the language you speak?
Where did you learn manners and etiquette?
Where did you learn how to act in the various groups in society?

The answer is in life itself! You have learned all of your social conditioning and attitudes through your environment. You act and react based upon the social conditioning of your environment, and that is based upon how comfortable you feel in relation to your environment.
However, what if your environment has also subliminally taught you some unhealthy attitudes and beliefs that you have unknowingly been using as a map of the world?

If that is a possibility…what effect may this have had on your life?

Some people say that what you do not know can't hurt you, but this is a lie! Also, as mentioned, if these attitudes and beliefs have been with you since you were young, how would you even know? It is very easy to learn a habit without even realising it!

Take the following story…

The story of sugar and salt

There was once a great king who had his food prepared for him each and every day by the cook. By request, the cook made a special meal each day, which the king enjoyed heartily as after eating the meal he felt very alive and energised. The 'secret' ingredient that the cook added to the meal was a healthy amount of salt. Salt (or sodium) has very important properties to the human body and is essential to survival.

One day the cook accidentally knocked the sugar bowl (refined sugar is an unhealthy compound that the body does not need, yet which millions of people are addicted to) into the salt jar and the two compounds mixed together. Since both sugar and salt are a white substance of similar texture, to the untrained they may appear quite indistinguishable from each other.

To this the cook felt at a loss of how to separate the two compounds. Upon assessing the situation the cook realised that he could not afford to buy any more sugar or salt out of their own money, so he decided to shake the jar of sugar and salt until it was mixed evenly together. It looked like the salt jar and although it now had a new taste, if covered up with other flavourings it could quite easily be disguised. So, the cook chose to start making the king's favourite meal with this 'new' mixture.

The first day the meal was served containing this new mixture, the king noticed a strange taste and was not sure whether he liked it or not. However, the king also noticed a seemingly pleasant high feeling (the sugar rush) and decided that the change in taste was actually worth it due to this new feeling. He couldn't work out the reason for the high, but as he liked the feeling he was not overly concerned. He noticed it gave him a quicker boost of energy than normal. Just out of curiosity though, the king asked the cook why he felt this 'rush' and why the meal tasted different. Of course the cook claimed that it was the same mixture as normal, but then redirected the king's attention to the high feeling he had and says that he could make more if the king wishes. The cook distracted the king from his first question because he did not want to get caught for accidentally mixing the sugar and salt.

The cook was now a little worried as the king did realise the change, but realises that he cannot buy any more salt and also cannot separate the salt and sugar mix. However, the cook then remembered that the king did like the 'high' that he got from the sugar, and then the cook had an idea! What if he were to add more and more sugar to the meal every day to give the king a 'high' feeling in hopes that he would become so consumed by the 'high' that he would forget about the new taste? So, he attempted this method.

Each day the cook added an increasing amount of sugar to the king's meal and soon enough the king became hopelessly addicted to the sugar rush and started to demand more and more of this 'secret ingredient'. To this the cook happily obliged, believing that he was now off the hook for any blame from mixing in the sugar.

However, as sugar is unhealthy (which is a fact for anybody), the high consumption (now driven by the king's addiction) has started to affect the king's health (diabetes) and he now feels ill and tired at many points through the day. Of course the king cannot understand why he feels so unwell – because, to his knowledge, he has been eating the same meal each day and nothing has changed. He thus blames his ill health on his age and continues to eat his 'new' meal!

Over the course of many months the king's energy deteriorates to such a low level that he has to rest and sleep at various points throughout the day, but again he just assumes that this is the way life is and adapts his life accordingly (in the human mind this is known as habituation). The people around the king begin to notice that he is doing less activity and he also avoids his friends because he feels that normal conversation has now become a struggle. His energy and lifestyle deteriorate, but still he keeps eating the meal because his new 'magic meal' gives him the high…or so he hopes. The reality is that the king is now caught in the trap, assuming that his new meal is the very thing that can cure his ill health, when in reality it is the new meal that is the cause of his ill health.

Sugar and salt mixed together may look the same, but will have a huge impact on a person's health, and how would a person know the difference if they were not told?

"Dripping water hollows out stone, not through force but through persistence."
Ovid

What have you learned without realising it?
How many people do you know who will continually say sorry for no real reason?
How many people do you know who have picked up unhelpful habits from people around them which then hold them back?

If we now look at the first story of Joe learning incorrect information from his tutor and then cross-reference that with learning life skills from others around us, it is possible to see how limiting beliefs and attitudes can easily be transferred to us as children. As children, we rarely question the information because we trust our peers to guide us. However…what if they have learned incorrect information and then passed it on to us without realising?

The bitter reality!
Although it would be easy to write a book of meditations that focus your mind on a beautiful garden with lush green grass on a summer's day, it would be doing you a huge disservice. Genuine personal development is not always about looking at the pretty things in life, but is rather about looking at reality, the good and the bad!

So far in this chapter my aim has been to suggest that you start to question things. Question them on a deeper level than you may have questioned them before. Believe it or not, there is a game going on behind the scenes for millions of people and most of them have no idea it is there! This game could also be more bluntly known as a battle…a battle within!

I remember once reading this quote:

"If you know the enemy and know yourself, you need not fear the result of a hundred battles. If you know yourself but not the enemy, for every victory gained you will also suffer a defeat. If you know neither the enemy nor yourself, you will succumb in every battle."
Sun Tzu: The Art of War

Given I mentioned that the only path to inner peace is through coming to terms with all parts of who you are, this quote may sound like a paradox. Surely we should not advocate a battle within and especially not a 'war', right?

However, the truth is that if you are feeling any form of low self-esteem, depression or social anxiety, it is because there is 'already' a battle going on within you. The battle is happening because there are different parts of your mind that are in conflict with each other. Any emotional discomfort you ever feel is your mind trying to balance out the confusion. As we all know too well, sitting in the middle of this confusion can be quite an arduous process.

So, in regards to the Sun Tzu quote, to find the inner peace, confidence or whichever outcome you want, you will first have to understand the conflict that is already going on within you. Once you understand the conflict only then can you begin to resolve it.

"True wisdom comes to each of us when we realize how little we understand about life, ourselves, and the world around us."
Socrates

The con trick – the ultimate illusion of the mind!

Millions of people all across the world are unknowingly caught up in an internal battle of different parts of their mind. Yet if 'self-acclaimed positive thinking gurus' are right and we just need to sit and meditate on a bright future and all will be well, why is it that millions of people seem so unable to break free from their inner battles of low self-esteem or low confidence?

"The greatest trick the devil ever pulled was convincing the world he didn't exist."
Quote from the film: The Usual Suspects

What if there is a belief system within you that is hiding in a place you would never think to look? Or what if it has been with you for so long that you have just become used to it and no longer question it?

To look at the bitter truth, if you are feeling any form of anxiety such as depression, stress, anger, jealousy, low self-worth, feeling of no value, wanting to hide from the world or many other feelings of disconnection, then you are caught in what I will define as 'the con trick'.

It is the truth that millions of people are caught in the con and succumb to its power each and every day, but most are not even aware of it. However, although many of these people will take great steps to avoid the pain that comes with the con, most of them are completely unaware that 'fighting' the con actually increases its power over them.

From here on in, the entire book will be centred on and around the con trick and will aim to show you the enormous power it has over so many people in the world. The con trick is the most elusive social emotional coping strategy the human mind has ever created!

With that said, it is purely a human trait; animals do not get caught in the con due to the structure of their physical brain. Be assured that the con IS NOT as obvious as you may think and hides many levels deep within a person's mind, lifestyle and emotions. It is essential that each chapter is completed sequentially and fully understood before progressing, as the entire book is like a jigsaw puzzle. Any missing pieces (or chapters) will result in an incomplete picture.

Con: (Confidence trick)

To swindle (a victim) by first winning his or her confidence; dupe.
Of, relating to, or involving a swindle or fraud.

In order for a con trick to be effective, the victim must be under no illusion of any scam. They will believe their adversary to be honest and trustworthy, with only their (the victim's) best interests at heart.

The very art of a con is to ensure that the person being conned is convinced that the other who is conning them is seen as their best friend! In life we want to be able to trust our best friend and hope that they are the support we need when we are in a vulnerable position. So if that was being insinuated, who would want to go against that? Who would want to give up on something that brings them perceived happiness, success and a feeling of security?

However, if there was a possibility that you were in a con, wouldn't you want to know? Wouldn't you want to know the difference between your best friend and somebody who is posing as your best friend just to con you?

The reality of the con is not as obvious as you may assume!

If what we have just covered feels quite elusive or even confusing at the moment, then do not be too concerned. The entire book will go on to explain the structure of the illusion that has just been discussed.

It is not the nicest thing to hear, but millions of people are being conned each and every day. The con will target anybody who is open to it, from the financially poor to the richest person on earth, from the extremely obese person who comfort eats through depression to the gym obsessive with the body of Mr or Miss Universe.

Each and every time they are conned, unless they take action to become aware of what is happening and alter their mindset, their resilience to the con becomes weaker and weaker. Eventually the habit process will take over and they lose the awareness of it ever being there in the first place.

However, do not just let me say such a statement as a declarative thought; allow me to back it up with sound logical psychological explanations, models and research.

Some say "Ignorance is bliss", but in reality ignorance is far from bliss (as you will learn in upcoming chapters). Living in the con though will be taking much more from you and your life than you may realise, your friends and family included!

How open minded are you prepared to be?

"The greatest trick the devil ever pulled was convincing the world he didn't exist."
Quote from the film: The Usual Suspects

The con: A deeper view

The ages have been host to many a social barbarian who has rampaged through the world causing chaos and strife and leaving many lives in torment and loss. People who are outwardly aggressive and manipulative, striking terror into the hearts of their victims with their wrath are easy to see because their actions are so obvious. Although many people feel that they lack the confidence to stand up to the office bully who makes the trip to the photocopier a nightmare, it is possible to give the loud aggressive people a wide berth and therefore avoid their attack.

However, the confidence trickster is not noticeable in a crowd. In fact, the very essence of the game they play requires their game or manipulation to be so well hidden that we have absolutely no idea of what is happening. In many cases we will also convince ourselves that they are OUR best friend and there to help us in times of need.

Each time a con trick is performed, although it can sometimes be completed in a few seconds, it wraps itself more and more around the layers of your mind and emotions. It effortlessly flows around like water to avoid detection at all costs. Although it may appear simplistic, its structure is extremely complex and its execution highly efficient. It relies upon the victim believing that the con is not really a con but a benefit to their lives in some way, yet really the reverse is true. Then, if there is even a trace of awareness of the con in the victim's mind, the victim is usually too involved in the game to accept that it has gone this far. Usually, by the time the victim has become aware that they are in a loop, they feel too self-conscious to admit that they have been tricked. Surely 'they' should have known better and been more streetwise. An insult to their intelligence no less!

Regardless of what many people may claim about openly admitting that they have been tricked or 'outwitted' by another whom they trust, it is not something that the majority of people are prepared to fully accept.

A con? You mean like street crime?

For many people when they hear the word 'con', it may conjure up an image of a quick-talking street hustler out to get some quick cash, but this is far from the level that is being discussed here. The con trickster on the street is much easier to recognise and even if we fall prey to them and feel the discomfort of dented pride, we can always give them a wide berth the next time. Indeed, the con trickster I am talking about is much more elusive!

The con trickster I am discussing here is by far the most powerful controller ever known! You may have one in your life right now, and if you do they will be preying on the deepest levels of your emotions. These are emotions that you (when you are in the con) will not even be aware of. This happens because they are usually hidden from conscious reality and buried far deeper than we as a human race are usually taught or educated about in school or education centres.

In regards to the con…our greatest strength is also our greatest vulnerability!

The deepest drive of any human being is to firstly create a sense of a safe and secure environment and then naturally progress towards loving and harmonious relationships with others. The relationships we desire may be of a romantic nature, an interdependent working relationship or simply a good friend who knows our 'inner demons' and accepts us just as we are.

Relationships are vital for anybody who wants to create a healthy world and a connection where there is trust. To know that we can trust and be trusted can bring a strong sense of confidence and security whilst we grow and explore life. These stages are eloquently illustrated in Maslow's hierarchy of needs between stages 2 and 3, which we will discuss soon.

It is this longing to connect to others who reflect our best interests that can give us the perseverance to work through challenges when we feel like giving up. However, it is also this same natural drive that can be manipulated and used against us in the con!

Although this longing is in part a desire to connect to other people as a survival instinct for the protection and the continuation of the human race, it is also something much greater than that and is not even fully understood by the greatest minds of science. Yet it is still something that we cannot turn away from nor dismiss. Many people try to through various different methods of distraction such as drugs or work, but as it is part of the human make-up created through thousands of years of the formation of the human brain, it is simply impossible to ignore.

Looking at the human drive in this way, it is easy to see that if the drive to connect to others was threatened (by the con trickster), the human mind would naturally take steps to reconnect to the other person and restore harmony. When harmony is restored the mind will once again be at peace. However, it is this reaction that the con trickster is using to gain power over the person. In essence, our own natural drive is being used against us.

The reason this 'trick' is so powerful is because the human mind will move away from pain. So…if the con trickster 'creates' a pain without us even realising and then offers 'their' solution to the pain, we may take their option without ever being aware of it!

Does this sound a little over the top? Well, let me ask you some questions…

- How many people do you know who have bought something that they did not need only to question why they did so days later?

- How many people do you know who have had sex or a one-night stand and have been totally confused as to why they did that?

- How many people will do things for other people that they do not really want to do as it is costing them too much time…but they keep on doing it?

- Or how many people do you know who stay in a job they hate but do not leave?

Why do people do things that they often do not want to do but seem unable to break free from repeating the actions? 'Surely' (as we are often taught) it is just a simple case of will power and staying focused? Yet how many of these people who end up in situations that they seem ensnared in HAVE tried to use their will power and it didn't get anywhere?

Without understanding the strategy of the mask…will power is virtually useless against the con trick!

My aim through this book is to show you a very clear self-reflection of whom you are and who you are not. The exercises will ask searching questions and will ask you to look within to discover any internal conflict that may be residing within your mind. The purpose of doing this as mentioned is that in order to create harmony, we must first understand the 'con'flict.

"An eye for an eye will only make the whole world blind."
Mahatma Gandhi

Depending upon where you are in your journey of self-discovery, even thinking about taking a reflective look at the 'real you' can sometimes have the effect of creating emotional discomfort. As discussed before though, if it feels uncomfortable it may come with the desire to avoid it and focus the attention on a more pleasing aspect of life. If this happens you may find that you walk straight past the door to the solution you seek.
Why do people avoid what they don't want to see? Because often as children we can be taught the phrase…

"What I can't see can't hurt me, right?" Or
"Out of sight, out of mind."

But is ignoring the 'hidden self' the best option? If we simply brush it under the carpet and forget about it, will it just go away and not affect us? In a word, NO!

As mentioned, in my own journey I was taught this attitude of 'think positive' by many of the self-acclaimed 'gurus' in the personal development world as I worked through my own depression. Book after book reiterated that I should focus on what I wanted and ignore the anxiety. Although there is an extremely vital place for focusing on what you want to achieve in life, there is something much more important to focus on first…namely…the mask and the con!

The truth is that avoiding your supressed anxieties is no different than leaving your non-waterproof mobile phone outside in the middle of a thunderstorm and pretending that it is not raining. You can deny it all you like, but your phone is still going to be damaged!

Facing reality

As we go through this programme you will see how easy it is for people to become endlessly trapped in the con and loop within the same pattern week after week, month after month and year after year. You will also discover that it is low self-esteem and self-doubt that give the con so much power over people's actions and reactions. The more anxiety, self-doubt or low self-esteem a person holds, the more control the con will have over them. We all have emotional vulnerabilities in some area of our lives whether we admit to it or not.

The more you fight, the weaker you become

It is essential to note at this point (and as you will become more and more aware of as you work through this book) that the con trick cannot be beaten down with aggressive power! It cannot be forced into submission and it cannot be ignored without negative consequence. The more a person fights any form of anxiety in anger or frustration, the weaker they will become to the con's power and manipulation. The weaker they become, the more vulnerable they will be in not only that situation, but also future interactions.

"A mind is like a parachute. It doesn't work if it is not open."
Frank Zappa

You can't cut corners

True lasting success in any area of life does not come from getting the quick fix. Success comes from understanding how to create the most potent strategies and then taking action to acquire the life you want! It has been observed many times that those people who suffer in financial poverty and then win millions of pounds on the lottery can end up back in financial poverty shortly after - why? Because they gained a quick fix but did not learn how to create it themselves, and it is the same with education!

At school I remember a teacher once saying to me…

"If you cheat you are only cheating yourself."
To me at that time though that was a lie! If I cheated on the school exams and passed…I received praise! Yet life is not like the organised school! If you cheat in life, then you 'do' cheat yourself!

Cheating life, cutting corners and getting the quick fixes are all the same, and trust me, you will never win. However, the con trickster will be more than happy to step in and start playing their game. The only thing is though, how will you know if they are getting inside your head? Well, this is what I am going to explain! There is a way to stop the game, but you will need to study this book intricately. Remember…do not cut corners!

In life it is impossible to get lasting success by cutting corners. Yes, it is true that shortcuts can make success more efficient, but missing out vital steps which leads to missing out vital knowledge will only lead to failure and more loss in the long run.

"The truth is incontrovertible. Malice may attack it, ignorance may deride it, but in the end, there it is."
Winston Churchill

Chapter summary

Be aware of your beliefs!
Your beliefs are your interpretations of the world in which you live. You have learned these beliefs from the environment that you have lived in. During this time, although you will have learned useful beliefs, it is also possible that you may have learned unhelpful beliefs.

Blind trust?
During the course of our lives we will have many teachers. However, just because a teacher may have a very official title does not necessarily mean that the information they teach is 100% correct. Everybody can make mistakes. Therefore, it is recommended that you start to take a reflective view of the people you have been taught by and cross-reference the information with what you already know.

The school of life!
Although many of us go to school to learn Maths and English, the school of life will teach us much more than we may ever realise. The school of life will teach us personal habits and attitude traits. It is said that we

become a reflection of the five main people in our life. Take a moment and reflect on what you may have unknowingly learned from your subliminal environment.

Sugar and salt!

In life it is so easy for poor habits to become intertwined into our life and then we start to act upon them without even realising it. Take a moment and ask yourself how many habits or traits you have adopted because it was what everybody else has done. This could be smoking, working long hours (a common work culture today) or certain habits in your relationships that you do not feel comfortable about but you just go along with.

See reality!

There can be many things in life which we would rather avoid because they feel unpleasant, but avoiding them if they can negatively affect our lives will not help us grow. Take a look at all areas of your life and check to see if you are observing reality or a glossed-over version of reality. Sometimes the truth hurts, but if you have weeds in your garden the only way to remove them is to firstly acknowledge them!

4

Discover Your Mind!

Know thyself!

Before we even begin to start working through the mask and the con, it is essential that we first take a few more steps to understand the enormous power that is contained right in your very head…your mind!

It is essential to discover the vast complexities of how your mind perceives and constructs the world in which you live. Without this knowledge the mask and therefore the con would be able to keep their power and remain in the shadows. However, it can be surprising just how many people do not make the time to understand their mind and yet still expect to have control over their lives. If this preparation time is not taken, it is unlikely that there will be a significant impact. If this happens…knowledge of the mask and the con would be virtually useless because the key to unlocking them both would not be there.

Be aware of your vehicle

It is possible for many drivers of motor vehicles (who are totally dependent on their car, van or motorbike) to break down and then not have sufficient knowledge to repair the most basic of malfunctions. It has been known for people to run out of fuel and be totally clueless of how to fill the tank, or even get a puncture resulting in a flat tyre and not know how to repair it. If they are not a part of a roadside recovery agency this situation can then have a huge impact on their day.

However, contrary to social criticism, not knowing how to repair basic malfunctions does not mean that the driver is stupid or of lesser intelligence. Not knowing how to repair a car simply means that they have not studied it or learned how to repair a malfunction. If a person does not have sufficient knowledge, they will not know what to do. If we have not learned something, we cannot refer to it in the mind. Although this cause and affect situation is obvious, it still leaves our poor driver stood by the roadside, unable to carry on with their day.

From an onlooker's point of view who does know how to rectify these apparently simple malfunctions, it may appear to them that the driver 'is' in some way of lesser intelligence. However, as stated, it is simply that the driver did not take knowledge of repairing malfunctions into account, or maybe they have seen learning the required knowledge of mechanics as irrelevant to their life. This usually happens through either a lack of education or they have not seen that learning the information as relevant, or yet it could simply be that they are naïve to the fact that the breakdown could happen.

However, we can see in this example that failure to adequately prepare for a vehicle breakdown can have much more of an impact on the driver's life than just a flat tyre. Some of the after-effects could be being late for a business meeting, being unable to pick up their partner from a restaurant or being stranded in a potentially dangerous environment.

Remember, every time a person tries to cut a corner to get that 'quick fix', life could easily take a turn for the worst, leaving them to face the consequences. For every action there is always an equal and opposite reaction!

To every action there is an equal and opposite reaction.
Newton's third law

The survival drive – The pain-pleasure principle

'We may lay it down that pleasure is a movement, a movement by which the soul as a whole is consciously brought into its normal state of being; and that pain is the opposite."
Aristotle

Just the same as any other living creature, the human mind will seek to gratify for enjoyment and growth (pleasure) and move away from that which could be a threat (pain). This is known as the pain-pleasure principle.
The reasons for which we seek pleasure and avoid pain are many, but the main one is simply for our survival. The body in itself is fallible and therefore at constant risk. This risk could be harm from illness, physical threats or internal threats by the release of too many stress hormones. We can see this internal threat react in full form when a person who is in a highly anxious state for long periods of time becomes ill and requires medical attention.

Firstly though, if we are to understand how the pain-pleasure principle functions within our physiology, we must first discover what these two terms actually mean.

What is pain?

Pain is any form of suffering that we encounter which is either potentially damaging to our health or is actually causing us physical harm. However, the term 'actually' can sometimes be a challenge to define, as you will see in this chapter. The reason it can be a challenge to define is because it is our perception that plays a large part in what is defined as pain. Perceptions, as we recall, are made up of beliefs.

For example, let us define the word "suffering". What exactly is suffering? To one person that may be not being able to smoke a cigarette for 20 minutes, but to somebody else, suffering (or reaction to the perceived pain) may only begin after being physically beaten for hours in a violent act.

You will notice that this is completely different to the term of 'physical pain', which is actual physical damage to the tissues. Physical pain can damage the nerves and cause a shockwave of pain through the nervous system and spinal cord. It will do this so the brain knows that the physical body is in danger.

In a natural and healthy state, the human mind will automatically move away from pain for self-preservation. Yet surely when a boxer is being repeatedly physically beaten round after round their mind will see this as pain, right? Logically this would be true, yet in many cases of boxing and other high-aggression sports, when the participants are receiving physical damage (resulting in injury and trauma), the participant will continue despite knowing that further damage can occur. Logically this type of action wouldn't make sense, so why do they carry on?

Looking at this situation more in depth, we can see that if the boxer 'perceives' the result of the action that they are performing as a rewarding experience then this will be seen as pleasure. The resulting pleasure they may perceive could be the recognition, a financial reward, a bond between friends or many others. So, if the emotional payoff they receive becomes of a higher priority to the boxer's perception than the physical pain, they will then see the act as rewarding and continue with it.

However, the question must then be asked:
What would happen if the reward (pleasure) was to then be removed from the situation?

By this I do not mean what 'other people' may see as the payoff for the boxer, but what the boxer sees as the payoff. For him or her it may not be about the financial reward, but rather the praise, recognition or being

able to feel that they have beat their school bully (as we will see in later chapters).
If the reward that 'they' sought after was suddenly taken away from them, the pleasure drive of the situation would then evaporate and their attention would become more aware of the physical reality again (the physical damage).

Although this pain had always been there, they chose to ignore it as they were distracted by the pleasure drive. Once the pleasure drive is removed the physical pain and damage they suffer will start to once again become a priority. It is then more than likely a natural survival drive to preserve their health would arise. They may then find themselves quickly losing motivation to carry on with the fight or to stop their opponent as urgently as possible (to stop the pain by avoidance or removal – fight or flight).

So pain can therefore be defined as:
A situation in which the person themselves perceives current actions to be harmful to their psyche and/or physical health where any other reward is lower than the risk.

What is pleasure?
In essence, if we take Sir Isaac Newton's third of law of motion into account, which states that…

"For every action there is an equal and opposite reaction"

…we can then observe that pleasure is something which is a perceived benefit to that person's health or emotional well-being in some way.

It is at this point though that we also have to take into account that in some situations what a person believes is pleasurable can actually be quite toxic or damaging to their health. In essence though (like pain), if the person believes it to be a pleasure to them they will still follow the drive.

It is looking at life through this viewpoint that allows us to answer some perplexing questions, such as why some people will stay in seemingly unhealthy situation - situations such as living with partners who are extremely violent, a person who continually takes harmful drugs or even a person who may abuse their physical bodies through methods of cutting or burning their skin. Cutting and other methods of damaging the body can be quite extreme, but in each case the person will still be deriving pleasure from the situation they voluntarily create (more on this through the book). As mentioned though, this is a situation they 'voluntarily create'. Acts of violence that are bestowed upon people who do not wish it to happen will not see the attack as pleasure and therefore it will be pain.

Indeed, the above situations through the eyes of an onlooker may cause confusion. For some onlookers it may be almost impossible for them to understand how a person can possibly be deriving pleasure from staying with an extremely violent partner or cutting their skin. Yet if we look deep enough into that person's reality who is receiving the harm, rest assured there will be some pleasure for them. Also, in each case it will far outweigh the perception of pain or actual threat.

So pleasure can therefore be defined as:
A situation in which the person themselves perceives their actions to be beneficial to their psyche and/or physical health where the pleasure is higher than the pain.

If we take a step back and review what we have just discussed, we can see that there is a huge similarity in both of these scenarios;

"It is the person's perception that derives whether a situation is painful or pleasurable."

The confusion of the onlooker
How many times in life do we hear of a person being completely confused as to why another person would do something which is harmful? How many people are stunned to hear such stories of the

person who has a lung infection and carries on smoking or the person with diabetes who still eats junk food? To an onlooker the actions of another person may seem confusing, though rest assured there will always be a method in their perceived madness.

Remember, in many cases it will be the perception of pain or pleasure which will drive the person to take action rather than the actual reality they see.

If an onlooker is to truly understand why a person is taking an action which is harmful to their health, then it is essential that they look through the other's eyes rather than their own perceptions.

The brain and the mind

The human brain is by far one of the most complex organisms known to man. Each and every day billions of electrical and chemical reactions surge through this relatively small piece of architecture that sits inside the skull. Your brain is so complex that science has yet to figure out the full potential of its capabilities.

If we take a metaphorical view of the difference between the brain and the mind we can describe it as follows…

Your brain (which is the physical part of your body) can be likened to a computer. A computer is a physical component consisting of a protective case, wires and a processor etc. In a computer the electrical impulses will flow around it, making physical components move. This is known as 'hardware'.

Your mind, however, is something different from your brain. The part of you which is classed as your mind is simply your perception of the world that you see through your brain's neurological feedback.

So, if your brain is like a computer, your mind can be likened to operating software such as Microsoft Windows on a PC (or personal computer). This is known as 'software'.

Now even though the great minds of science are still mapping out the vast regions of the brain and therefore unable to define its true potential and structure, **the mind** and how it functions is not as complex as it may first appear.

Although I have just claimed that the 'mind' may not be as complex as it may appear, it then begs the question of why so many people can go through their day and experience a whole rollercoaster of emotions. Each and every day some people may experience wave after wave of emotions, which can leave them feeling confused and unsure of how to gain control. To a person who is unaware of how to gain control it may appear as if their mind is acting irrationally, however it will always be using profound logic. Just because a person may not understand why their mind is acting in a certain way does not mean that the mind is acting irrationally.

At this point I ask you to recall the last chapter where we discussed things we may have been taught which are incorrect, and the term irrational behaviour is one of those. However, it is vital to note that although many people may feel like their mind has a life of its own and that it may seem to take action of its own accord, in reality it is actually functioning from a very sound and logical pattern. This can be similar to the IQ tests that ask us to look at a series of boxes on a screen to figure out the sequence and then fill in the last box with the correct answer. If we do not understand the process then we cannot fill in the last box, but as soon as we do understand the sequence the last box is easy to complete. Just because a person may not know how to consciously work their mind does not mean that it is not functioning correctly.

Be selective of what you hear

Although there are many truly amazing people out there who are providing education in the realms of social and emotional learning, it does not always mean that 'everybody' who provides education and advice is correct! Remember…question everything!

Personal experience – Given the wrong medication!

I had an experience many years ago where upon a motorbike accident I tore a muscle in my back. I went to the local medical practice for a painkiller that was stronger than the over-the-counter strength due to the pain being so intense.

When I spoke to the doctor he wrote me a prescription for the painkillers, but also suggested I try another tablet at the same time. I felt a little confused and asked what it was; his reply was that it would make me 'feel better'.

Long story short this second suggestion turned out to be an anti-depressant to stabilise emotional levels and not my physiology (as I found out upon further research). Completely confused (as at the time I felt fine emotionally) I asked why he'd suggested I take this 'other tablet' (which had been suggested quite vaguely). His reply was that 'he felt' that in the conversation I seemed to be depressed about the pain. This was simply not true!

Fortunately, my awareness of the situation was alert so I only took the painkillers for the injury and left the anti-depressants. Nevertheless, I found it quite unnerving of just how easy it was to be prescribed anti-depressants when I had no reason to be taking them. I didn't ask for them nor did I need them, yet they were still prescribed. Either the doctor thought he was doing his best to help me, or there was something else going on behind the scenes! That last part may sound quite dark and is intended to, as wrongly prescribed drugs are no laughing matter. However, when I asked him why, he said that 'he thought' it was in my best interest to take the anti-depressant and that it could have helped me, but his view of my situation was incorrect.

How many of us give automatic authority to the doctor's knowledge (or other perceived authorities) without questioning it? Let's also ask, how many other people may have been misdiagnosed across the world - medical or otherwise?

Everything has its place

Do not get me wrong in regards to anti-depressants; personally I am not completely against them as sometimes when working with clients the intervention of drugs has helped calm their anxiety quite considerably. In the 'calmer state' their underlying emotions can be worked with and the therapy can take more of an effect. However, all I am saying in regards to the above scenario is to be aware of why you're taking them, who's prescribing them, and be sure to assess whether you have other alternatives.

Although the above scenario happened in regards to a misdiagnosis of my own emotional state resulting in a drugs prescription, it is still possible to hear many people making claims about their own emotional state that are incorrect too.

We can hear people claim that they have a chemical imbalance of serotonin that needs medical support, but in reality it may be that they are in a job they can't stand or that they are staying in an abusive relationship and can't see a way out, and so their 'chemical imbalance' is simply the body continually protecting itself.

We hear of some people that claim depression is disrupting their sleep and take medication to help, but in reality they don't sleep as they are staying up late at night on chatrooms and social media as they feel lonely.

Or what about those people who blame themselves endlessly for having 'irrational' behaviour that apparently 'makes' them act in a way they don't like and then upsets their life, while really the truth is that their mind is just acting and reacting to a set of preconditioned thought patterns that they are not consciously aware of?

"The reality of the other person is not in what he reveals to you, but in what he cannot reveal to you. Therefore, if you would understand him, listen not to what he says but rather what he does not say."

Kahlil Gibran

Discover your mind

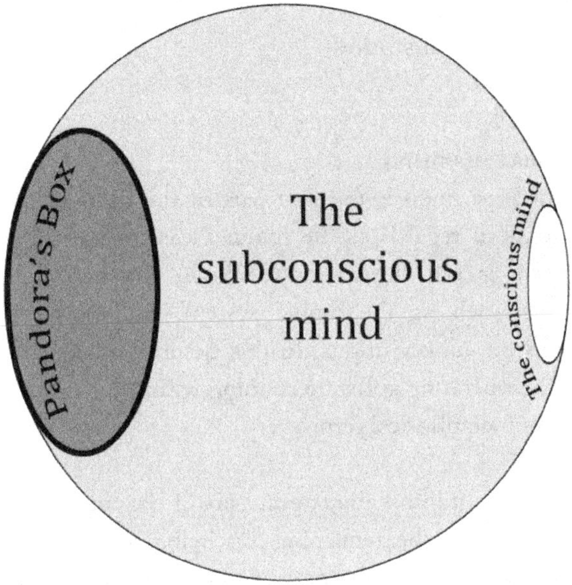

The topic of the mind is a huge and vast area which, if explained in its full purest form, it would take several books to even scratch the surface. Fortunately, to discover the con and uncover the mask the process of understanding the mind in its full form it is not necessary. Also, in all honesty, covering too much detail in regards to the mind at this stage would actually restrict learning. This is because too much information can cause the mind to overanalyse and fall into the trap of what is known as analysis paralysis, which again basically means that 'too much' information can make something so complicated that it is difficult to understand.

So, for maximum benefit we will cover the 3 most important parts of the mind.

1. **The subconscious mind**
2. **Pandora's Box**
3. **The conscious mind**

The subconscious mind

The subconscious mind is the first part of the thought processing units we will discuss in regards to the mind. Please recall once again though that the brain is not the mind; the brain (physical) has scientifically defined areas such as the limbic system, the amygdala, the corpus callosum and the hippocampus. In this description though, this mind is likened to the operating software running within the brain, hence we will discuss this in metaphorical terms.

The subconscious mind is the largest part of the mind and comprises an estimated 95%, with the remaining 5% being the conscious mind. The subconscious mind is the first part of our mind to develop and it is said that we function on a purely subconscious awareness until the age of 7 – 8 years old. After this age our conscious mind begins to form, bringing us further options of thought and ability.

The subconscious can be likened to a database of all of the information that we will experienced on a day-to-day basis throughout our lives. However, given that the human **brain** is enclosed in pure darkness (as it is in the skull), we must ask how the mind makes sense of the information the brain has correlated. Although at first glance this may appear to be immensely complicated, our mind will process information on a much simpler level than we may assume.

As mentioned, the brain itself is enclosed in darkness and therefore cannot attribute light, shape or colour to anything it processes, so detail is given to stimuli through electrical and chemical stimulation. To gain information on the world around us the brain and the mind work in harmony with each other, and the process is as follows…

1. A child will move about physically until they come into contact with an object. For example, a dog.

2. If they have never experienced a dog before, their mind will have no reference of what a dog actually is, so is therefore unable to tell what the object is.

3. The physical brain cannot think for itself and is merely an information-processing unit of all our 5 senses - sight, touch, hearing, taste and smell. So the eyes, nerve endings in our skin (touch), ears, taste buds (tongue) and olfactory (nose) all assess the all of the external information the child will come into contact with.

4. The information that our body senses is then sent to our physical brain through a path of electrical and chemical stimulation and is subsequently processed by the brain as to whether this information is one of two things: 1) is it a threat or pain? or 2) is it healthy or pleasure? (survival)

5. The mind will then interpret the brains recorded information of the physical world (pain or pleasure) and convert it into a reflected emotion which then the mind can understand. It does this by using the following scale...

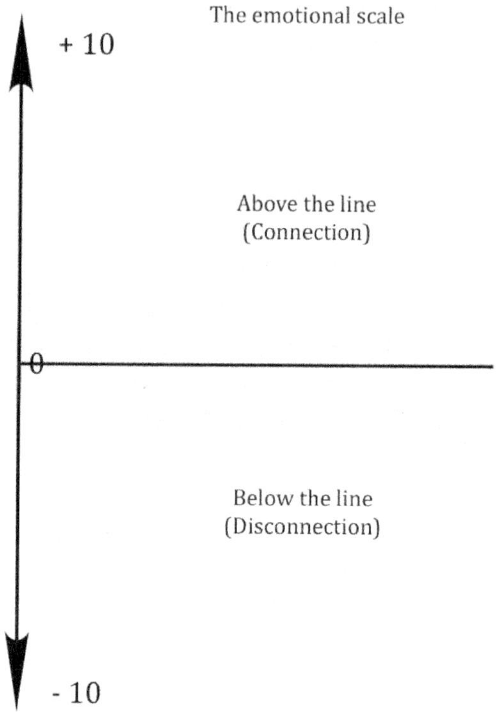

As you can see on the scale there are 3 points of reference:

The top: + 10
The middle: 0
The bottom: - 10

This scale is a rating of 'our perceived' emotional association to a physical experience. The highest is +10 and is perceived as the most pleasurable emotion. The lowest is -10 and is perceived as the most painful emotion (at this point please recall the information on the pain-pleasure principle).

6. The mind will then use all the information that the brain recorded to assess where the stimulus (or experience) belongs on the scale. If for example the sense of touch receives a pain stimulation (from a burn) and then releases stress hormones, the mind will then associate the experience of placing the hand into a stimulus, which is for example visually orange (fire) with feelings of extreme heat and a smell of smoke, as a painful experience. It will then register it in the lower section of the chart as an unhappy emotion (fear for example).
   If however a child was to eat a sweet and the sugar was to release pleasure hormones into their system, the sweet (taste) could then be registered on the scale in the higher section as pleasure (or happiness) (as we saw with the king and his meal earlier). There are obviously a great many more sensory stimulations that go into defining each experience than we have discussed here, but this is just intended to give you an outline of the process.

7. In relation to the first experience (the dog), the child may store any number of associations to this stimulus including how this particular stimulus (the dog) is in relation to the environment. In reality the brain itself will never have any idea of what a dog actually is.

8. The mind then associates the physical sensation of pain or pleasure to an emotion in relation to the dog (joy, anger, curiosity) and can therefore understand what it thinks the brain has recorded (this is where the confusion can begin). This is (for example) why some people are afraid of dogs and others are not.

9. Once the brain and mind have stored the reference point to the stimulus known as 'dog', the child has then created what is known as a **belief**. A belief is a person's internal map of the reality that they perceive. Beliefs are not actual reality, but what that persons mind believes is reality based upon their pain and pleasure responses.

A belief is comprised of two parts:
Part 1: The physiological memory of the stimulus (the sensory image = brain)
Part 2: The emotional association of that image (on the above scale = mind)

10. Once the belief system has been created in association to that stimulus, it is stored within the subconscious mind and then used as a reference point by the protector self (to be discussed soon) for future situations which the person encounters. If you will, when the mind forms a reference/belief it can be likened to recording a video of that moment in time of information and then placing it in a library (the subconscious). Then, when the person comes into contact with a similar stimulus again in the future, the mind (which is like a librarian) searches for the video containing the most stimulating memory which is 'like' this current stimulus.
    Once this recording has been located, the mind replays the video to gain what it thinks is a correct assumption of what this stimulus (today) means. The mind will then use the information that it sees on the video to assume whether this current day stimulus is pain or pleasure. However, as you can see, if the information was learned incorrectly then the mind can store an incorrect belief while 'assuming' it to be correct. This can result in the mind using an incorrect map of the world. We saw this with Joe earlier when his tutor taught incorrect information. This is where the mask and the con can create confusion from creating actions based upon this distorted reality.

So in a nutshell the brain is a neurological storehouse likened to a library full of videos of pain or pleasure. The mind then interprets these stimuluses in what it thinks is correct. These videos are then referred to by the mind when it replays them. The purpose of this is to assess and compare each and every stimulus we encounter every second of the day to determine whether it is a threat or not (pain or pleasure). The subconscious mind will assess today's world by comparing it to the past recorded videos.

For the majority of our daily lives our minds are using previous experiences to assess whether the current stimulus is pain or pleasure. This is why some people can have a panic attack upon seeing a house spider when in reality there is no physical danger. Indeed, it is their association of the spider that has been classed in the pain (or threat) part of their scale.

Pandora's Box

The myth of Pandora's Box - A Greek story of the God's

One day Zeus had given the order that man did not deserve fire, but Prometheus gave man the secret of fire even though Zeus had told him not to. Prometheus did this because he knew man needed fire for food and warmth. Zeus was furious that his order had been ignored. As punishment, Zeus chained Prometheus to a rock for many years to come.

However, Zeus wanted yet more vengeance and went after Prometheus' brother, the gentle, kind-hearted Epimetheus. Zeus did not chain Epimetheus to a rock, but had a different kind of punishment in mind.

Zeus ordered the maker of things - Hephaestus - to make Zeus a daughter, and so Hephaestus made a beautiful woman out of clay. He brought her to life, and then brought her to Zeus. Zeus named his beautiful new daughter Pandora.

Zeus knew that Epimetheus was alone. Zeus told Epimetheus that he had chained his brother to a rock, but Zeus felt sorry that this punishment had left Epimetheus without the company of his brother. So Zeus gave Pandora in marriage to Epimetheus.

Epimetheus was kind-hearted, gentle and thoughtful, but also suspicious, and although he loved Pandora he assumed Zeus was tricking him.

As a wedding gift Zeus gave them a box (though some say it was a jar), however the box was locked and it came with a note. The note said: "DO NOT OPEN." Attached to the note was a key.

Shortly after the gift had been given, Pandora's curiosity got the better of her and she opened the box. Suddenly, as she raised the lid, all the evil spirits of the world flew out - envy, sickness, hate, disease, shame and guilt, and then they plagued the world. Pandora slammed the lid shut, but it was too late as they had now escaped from the box.

Epimetheus heard her weeping and came running. Pandora opened the lid of the box to show him that it was empty. However, just before she slammed the lid shut again, one last spirit came out - the spirit of hope. The spirit of hope then began to renew the faith in all the people plagued by the other evil spirits. The spirit of hope allowed the people of the world to find confidence to carry on when times were hard.

The hidden part of the mind

As we discovered in the last section, the brain processes all the information its sees into the library inside and then the mind uses that information as a reference point. The mind will then guide us around the world by moving us away from that which it sees as pain and towards that which it sees as pleasure.

However, some situations that we encounter may be so painfully traumatic that although the brain has processed it, the effect or the emotional reaction of the experience causes too much pain for the 'conscious mind' to process (the conscious mind will be covered shortly). This may also happen if the mind has no information on how to cope with the trauma. In these situations, for example witnessing an extreme act of violence or an experience of extreme abuse, the subconscious mind has created a separate section, a hidden box in the mind if you will. The purpose of this is to in effect 'bury' the painful experiences away from the library. If the traumatic memory is buried (or supressed), the main part of the mind can no longer use it as reference. If it can no longer be used as reference then the mind will assume it is protecting the person's consciousness. If you will, imagine Pandora's Box as a cellar beneath the library - the event has still been recorded, but it is not accessible by the conscious mind.

The purpose of Pandora's Box is to protect our conscious awareness from re-experiencing too much emotional trauma all at once. This then allows us to continue our daily tasks without the intrusion of an extreme emotional reaction from remembering the original stored memory.

However, we also need to look at the following two references to how an experience may be forced into Pandora's Box...

Reference 1: The situation is actually threatening

If the situation is actually harmful to the health then it can be neurologically stored as danger. An example here would be if a person had nearly choked to death on a certain piece of food and then had a severe reaction to or phobia of that food in the future.

A trauma may also be supressed if a child is in actual physical or emotional danger in their home life by their peers.

Reference 2: A misinterpreted scenario

To understand this reference we need to recall that in some cases it is the person's perception which creates the pain-pleasure reaction, and thereby the mind can sometimes assume that the pain of the situation is much more threatening than it actually is.

Take the following example. A man and a woman are experiencing a particularly difficult time in their marriage and having an argument. Hurtful words are being thrown about when their 4-year-old child walks in the room to try and stop the argument by shouting at them to stop. If a parent in their confusion and frustration was to say to the child that it was 'the child's fault' that the man and woman were having an argument, then the child may believe this to be a pure fact. The truth would be that it was the parent's inability to control their emotions and not the child's fault. However, if the child blamed themselves for the situation, it could have a devastating effect for years to come.

Each person's story is different

Although in the above example I used a particularly unpleasant experience, many children can receive trauma in many ways. A trauma is anything which 'that person' sees as a trauma as they are unable to cope with it. It is irrelevant if another person sees it as a trauma or not. If 'you' feel upset about something you have experienced, then it is a trauma for you.

If your mind felt the situation at the time was too much to handle, then it may have stored it in your Pandora's Box without you being aware of it.

As I mentioned earlier in this book though, you MUST be able to own your story and your experience (though it requires strategy).

If you have an experience stored as a trauma, then it is a trauma for YOU. It is not important at this stage what anybody else tells you what you should be feeling (such 'as it wasn't that bad' or 'don't read too much into it') as that is their denial or ignorance. If you have had a traumatic experience - real or over-amplified by the mind - your experience is STILL trauma and you must own that! The truth for both of the above references (real or over-amplified) is that your mind will be assuming the situation or experience is real (replaying past videos) and will react in accordance. It is just doing its best with the information it has access to and no amount of pretending otherwise will change that. However, as you will see through this book, these stored true or misperceived reactions **can** be updated and resolved.

The protector self (the mind's guard)

The subconscious mind is responsible for the perception of the pain and pleasure drives that we discussed earlier. However, as the subconscious mind has no ability to control itself it has created its own guidance system to support the entire structure. Here I will introduce another powerful part of your mind, which I call the 'protector self'.

The protector self is the part of your mind which deciphers whether there is an urgent need to protect the conscious awareness part of the mind from recalling a memory of threat or overwhelming pain. It will do this if it assumes there is too much danger (real or perceived). The protector self is also one of the main reference points in relation to the mask and the con.

The protector self has its own internal referencing system, which I will call the internal cinema screen. On this screen the protector self will

watch replays of the recorded videos to predict whether the situation in front of us in 'real time' is a threat or not.
Through this the protector self will compare what is perceived in the 'real' world to that of the internal memory system to determine whether something is a pain or a pleasure. If the protector self assumes that the current-day situation (for example a business meeting) is a threat by comparing it to the last most stimulating or associated memory, it will then immediately try to move that person away from the perceived threat. We see this when a person puts their hand near fire and usually pulls it away even before they realise what has happened - the action was driven by the protector self.

The same is true for that of pleasure. If the mind observes something which it believes will be pleasurable, it moves towards the source of its observation and will keep trying to gain pleasure. Sometimes, even when the source of pleasure is removed or denied, the mind will keep repeating the pattern. We see this when a person is rejected by a partner (or a marriage break) and then the rejected partner keeps attempting to restart the relationship. Even though they know in their conscious mind the relationship is over, their protector self has become confused (and the subconscious is in denial) and is attempting to reconnect. It is however the subconscious as a whole (not the conscious mind) which is still trapped in time and has not updated or come to terms with the situation today.

To build on the image even further, please imagine the following…

1. The subconscious library is now stocked with a range of videos containing information on what the mind assumes is the world based upon the pain-pleasure experience.

2. The protector self is sat in the subconscious mind and looks at the world through our eyes (today's reality), assessing the stimulus we encounter.

3. When the protector self sees something through our eyes (a dog for example), the protector self will go to the library and look for the video of information that represents the image it sees (an 'association' of the dog).

4. The protector self will use the information from the past video (played upon the internal cinema screen) to determine if this current experience means pain or pleasure. If the video recording says that the dog is pain, the protector self will move away from the dog. If the video says that the dog means pleasure, the protector self will move towards the dog (to pet or stroke it).

5. With all these experiences so far the protector self will allow the memory to flow into the awareness along with the emotional feeling of pain and pleasure. So, for example we may remember a dog biting us (pain) or happily playing with the dog (pleasure).

6. However, if our protector self encounters something that is associated to a memory that is stored in Pandora's Box, the protector self will hit an alarm to release a powerful surge of stress hormones into the body to move us away from the threat urgently. Yet if the memory is buried in Pandora's Box the protector self cannot show us 'why' (consciously) we are moving away from the situation, but will just move us away. When people have this reaction and cannot attribute any memory to it, they can sometimes class it as irrational behaviour. As we can now see though, the behaviour is not irrational to your protector self as it is functioning from what 'it' sees as reality. Your protector self is therefore functioning perfectly well, but it is just referring to information that has not been updated and is not accessible to the conscious mind.

Again, please note that 'updating' this information requires much more strategy than simply writing down your goals and a few meditation sessions. Suppressed memories within Pandora's Box can be (in some cases) extremely complicated (but not beyond repair). Each memory could be compounded by many emotional structures weaving a tapestry of apparent confusion. If you have had no training on how the mind works, finding your way around this maze can sometimes appear to be an endless challenge. There is a big difference between knowing this information and living it!

A little more on the subconscious mind

It is said that the subconscious mind can process many millions of "bits" of information each second. Such information would be physical things such as the heartbeat, breathing, digestion, talking, and muscular movement. It is also aware of the emotional side such as awareness of safety, awareness of emotional overload, the control of guilt, shame or love and all of the other stimulus and motor functions we experience every second.

However, although all of this information is being processed continually (even as we sleep), most of it does not filter through to our conscious awareness. The conscious mind as we will discuss in a moment is much smaller and therefore unable to cope with such demands. If this information was to filter through to our conscious mind it would be completely overwhelmed and thus unable to function.

The subconscious is powerful beyond our wildest dreams and the greatest minds of our time are still making new advancements in relation to its complexities. To date nobody really knows what its potential is truly capable of. However, as you will see through the pages of this book, it is our guide and master unless we discover how to gain control.

The subconscious mind is very functional in its processes and does what it has learned to do. It will also keep repeating a learned function or a protection programme until it is taught otherwise. The purpose of this auto-repeat function is to be assumed for efficiency. A set response or repeated pattern to a certain stimulus is classed as a reaction (re-action), which broken down in sections simply means 'a repeated action' or loop.

Although the subconscious is immensely powerful, it is still only following rules. These are the rules determined by pain and pleasure defined by past experiences stored in the library. Again this is not actual reality, but what the mind has assumed is reality. Thus it is just like a computer programme following a script of predefined guidelines. However though, it is essential to know that the subconscious does not have the ability to change the information stored within itself. This means that if there is a limiting belief stored within the Pandora's Box within the subconscious, it is in fact cut off from the very part of the mind which can update the memory (the conscious mind). **Yet disconnection will only happen as long as the mind is experiencing internal conflict.** Once the strategy of re-linking the two minds together has been learned (inner harmony), the mind can naturally update any stored trauma.

NB: *I have personally heard some therapists, authors and even medical doctors claim that it is a 'fact' that some traumas are so deeply rooted within the mind that they are unable to be released. In other words, they are claiming that some people are doomed to walk the path of anxiety for the rest of their life. In my opinion I believe that any trauma can be worked through providing the correct support and strategy is used, thereby allowing the person to live a full and wholesome life. Not only have I personally seen profound breakthroughs that myself and my own clients have created, but there is also phenomenal evidence nowadays that proves that the mind is capable of resolving extremely deep traumas. For further study on this area please refer to the fantastic book 'The brain that changes itself'. Also, another ground breaking therapist to refer to is one of the most profound trauma therapists that I have seen, Dr Peter Levine.*

Yes, it is the truth that some people are so intertwined within their coping mechanisms that it feels almost impossible to break free from the reactions, but again with the correct support big changes can happen.

When discussing this area though we also need to take into account so many other areas such as hormone balance, lifestyle, and the effect of drugs or alcohol. However, my message to anybody reading is do not let anybody tell you that you are stuck in the loop forever if they have not tried 'every' possible option! Again…QUESTION EVERYTHING!

The conscious mind

The conscious mind is the last part of the thought processing units we will discuss in regards to the mind. If controlled by our focus the conscious mind can exercise a great power over the rest of the mind and it can be very powerful in its nature. However, even with all the power the conscious mind has, we still need to remember that it is only 5% of the total mind and therefore at a great disadvantage in relation to control. The conscious mind's function is to bring our perception into the here and now, present tense, not in the future or past (like the internal cinema screen). Consciousness can be classed as the quality or state of awareness that we experience in that moment - to see current situations as they are rather than what we may assume they are based upon our projections of the internal cinema screen from recorded videos.

An example of the conscious mind taking ownership of our mind would be as follows:

A person with arachnophobia (the fear of spiders) is sitting in their lounge and has started to notice that they feel anxious. They are not too sure of what has triggered the anxiety until they notice out of the corner of their eye a large house spider on a chair opposite to them. The person's immediate reaction (from the internal cinema screen) is that they start to panic and their body feels very tense. This reaction is purely subconscious as there is no actual danger from a house spider.

To gain control the person stops and takes a deep breath, then brings their conscious mind into full awareness and sees the situation for what it actually is. Whilst in conscious awareness they can see the actual reality rather than the projected reality. Once in this state the person then realises that the 'huge spider' is not actually a spider but simply a clump of black hair from their dog. However, their subconscious mind created a 'hallucination' of a big spider and then reflected that upon the internal cinema screen and forced it into the person's imagination. So, to the person's perception (in that moment) the spider was real for them.

By gaining conscious (present tense) awareness their body then stops releasing the stress hormones as there is no longer a threat. Their physiology starts to return to normal and they can continue on with their day.

Now even though the conscious mind has the ability to bring our attention back to the present moment, it is still only an estimated 5% of the total mind. As such, its strength and control in relation to the rest of the subconscious is lesser in comparison. Therefore the conscious mind's power can be quite limited when it tries to use 'its' power to continually maintain a present-tense focus.

We can see this in such situations where a person may be having challenges in a job role. An example here would be if the person was having a challenge with another member of the team and it was continually on their mind creating stress.

The scene may unfold as follows…

1. The stressed member of staff is worrying about their team member and the stress is starting to negatively affect their health.

2. The stressed member of staff then starts to use visualisation exercises to bring them back to the present tense to ease the stress (as in the above example with the spider/dog hair).

3. This may work temporarily, but the stress keeps returning to the confusion of the stressed member of staff.

4. The stressed member of staff is unaware that their protector self has been using the subconscious mind or Pandora's Box as reference and is panicking that being in the 'present moment' is going to ignore a deeper 'assumed threat' (from the internal cinema screen / a past looped belief).

5. If the protector self assumes a greater threat from the conscious mind taking over it may choose to continually override the conscious mind to protect the member of staff from the 'assumed threat'.

6. Although the protector self is misperceiving the situation by referring to the past, it will still believe that it is correct in doing

so; as the protector self has access to more of the mind than the conscious mind, it can and will override it if it feels threatened. If it feels threatened it will take steps to protect itself from the 'assumed threat' (the replayed video tape).

This is one of the reasons that just using 'thinking positive' and simple 'mindfulness' techniques can often only offer a quick fix if they are competing against a deeper past associated belief within the subconscious mind.

Being present is essential!

Although I have just discussed that the protector self may panic if it assumes the conscious mind 'being present' is ignoring a potential threat, it does not mean that we should simply just give up trying, but also to use subconscious strategy too.

When working through the mask and the con it is essential that the mind remains as present and focused as possible to gain the greatest clarity of the situation. This is the reason for making continual notes, as doing so will anchor the mind to the present moment and can stop what is known as the 'hijack'!

A **hijack** is where the protector self will override the conscious mind in order to keep the person safe from what it assumes is a threat. We can see a hijack happen when a person is trying to reassure themselves in a stressful moment but their mind keeps refocusing on their worries.

More about the conscious mind

The conscious mind is the analyst part of the thinking process. It has been said that it processes about 7 bits of information per second (+/- 2 bits) of the millions of bits of information that are in the environment focus at any given moment in time.

The bits of information available are things such as the clock ticking, body temperature, breathing rate and somebody shouting in the distance. However, when our mind needs to be focused and concentrate on the task at hand, many of these bits of information are screened out by the conscious mind.

The conscious mind is the part that allows a person to experience and become aware of the selected information it chooses. Once it has selected the most relevant information it will then move that into focus so that it can be acted upon.
However, if the hijack is triggered, the protector self will override the conscious present-tense awareness and force the internal cinema screen projection into the mind's focus. This can be distressing if it keeps happening and can cause confusion between the two apparent realities. This reaction is what many people may class as 'irrational thought' patterns, though the reaction is not irrational, it is just that the protector self assumes the internal cinema screen projection is more important or vital.

The searchlight

Another metaphor for the conscious mind could be a helicopter scanning an area of a forest in the dark. There are many bits of information that the helicopter could pick up such as the types of trees, woodland animals, rocks and lakes etc., but if the helicopter is specifically looking for a camp fire for risk of causing more damage it will screen out anything that it is not looking for. This does not mean that it will not see all the other information (trees and lakes etc.); it just means that it will not shine the main searchlight on them. This then allows the focus to remain on the camp fire. This is known as conscious screening (or selective attention / focus).

So just to reiterate, the conscious mind can make decisions and does have some power. The problems occur when it is in conflict with its more powerful counterpart (the subconscious). In this reaction confusion may occur as it feels as though two parts of the mind are fighting for power…and in effect, they are! This can give a person a push-pull feeling as their mind is trying to accomplish two actions at the same time. The conscious is attempting to be present and the subconscious is reacting to the replay of videos from the internal cinema screen. The push-pull feeling of confusion is very common and is the result of the two minds attempting to gain control of each other. When this conflict is occurring in the mind, the protector self can feel that there is a threat and protect the person by releasing stress hormones into the body. These stress hormones will speed the body up, which can in some cases can cause further stress reactions.

Can will power change a habit?

An example of when the conscious mind attempts to overpower the subconscious mind is very apparent when a person makes a decision to change a habit. The reason the habit is there is because of a pattern stored within the subconscious mind (the desire to smoke cigarettes, for example). However, when the conscious mind attempts to change or overpower the subconscious drive, although it can do it temporarily, the subconscious is too powerful and has more control. Eventually the subconscious regains control and the old habit remains. An example of this is the famous 'New Year's resolution' in which a person desires to change a habit. The reason most people do not succeed at changing their habit is because they are using conscious willpower alone. However, willpower from the conscious mind 'only' is often doomed before it starts.

Take for example a person who 'wills' themselves to stop smoking and they focus upon this 'new' habit 3 times a day for 20 minutes at a time. This can be recognised as a dedicated effort (60 minutes out of a busy day). However, on the other hand the subconscious mind will focus on keeping the habit continually throughout the day and night much more often than the conscious mind. Also, the subconscious has linked lots of pleasure to the habit or it would not keep doing it.

Therefore the only way to change a habit permanently is to change the subconscious belief (or a Pandora's Box loop). To attain this level of connection it will require that the subconscious is allowed to 'consciously realise' why the habit is there and 'why' the mind is gaining pleasure from it.

Another example of the conscious and subconscious conflict for power would be to imagine a five-year-old boy holding his father's hand (the dad is a 20-stone muscular wrestler). The little boy can pull his dad's hand and his dad walks, but who's really in control? If the little boy stepped into a busy road the dad would simply pull him back, giving the little boy no control.

However, another point to note and which is in direct relation to the mask and the con is that habits may be intertwined with other habits or coping mechanisms and then buried many levels deep. Smoking or eating too much sugary food for example may be created because of 4 or 5 compounded levels of coping mechanisms (or masks).

Take the following...

- ⇓ A person could smoke cigarettes to feel they release stress
- ⇓ They may be stressed as their body is too sensitive to stress reactions they feel each day
- ⇓ They may be sensitive as they eat too much sugar which then affects their hormone levels
- ⇓ They eat sugar as it gives them a quick boost of energy in the day
- ⇓ They may need the quick energy as they are tired in the day
- ⇓ They may be tired as they stay up late on social media
- ⇓ They stay on social media as they are lonely
- ⇓ They are lonely as they do not socialise with real people
- ⇓ They may not socialise because they believe they are not good enough as a person

The list goes on...

Here we can see that if the person tries to give up smoking, their protector self may see the end result of having to face up to the anxiety that they don't feel good enough.
So in the above case, to simply 'stop smoking' may cause more stress than the smoking, so the smoking continues as it is the lesser of the two evils to the protector self.

State recall

At this point it important to recall how the two minds (conscious and subconscious) differ in the way they see the world. As we have covered, the conscious mind sees today as it is, however the subconscious sees a very different world.

Have you ever noticed that many people upon connection to their anxieties may feel so overpowered or overwhelmed even though 'logically' there is no apparent reason for their reaction?

One key difference between the conscious and subconscious is that the subconscious has no understanding of 'time'. All it sees is the video recording on the internal cinema screen and reacts from that. If the internal cinema screen was up to date then the subconscious mind would function from 'today's' environment, however in many cases it has old and out-of-date programmes.

Take for example the following;

1. A person was bitten by a dog when they were 4 years old.

2. Their mind has stored this as intense trauma and it was then suppressed in Pandora's Box.

3. The person now 20 years on sees a dog that looks similar to the dog that bit them when they were 4 years old.

4. Their protector self, unable to understand a time difference, may now assume that this 'new' dog is the same one that bit them and start to react stressfully.

5. The reason the protector self reacts so stressfully is that it has performed a 'state recall' and assumed that the person is still the same age and competency as when the dog bit them (4 years old) (an internal cinema screen reaction).

6. The person's conscious mind now describes this 'stress reaction' as 'irrational' and is confused.

If a memory has not been updated, the protector self will assume that the image on the internal cinema screen is the current reality and protect itself accordingly. The memory could be stored so intensely that the mind could continually replay that video each time the person sees 'any' dog. As the subconscious mind has no idea when the initial bite happened, it could assume that it was recently and act as if it was still an immediate threat.

This is why some people can observe something from their childhood and immediately feel like they are a child again. When an intensely stimulating video plays from the subconscious mind, if it overpowers the conscious mind (hijacking) it can return the mind to the exact same emotional state as when we first experienced it.

When I have been coaching in 1-to-1 sessions I have witnessed clients' voices and body language change to that of a frightened child when talking about a traumatic situation from when they were very young, for example an act of violence or sexual abuse.

Another trigger that more people may be able to relate to more easily (and one that usually brings a smile in class) is when one of our parents may say something to us as a full-grown adult and we may automatically react like a child or even have a stroppy tantrum. This is where some people may say they are acting irrationally, whereas in truth it is simply that the subconscious mind has replayed a video in relation to that parent, put the mind back in the most recorded state (if it was to shout at a parent, for example) and then re-triggered that reaction. However, in many cases this happens so quickly that the conscious mind doesn't even realise what has happened!

The subconscious is almost childlike in its simplicity. It is very powerful, but when in the grip of old out-of-date belief systems (videos), without the guidance of updated videos, it could quite easily seem to end up out of control. Through this book I will cover options of how to create a harmony between these two parts of your mind and then gain power over your reactions. To gain inner peace it is essential to end the battle within!

Chapter summary

Know yourself

As we are rarely taught profound learnings about the human mind in school, many people can feel quite confused when their mind acts or reacts in a manner which they do not require it to. This can sometimes be classed as irrational behaviour or irrational thinking. However, the mind is not irrational - it is just that the person may not understand why it is acting the way it is.

The pain-pleasure principle

The mind will naturally move away from pain to protect itself and towards pleasure for growth. Through this process it can allow the greatest opportunity for the survival of the self. However, due to the formation of the mind a person can override these drives by forming a 'belief' of what they see as pain or pleasure.

If the mind can create a confusion of what it thinks pain or pleasure is, it can on one hand be an advantage, but on the other it can be extremely dangerous.

Take a moment and become aware of the 'hijacks' in your life. Every time you are trying to focus on something and your mind completely or partially blocks your attention, you will be experiencing a hijack. When you do feel your attention suddenly taken, look within to see if you can feel what triggered it. Was it something you thought of or was it in your immediate environment?

The brain and the mind

Here we discussed that the brain is the physiological part of our body and is likened to a computer. The mind then runs through the brain, interpreting the physiological stimulus into images and emotions.

The three parts of the mind

The mind is comprised of 3 parts as a metaphorical process. The subconscious is the storehouse of all of the memories interpreted by the brain. Pandora's Box is the suppressed part of the subconscious to stop overwhelming memories hijacking the conscious. The conscious is the present tense and today-based focus and attention.

The protector self

The part which I call the protector self is the guardian between the three parts of the mind. The protector self's function is to restrict any traumatic memories from surfacing and to also automatically move a person away from pain and towards pleasure. At times it may feel as though the protector self is acting in a manner which is unhealthy, but the reason for this is that it is using old or out-of-date images on the internal cinema screen.

Take a moment and become aware of your protector self in daily life when you find yourself wanting to avoid certain tasks but may not be aware why. Any time you find yourself feeling that your behaviour is 'irrational', it will be your protector self hijacking you.

Belief patterns may not be straightforward

Although many people still subscribe to the idea that belief patterns are relatively easy to change and it may only require 30 – 60 days, this can often be an illusion depending upon the structure of the belief. As the mind is only concerned with moving away from pain and towards pleasure, if there is an unhealthy habit in place, it therefore must mean that the mind is deriving some form of pleasure. Many people may claim that the cigarette is addictive hormonally and although this can happen, there may be more to it. If the cigarette is covering up a suppressed pain, to the mind the pleasure association being created by the cigarette is covering up the pain. Therefore, the protector self may assume that the cigarette is actually creating pleasure (by the removal of a deeper pain - the lesser of two evils in perception). Therefore, if the smoking declines the protector self may attempt to keep the habit to cover a deeper pain. This is one reason why so many habits seem so difficult to break.

Take a moment and list all the times that you have tried to break a habit and it has not worked and check if you can actually recall the 'real' reason you didn't attain the result you wanted.

5

Belief Structures

As we have covered a lot of information so far, it is important to start bringing everything into alignment by using a visual images, or if you will into storyboard sections. The reason for this is that it is easier to remember a story than lots of facts that may not seem to correlate without prior knowledge of the brain and the mind.

Rather than reviewing the actual brain and how it stores the information through electrical and chemical impulses, we will now focus attention on beliefs. These are the core as to where the whole system starts to appear to misalign.

Automatic beliefs as you may recall are structured in the following manner:

1. The brain interprets the actual information we encounter through our 5 senses.

2. Those impulses are then stored in the brain and neurology but we have no way to interpret them as they are just stimulations moving us away from pain and towards pleasure.

3. These impulses are reinterpreted by the subconscious mind into videos and visual images of what it 'assumed' happened.

4. If any of these impulses are deemed too intense for the consciousness to handle, they are moved into Pandora's Box and suppressed. The subconscious assumes that they are too intense by the skills and adaptability we had in relation to handling the situation in regards to our safety we had at the time of the challenging situation.

5. The videos are classed as beliefs and are stored in the subconscious mind as what the mind assumes is a factual representation of the world. Only the most stimulating or high arousal experiences are stored as the main beliefs.

6. When we encounter a situation today the protector self within the subconscious mind will then put the video in the player of the closest association to this situation and project the video onto a screen (our internal cinema screen). Then the last most stimulating experience closely representing this experience today will be used as a reference for how to act and react to the 'todays' experience in the current moment.

7. Although the mind may not allow access to the Pandora's Box memories, it will still use them as a reference for today's experiences. This can then create confusion in many situations.

Perception is reality

The above understanding then leads us to the next part, which is classed as **perception is reality**. This in base terms means what the protector self 'perceives' on the internal cinema screen (which is from the videos stored in times past) will appear as real to us in the current moment.

An example of this would be if we were to see a spider and have linked pain to the image. The protector self viewing this on the internal cinema screen would cause a re-action and move us away. The anxiety of spiders will appear real to us even though we may not consciously understand why (as we can only view life through the conscious mind).

Even though in reality we actually have nothing to be anxious of (from a house spider), the anxiety will remain in a reactive state until we do either one or both of the only options.

1. To remain completely conscious at all times (which is immensely challenging due to the thousands of other stimuli in our daily lives).

2. Update the video within the subconscious mind. Again, depending upon the intensity and complexity of the belief this can in some cases also be very challenging as it may be wrapped around a few or many levels of compound coping mechanisms. Therefore, to only work on what is consciously apparent may make no difference at all.

The vortex of creating beliefs

Although the brain and mind are doing their best to keep the 'self' safe and healthy at all times, sometimes the assessment of the situation can be a little too assumptive. The brain is a recording machine and as such will just take in all the information it sees.

So if for example when we are small we may see another sibling scream and panic upon seeing a house spider. If at that moment in time we are vulnerable and have no reference to what a house spider is, we may see this intense emotional reaction by our loved one as something that we should also store as a potential threat. Then, if the subconscious mind stores this as the fact, we will then react in future as if it is, but may feel we have no real reference of why the spider causes the reaction, i.e. the spider did not actually hurt us.

Beliefs are not facts

Bringing all the information we have discussed so far into the light, it is now clear to see the confusion that misinterpreted beliefs can cause. This confusion happens because:

The protector self assumes the stored beliefs to be real and factual and acts upon them as if they were real and factual!

The definition of a 'fact' is something that can be proven to be true, such as a distance, mathematical equation or any measurable situation. However, even though a belief is a recorded situation that may have been based on truth at the time it may not be permanently a fact. For example…

- The measurement of one kilometre will always be that length and therefore can be classed as a fact
- A belief such as "I am a failure" cannot be a fact as not everybody would agree and is subject to opinion.

Other examples of beliefs would be:

"I am good enough"

"I know my home will be there when I wake up in the morning"

"People will smile if I smile at them"

"If I raise my voice people will hear me more clearly"

However, this is not to say that all the above beliefs will be true for everybody, because beliefs are created from experiences. Therefore a person's beliefs can only be in relation to what experiences they have been exposed to.

As the subconscious mind cannot see the world (but rather just as a mass of sensations, it can only do its best with what it has to work with. A belief if we recall is made up of 2 parts:

Part 1: The physiological memory of the stimulus (the sensory image = brain)
Part 2: The emotional association of that image (= mind)

So remember, beliefs are not reality, but what we internally perceiving as reality!

The law of expectation

The law of expectation is one of the most powerful and governing belief structures in the human mind and it can set the structure of a person's life and determine the level of success in any given area that they apply themselves. This law states that:

We subconsciously expect to happen what we believe to be true, and dismiss other options.

The reason for this is that the subconscious mind will always align to its internal reference points (beliefs) because that is the mind's best assumed option of survival and efficiency. This is however assuming that the belief is the best option for that time and the most fitting. Though, as we noticed it is possible for the subconscious to store outdated beliefs and still assume that they are the best option. Though this can cause conflict in the emotions, as we can see in the next example…

The innocent child

Take a small child who is completely dependent on their parents for survival and was then humiliated when they were too young to be able to defend themselves. For this to happen the parents may have intimidated the child with threats that if the child did not accept the insults and act submissively, then they would disown the child which would cause the child to starve or be unwanted (a dark threat to a child and an example I would prefer not to use as an author, but it gets the message across). The child faced with this traumatic situation may then form a misguided belief that…

"I have to accept abusive from others as I am dependant on them for my survival"

If the child had only ever been exposed to abusive people as opposed to kind people, they may form the belief that ONLY abusive people provide them with food, shelter and water. Also that as a person they have to obey their peers as they are not good enough to look after themselves.

"Our environment, the world in which we live and work, is a mirror of our attitudes and expectations."

Earl Nightingale

If the child was to store this belief in their subconscious mind (or more likely Pandora's Box), the child (now an adult) when looking for a job or buying a house will be using the reference of the belief (if they have not updated it) that "I have to accept abusive from others as I am dependant on them for my survival" and start to act in accordance to this parameter (and actually align) to find people who display these characteristics. Beliefs are our reality!

From an outsider's point of view this may seem like insanity, but to the person's mind (which is simply following what it thinks is correct and the best option for survival at the time the belief was formed) it is just simply following an old belief process. The mind may seem limited by using this process, but in reality it is the only representation of the world it knows. It is just that their beliefs in their mind will appear to be making errors if they have no knowledge of how to update it.

A metaphor for this would be a person buying a computer for the first time and adding a file or a downloaded programme into the main driver system in the computer which can make it seem to act erratically. The computer is actually acting correctly in accordance to the new parameters which it now follows – even though it can in some cases leave the computer unusable to the operator. The computer is not faulty, it has just been altered by the computer's owner who was not aware of what they were doing or had no knowledge of what results their actions would create.

Your mind works perfectly, no matter how anxious, self-doubting or emotionally confused you may feel sometimes. Erratic emotions are simply misaligned out-of-date belief patterns stored in the subconscious databanks!

The self-fulfilling prophecy loop

As our minds are made up of collections of beliefs, naturally the protector self will attempt to predict the outcome of a situation that we encounter in order to keep us safe from harm, however this predicting can sometimes be the very thing that causes further pain and confusion.

For example let us take Joe from the story earlier who was taught the wrong information before he moved to London and was then sacked from his job because he made a mistake. From that experience he may have formed the belief of:

"Employers will reject me because I made a mistake"

The error of the belief here though is that:

1. He is assuming that 'all' employers will reject him (generalisation)
2. That he made a mistake and that will be permanently held against him

However, although some employers may reject him, obviously the belief is incorrect as it is only based on one experience, but let us look deeper at what may happen with Joe in another interview if he held this belief and see how the self-fulfilling prophecy unfolds:

1. Joe decides to apply for another job.

2. Joe believes that interviewers will reject him (his current belief).

3. He applies with ABC company, but when he rang up the company secretary to ask if there were any jobs available, his internal cinema screen was flashing up images of his last job and he is now worried that this company will do the same. Applying for this job is now seen as a potential pain or threat by his protector self.

4. The company secretary noticed Joe's voice had a flat tone to it and assumed he was nervous, but also held in their mind that he may be of low quality energy. The reason Joe's voice was flat was because his protector self was trying to move away from the potential pain (on the internal cinema screen – applying for the job only to be rejected).

5. Joe got the interview but during the meeting his body language was slumped, his voice was flat and he didn't look enthusiastic (law of expectation). Again, the reason for this was because his internal cinema screen was using the belief "Employers will reject me because I made a mistake" and is now assuming that the owner of ABC company will reject him too. So, in this assumption he is preparing himself for the rejection by acting in apathy.

6. The owner of the company sees Joe's low energy as an indication that he would be a poor quality member of staff and tells Joe that he has not got the job (self-fulfilling prophecy).

7. Joe justifies this with the belief "Employers will reject me because I made a mistake" when really it was his body language and tone that caused him to get rejected.

The self-fulfilling prophecy is a situation in which we create the outcome that we assume is going to happen based upon our prediction of the future. This information is derived from past experiences. We could then 'blame' the outcome on the current situation (Joe could assume or make the excuse that the employer was hiring from within or he wanted to employ a female) but in many cases the outcome is created from our own hidden beliefs and actions.

Is there more to this though?

Is the mind really this straightforward though? Is it just a simple case of unlocking one belief pattern and then the rest goes away? Well, as I mentioned, personally I feel this is what a great deal of the personal development world would have us believe. However, what if what we 'think' we are looking at isn't what we are actually looking at? For every cause there is always an effect. We can assume that a belief may make us act in a certain way, but what if the effect we experience is not as straightforward as we assume? What if our actions and reactions are actually being driven from a seemingly unrelated event that would appear to have no logical pattern of connection? Well, in many cases this is what is happening. Welcome to Life Beyond the Mask!

Chapter summary

Beliefs are not reality but what we perceive as reality

It is vitally important as you read through this book that you keep in your mind that a belief is not reality but what we perceive is reality. Although it is the truth that some beliefs may be based upon a fact, that is different than all beliefs being fact.

Take a moment and list out all of the beliefs which you believe to be the truth but are actually holding you back in life (e.g. I should be perfect). Then reflect upon what impact each of these beliefs are having in your life.

Overly painful or unresolved memories are suppressed into Pandora's Box

The mind is always doing its best to keep your conscious mind protected from overwhelming pain. If you faced a situation in your past where you did not have sufficient resources to deal with the emotional pain at that time, then your mind may have supressed the memory and may still be referring to it, believing it is relevant today. The only thing is that it may still be looping in that time, thinking it is today.

Take a moment and ask yourself of any situations which have happened in your life which although you feel you could cope with today (or not) would have been too overwhelming for you as a child and therefore may have been supressed. Only do this if it feels comfortable to do so. Some of these practices may require further support.

Acting upon a belief

There are two action potentials that we can have; the first is a reaction and the second is responsibility. A reaction is also known as a repeated action and is a programme where the mind will automatically act upon a belief which is stored within. A responsibility action is simply where a person can step back in the moment and choose what they want to say or do without feeling pressured. This can be broken down into response-ability.

Take a moment and observe the situations in life which cause you stress. Review each of these in turn and ask yourself if when in these situations you are reacting or able to be response-able.

Law of expectation

The law of expectation deems that we expect to see in our world what we believe is going to happen. For example, if a person expects other people to treat them with respect and somebody was rude to them, they may justify it as the other person was having a bad day and that they will be nicer next time. The mind can also screen out information which contradicts what they believe to be true. This can also be known as cognitive dissonance.

Take a moment and ask yourself which expectations you have about life, both positive and negative.

Self-fulfilling prophecy

The self-fulfilling prophecy deems that we will subconsciously create the outcome that we expect to happen. If a person walks into a networking event and expects to be rejected they may unknowingly start acting very dry or flat in their tone of voice, which may not feel appealing to other people and can then create a disconnection. The opposite can also happen, where a person is so convinced that they will succeed that they again unknowingly take actions which create the expected result.

Take a reflective look at your life and ask yourself what actions you may be taking which are creating results that you do not want. Then compare these to their opposite or positive actions you take.

6

Stress, Fear and Anxiety

The words stress, fear and especially anxiety are often used by millions of people all over the world to describe their feelings in challenging situations. Obviously it depends on whereabouts in the world you are and also who specifically you speak to, but one thing is for sure - stress, fear and anxiety reactions are reaching epidemic levels for many people.

Although many people will say that they feel stress, fear and anxiety…what exactly are they? And how are they created?

NOTE: *In this chapter I will be using the term 'adrenaline' to refer to the hormone that triggers the speeding up of the body and emotions (though the actual name for adrenaline is epinephrine). However, there are other hormones (and many other physiological reactions) that are also involved in the stress reaction. For this chapter I will be giving a basic physiological and emotional overview. Further study on the stress reaction is highly recommended for your own benefit.*

Stress reactions are normal!

Stress overload is a reaction that millions of people suffer from each and every day. However, that is not to say that all stress is harmful; a healthy amount of stress in the body is actually healthy for motivation and movement. The harm and discomfort starts when the stress levels become too high and force the body into overdrive or burnout. It is usually the after-effects of stress that are much more unpleasant than the initial stress reaction itself. Continual stress reactions can lead to sleepless nights, arguments, anger, loss of health and a list of other symptoms that have an adverse effect on health and wellbeing.

The initial reaction of stress (which is also known as fight, flight or freeze) is in itself one of the most valuable functions we have in our physiology. Yet if we do not understand how it functions within the body and mind, it can it be immensely disturbing to our daily life. In many cases it is easy to become its slave, running backwards and forwards to avoid its wrath and power. If the stress reaction is not understood and tamed, it can easily grow far beyond control through sheer exhaustion of the physical and emotional resources.

The feelings of stress are well known, but the understanding of how it affects the body and mind may not be as clearly understood. How many times have we felt that gripping tightness in the chest or shaky limbs as we watch the clock tick away, drawing us closer to that dreaded event that we would rather avoid? Or maybe it is our heart beating so loud that it feels like it may punch its way through our very ribcage? Or what about the common feeling of wanting to be sick or just to run away as quickly as possible and deal with the consequences tomorrow?

You are not alone!

Some of the above (and other) symptoms may be very common to many people in daily life. There are also a surprising number of people who can feel that they are alone in having these reactions. However, if you have ever felt that you are alone in experiencing these reactions, you are mistaken. The release of stress hormones into the bloodstream under situations of actual threat or internal cinema screen threat will happen in every human being alive, as stressful reactions are part of our physiology. This is of course unless there has been medical or nutritional intervention or a deformity of the adrenal glands / other organs.

Some people can find it quite surprising when they hear that trained fighters, police or the armed forces will actually be feeling these stress reactions when in challenging situations, but rest assured, they do! They may be able to handle their reactions and appear to the outside world as calm, but their body will naturally be releasing the stress hormones if they are in danger. If you would like to test this for yourself you could perhaps go and speak to firefighters, school teachers with challenging children or similar high-pressure roles. Of course, you will get the odd few of these that claim they don't react, but most of this may be bravado. Yes, it is possible that there will be a small percentage of these people who have become so used to feeling the effects (or they know they can handle the situation) that they release less, but many will still be in a reactive phase in the moment of threat. Again though, this can be cross-referenced with the chapter covering the pain-pleasure principle. Remember, it is the mind's perception which derives what is pain or pleasure.

The trigger

Throughout each and every moment of the day, the mind (including the protector self) is continually scanning the surroundings and assessing each situation carefully (whilst, if we recall, pattern matching with the recorded videos). When the protector self perceives a situation today to which it matches a potential threat to something in the past, the body (in order to protect itself more efficiently) releases adrenal hormones into the bloodstream. The adrenaline (and other hormones) will ask no questions; they just do their job, which is to speed up the body and mind. They do this in order to help the body to become stronger and escape from danger (a turbo boost, if you will). In many situations it is possible to physically feel this reaction before the conscious mind has even become aware of what is happening. This is the protector self reacting milliseconds before the conscious mind. The protector self can sometimes appear extremely sensitive to the environment and in some situations it may just be the slightest change in another person's tone of voice or a look that can trigger the protector self into action (releasing adrenal hormones). Again though, this can often be a cross reference of pre-recorded videos.

When the body releases a dose of adrenal hormones into the bloodstream, the adrenal hormones will force the body to speed up its physiology. This feeling could be likened to drinking a very strong coffee or taking an ephedrine drug. Although the purpose of the hormone is to speed the body up to take action (fight or flight), if the adrenaline is not used up by the body by taking some kind of physical activity or movement, the hormone will simply remain in the bloodstream until the body can get rid of it. This can leave the body feeling stressed and erratic.

The office worker goes nuclear!

An example of this may be if an office worker in a sedentary role was to be shouted at by an angry co-worker or manager. If their mind saw this as a threat and then started to release adrenaline into their bloodstream, their body would naturally want to either attack or run away (to use up the hormone).

However, in that role it may be seen by others around them to be socially unacceptable to move about or leave the office and their peers may expect the office worker to go back to their desk and carry on working.

If the office worker was to remain sedentary with a high dosage of adrenaline within their bloodstream, soon enough it would make their physiology and emotions act very erratic and disruptive (unless they 'force' themselves to remain still and quiet).

This explains why it is that some people can appear to be very calm for a long period of time and then suddenly explode in rage for 'apparently' no reason. What will have been happening behind the scenes is that the adrenaline and other hormones will have been steadily building up until the person could no longer cope. As soon as the overload stage hits the person, it can force their physiology to physically move about or defend themselves. However, if this happens many hours or days 'after' the event it can cause confusion to other people.

Post stress reaction

As mentioned, the adrenaline's purpose is to speed up the body and physical reactions to enable a higher physical power under a potentially threatening situation. However, once the adrenalin has been released into the bloodstream, if it is not used up through the form of energy demand through action, it will remain in the body until the body can remove it through the normal process of ridding the body of unwanted chemicals. This is similar to absorbing any narcotic drug or alcohol that the body will eventually remove though cleansing the blood, which will have to work its way out of the system

However, whilst the adrenaline remains in the body it will continue to perform the role that it has been designed for, which is to speed up the body. Unfortunately though, if the body has not burned off the adrenaline and then for example remains inactive, it can feel very overwhelming and uncomfortable for hours, days or even weeks after the event.

The continuity of the post-stress reaction can be quite distressing in itself. If the stress reaction is not understood, it can be quite confusing to the conscious mind as to why the body is still in a heightened state of anxiety many hours or sometimes even days after the potentially threatening situation has passed. This continual stress build-up can lead to sleepless nights, irritability, a lack of concentration, a loss of appetite and further increases of stress due to confusion owing to the adrenaline pushing the body to keep moving until it reaches overwhelm.

Before we look the causes of stress, it is important to understand and acknowledge what a stress reaction looks and feels like. Even a base understanding of this concept can usually have an extremely calming and reassuring effect on the person feeling these symptoms. As in many cases, when we understand something it allows us to feel in control and to potentially determine how long the feelings will last for, or at least understand why it is happening. As human beings with a natural survival instinct, we tend to feel anxious about that which we do not understand. One reason for this is that if there is no understanding of the situation, it is impossible to determine whether it is a threat to our health or not.

Situations like this will be continually observed by the protector self as a potential threat.

Am I just weak?

No, you are not weak for having a stress reaction! Under a stress reaction, it is possible to feel the physical feeling as being a symptom of physical and emotional weakness. The reason for this is because sometimes when a stress reaction happens it can leave the body feeling very shaky and the mind totally confused as to how to handle the situation. However, no matter how shaky, breathless or confusing it becomes, it is actually the body reacting to the adrenal hormones and preparing to deal with a dangerous situation more effectively. If too much adrenaline is released, it can have a perceived effect of the body being weak and vulnerable, however this is usually if the body is not used to being prepared or dealing with the reaction.

The cause and effect cycle of a stress reaction

As mentioned, the flight, flight or freeze trigger is a very normal reaction for human physiology and is written into our genetics as part of our survival drive. If we did not have this reaction to protect us, we would be severely vulnerable if a threat was to suddenly appear. The flight, flight or freeze drive is triggered through the protector self. When this reaction happens the information of the potential threat (which is happening today) will then be analysed by the protector self milliseconds before the conscious mind (the thinking mind). This is why a person may feel the reaction to the threat before they realise what the threat is (and whether there actually is a threat at all or imagined).

Yet as mentioned, for every cause there is always an effect. Even though it can feel very uncomfortable and confusing when in the grip of a stress reaction, surprisingly it is not the stress reaction that is the cause of the discomfort. It is indeed true that the stress reaction causes the most physical, mental and emotional pain, giving the impression that it is the stress reaction that is the area of concern, however a stress reaction is simply the end result of the initial trigger.

To give you a visual image of this please imagine a fire that is burning a plastic compound which produces thick black smoke. Although on the surface it may appear that the most important thing to stop is the thick black smoke (if it is going all over the walls and clothes), in reality the smoke would not be there if it wasn't for the fire. Even deeper than that, the fire would not be there if it wasn't for the heat/ignition, and even further the ignition couldn't happen if the plastic wasn't flammable. So in this metaphor, there are 4 stages:

Stage 1: The flammable substance (the Pandora's Box trigger) … leading to…
Stage 2: The ignition (today's trigger reaction to the video) … leading to…
Stage 3: The fire (the physical feelings of the adrenaline) … leading to…
Stage 4: The smoke (the fight, flight and freeze reaction)

Reverse engineering

So now let's reverse the whole process above and look at the most noticeable effect, which is the smoke, as in most people's lives during a stress reaction it is that which is the most prominent concern. We will cover stage 3 and 4 in this chapter as stages 1 and 2 are covered throughout the rest of the book.

Stage 4: The fight, flight or freeze reaction (the smoke)

As we discovered in earlier chapters, the mind will remove itself from what it sees as pain and move towards what it sees as pleasure. These "what it sees" are images from the perceptions that are created from beliefs (our internal map of reality).

When the subconscious mind observes a situation today which has been cross-referenced and associated by a belief (a past video) that it perceives as painful, it will assume the image today as a pain and as a threat (a trigger from association). The protector self will then be cautious of the situation today as it could be a threat to the health. If the protector self senses danger, real or imagined (both are the same for the protector self), it will trigger the internal alarm and aim to protect itself. The body will protect itself from the threat (to survive) and do one of three things…

1. Attack, intimidate or destroy the threat (fight)
2. Remove itself from the threat (flight)
3. Switch off completely to trick the threat into giving up the attack (freeze)

The above reaction is known as the fight, flight or freeze reaction.
As mentioned though, the fight, flight or freeze reaction is the smoke and therefore something that the outer world can see more readily. For the 'smoke' section we will focus more on a person's actions rather than what the physical feelings within are.

Although some of the reactions that I will cover may be seen by many people in the outside world as arrogant or a bully (for the fight), a coward or weak (for flight), or stupid or slow (for freeze), all of these reactions are performed for the aimed protection of the physical or emotional self.

A deeper look

As mentioned the fight, flight and freeze drive in the human body is where the protector self senses a potential threat (real or imagined) to the health of the body or life and then hits an alarm to release adrenaline into the bloodstream. The adrenalin will cause the physical body to 'speed up' in order to protect itself as that is the purpose of that particular hormone.

Firstly though, let us look at these three reactions - outward actions - in more depth.

Fight

The fight reaction is created to either intimidate a potential threat or to actually attack the potential threat. In this reaction if the threat is going to cause harm, then intimidating the other person can manipulate them into backing away, or actually attacking them will ideally disable their attack and thus end the threat.

The issue with this reaction though is in many social groups there appears to be a split. Some people want to react in a fight reaction (to shout out) but then feel guilty and suppress it. This unfortunately has the effect of internalising their stress and affecting their health in a negative manner. Yet other people use it to intimidate others on a regular basis and can sometimes be praised for their apparent power. In reality it is often that people around the person in fight reaction may be intimidated and are appeasing the person through anxiety (nobody 'truly' enjoys being belittled). Learning how to express the fight reaction in a healthy manner is an essential skill as suppressing it will usually only lead to ill health.

Some of the reactions a person may display in 'fight' mode are:

- Physically aggressive
- Talking over other people continually
- An intimidating stare
- Talking about physical violence when not required
- Doing everything for everyone (controlling)
- Being critical of other people / parental
- Continually trying to take control
- Patronising people in a group
- The know-all

It may be noticed that some of the above reactions may not seem completely aggressive such as doing everything for everybody, but the fight reaction can be subtle, using different forms of control. I will soon cover this in more depth.

Flight

Whereas the fight is about moving towards the threat to attack or overpower it, the flight reaction is about moving AWAY from the threat. The logic behind this is that if we avoid the threat it cannot hurt us.
Again, there can sometimes be a social confusion with the expression of flight mode. To some people they may feel that they are being cowardly or weak and can also be judged by other members of the social group as cowardly or weak, but this is not the case! Their reaction is simply a learned pattern derived from their belief systems (or the healthiest option). If their beliefs have not been updated from childhood, their reactions will be the only ones they have practiced or learned.

Some of the reactions a person may display in 'flight' mode are:

- Submissive body language
- A desire to run away
- Agreeing to everybody's demands (not setting boundaries)
- Overeating / comfort eating / binging
- High levels of alcohol or drug consumption
- Oversleeping
- Isolation
- Obsessive use of social media (not really connecting to people)
- Overworking

Again we can notice that some of these actions may be seen as justifiable depending upon where a person is in life, e.g. isolation may be working on a project or avoiding contact for personal reflection time.

Freeze

The state of freeze can best be described using the reaction of animals in a potentially life-threatening situation. As an example, if we take a cat that catches a mouse with the intention of killing it, the cat may toy with the mouse first, pawing it as it struggles. However, in some situations the mouse may simply go completely limp and act as if it's dead. The mouse isn't dead though, but rather faking a death to trick the attacker into becoming bored and walking off as the game is over. Once the cat loses interest, the mouse may 'spring' into life again (with the aim of startling the cat) and then run away when the cat backs off in surprise.

In the social world of human beings, although we may not play dead, some people may appear to completely shut down in perceived overwhelming situations. An example of this would be in a situation where a person may feel patronised or bullied by several members of the group and simply go very quiet and stare into space. If this reaction is out of character for them, the aggressive members of the group may feel guilty and stop the attack (although the exact opposite of this may happen where the attack become more severe).

Some of the reactions a person may display in 'freeze' mode are:

- Appearing extremely distant
- Unable to answer questions
- Unresponsive to questions or threats
- Aloofness
- Complete apathy
- Extreme lack of motivation

A quick review of the sugar and salt

In the story earlier about the sugar and salt we discussed how two completely opposite compounds can mix together but appear the same, and so it is the same with the smoke (the outward actions of the stress reaction) and everyday 'normal' behaviour.

We are going to discuss this in a lot more depth soon as it is such a large part of the mask and the con, but please be aware that the above actions can appear elusive.

For example...

- Being critical was listed in the 'fight section' which yes, although it can be an attack to intimidate another person into feeling 'worth less' and thus the attacker gains control, the critical person may also be genuine and offering a supportive viewpoint to help the other person grow or think more creatively.

- Submissive body language was used in the flight section. This could be a person aiming to appease a potentially threatening person by acting submissively and not defending their boundaries, or it could be a confident person making themselves appear less threatening to a person with low self-esteem.

- Being unable to answer questions was a point in the freeze section, which could be a person shutting themselves down in an attempt to stop an overwhelming bully, or it could be that they simply do not understand the questions as it is not their strength or area of expertise.

Keep this in your mind throughout this book as everything I cover merges into one whole picture as we progress.

Stage 3: The fire (the physical reactions)
As we are working backwards in the stress reaction pathway, we first covered the smoke, which is the outer effect of stress and the actions a person may take. Now we will work on the fire, which is to reflect the physical and emotional feelings that a person may experience on the inside when their protector self releases the adrenaline and other hormones to speed up the body.

As we discussed earlier, once the adrenaline has been released into the bloodstream, its purpose is to speed the body up to an optimum rate to protect itself. However, some of the physical and emotional reactions may feel very confusing for the person experiencing them if they are not aware of why they are happening.

Some of the reactions may be:
A pounding heart, breathlessness, shaking limbs and muscles, a dry mouth, bladder release, cold sweating, disorientation, light-headedness, feeling cold and clammy, distorted vision or slurred or stuttered speech! If you thought you were the only one who feels this way, think again - we can all have these reactions!

Under a fight, flight or freeze reaction, it is possible (due to the overwhelming surge of hormone release) to feel physically weak, confused and even more afraid, but again, it is the body becoming stronger and being able to deal with a potentially threatening situation more effectively. For example, the blood will pump faster to reach the muscles at a faster rate, the muscles will shake as the nervous system is speeding up ready to move faster, and the sickly feeling may be to expel food so the muscles can use the energy that would otherwise be used to digest the food.

As mentioned, the fight, flight or freeze reaction can also sometimes appear confusing to the person experiencing it because the adrenal release can also speed up the processes of thoughts. With a flood of thoughts and options all at once, the thought processing part of the mind may become overwhelmed and struggle to make any decision at all. This can be similar to a computer when there are too many processes at once and the little egg timer appears on the screen asking the user to wait. This lack of being able to come to an answer may again leave the person feeling helpless (this helplessness is another strategy within the con trick that is used on people).

In reality, there are no hard and fast rules to the way the adrenal hormones can make a person react when they come into contact with something that they perceive as a threat. It could be a mild nervousness to total panic, and the reaction is not the same in all situations.

A few reactions during fight or flight or freeze may be:

Physically

Crying! Crying is a way in which the body is trying to relieve built-up stress. Crying can be likened to a valve on a pressure cooker. When the pressure becomes too much, it releases the excess steam to stop the pan exploding (although there are other reasons for crying).

Feeling sick / wanting to use the toilet! This is a perfectly normal reaction, but can leave the person confused and sometimes feeling ashamed as some people see this as a very childlike bodily function. The purpose for doing this is that the body is trying to release excess food and waste from its system. When this happens it will free up the otherwise used energy for other functions such as running or shouting.

Shaking / trembling! This is when the hormones are stimulating the muscle fibres too much, trying to enable the muscles to have more energy to run away or to fight. However, trembling limbs can be immensely confusing and bring a feeling of wanting to sit down or even collapse.

Breathlessness! With there being an extreme demand upon the body to pump blood to the limbs, the lungs and diffusion (the body allowing oxygen into the blood) may struggle to keep up. The lack of ability to keep up with the demand may give a feeling of breathlessness.

Tunnel vision! This is where the peripheral vision (the outer visual field) may appear blurry. The purpose of this is to allow the vision to focus all its attention on the potential threat in the immediacy (in front of the person).

Panic attack! This can be the most feared of all the reactions to stress, as not only can it be the most physically painful, but it is also the most disabling and to some the most embarrassing. A panic attack is where the whole body can become so overwhelmed by adrenaline that it may try to perform too many functions at once and is literally overpowered by the energy wave and shuts down (freezes). Victims of crime have sometimes faced this as they stand there helpless and rigid while the criminal goes through their pockets. As discussed though, this can either be an overwhelm reaction or a freeze reaction.

Mentally/emotionally

Feeling worthless! Although this may seem a useless reaction, in some cases it is a very effective one. Feeling worthless in a crowd of people will automatically make the person shy away from contact. If the person believes the group to be an overpowering threat, but their conscious mind is in too much denial to admit that, then the underlying anxiety may override and force the person into submission, thereby staying safe. In truth though (as bullies only bully because they can) this may actually antagonize people into attacking the person for acting like a victim, but the mind will still perform this action if it believes it to be the safest option. Alternatively, this reaction could simply be a suppressed belief pattern of low self-worth or low self-esteem.

Needy of others! The purpose of this is the person is literally doing the best they can to gain support from others around them. When the mind feels overpowered it can either retreat into its shell, avoiding contact from others entirely, or can rally support from others for protection. This would not depend entirely upon the upbringing of the person, but rather their perception of it and how valuable they felt as a person in relation to others.

Confused! Confusion is an extremely common reaction, likened to a rabbit caught in headlights. The reason for this is that with the rush of the adrenal hormones, the mind speeds up to an extremely high rate and does its best to process many things at once, but if the person is not used to being in this state (pre-prepared), it can be overwhelming and very unsettling. This reaction can then lead to further confusion.

Worrying! Worrying is a feeling which is common for many people in today's society as they may not feel they can fully express themselves. The workplace is a very common one for this as employees may have anxiety of the 'boss' sacking them (real or projected) leading to a loss of income / rejection.

With worry, the mind is doing its best to process all the thoughts from the internal cinema screen which are going round inside it. The only way a thought can be fully processed is by taking action on the information it is trying to process and thereby gaining resolution, but if the person refuses to take action on the thought and just lets it swim around it will keep on doing so, trying to come to a conclusion, and the worry goes on.

Hate! Under times of intense fight or flight, the feelings of hate may start to arise. Hate is the extreme emotion of fear and anxiety and expresses itself in total disconnection from others, and in totally disconnecting from another the mind believes it can stay safe. However, hate can come with a destructive side, with a person wanting to destroy the threat as it is too much for their mind to handle.

NB: *The above is by no means an extensive list and the reactions can range from a few to a whole plethora in number. It is always important to be aware that if something does not feel right inside or there is a sense of wanting to escape, nine times out of ten it will be the fight or flight reaction that has been triggered within the mind and the 'red alert' alarm has been sounded.*

The reality of a stress reaction

Once the release of the stress hormones has been triggered, there is no reverse procedure. Likened to that of a drug being injected into the bloodstream, it has to work its course and be used up by physical action or the body's natural cleansing. Regardless of whether this reaction seems justified at the time or not, it is your reaction and the best option your protector self had access to at that moment in time. Many people blame themselves for reactions they experience, deeming them to be some kind of weakness. It can be viewed this way in many 'bravado' cultures because the 'disabling feeling' it brings with it could be likened to that of the so-called coward and therefore viewed as socially unacceptable. To see a stress reaction as a sign of cowardice is a misperceived view from lack of knowledge on behalf of the person observing. An essential note at this point though is that to deem a person 'weak' or a 'coward' for reacting this way is a form of leverage that the con trickster will use. Why these reactions may happen seemingly 'out of character' is what we will be discussing in further chapters.

Fear and anxiety - defining the terms

Over the years there have been many books, audio programmes, distance learning materials and training seminars designed to allow greater understanding around the concept of fear. The word in itself almost seems to appear as a separate branch of psychology today. Many of these materials have new exciting angles and flashy images, but no matter how it is dressed up, there is still only a finite amount of information that we need to realise and understand in order to gain clarity and control (and therefore power over our reactions).

The above statement, however, is in no way intended to disregard other materials in the marketplace; different authors have different views and perceptions of the world and seeing the world though many different eyes will allow each reader to learn the information in creative ways. Never assume that one way is the only way.

A fantastic book which helped me immensely when I was starting my journey is a book simply titled 'Fear' by Geoff Thompson. I personally recommend Geoff's books as they have had a big impact on my own growth!

For the purpose of this book though I will now give a separate meaning to the words fear and anxiety. To truly connect to the essence of the lessons in this book it is important that these definitions are kept separate.

In many cases of helping somebody understand their inner feelings and reactions it is the blurring of these two areas that has made a solution to stress almost a challenge.

The difference of Fear and Anxiety

Fear

The reaction of fear is a very potent survival mechanism and is present when we are in actual physical danger. In some cases it has been known for people to start to defend themselves by running away or attacking even before the danger has presented itself in clear form, such as that in a mugging or assault (also known as a pre-emptive strike).

In situations such as this, the body and mind work together and focus the entire attention on that of the immediate moment, such as an attacking dog, the car that is going to hit us or whatever threat is potentially going to damage the body.

Therefore, fear is a physical hijacking of the body to jump into action at that moment in time from an actual (not imagined) threat. The adrenal hormones surge through the bloodstream and a reaction of fight, flight or freeze takes place.

Throughout the course of our lives, we are all more than aware of the feeling of fear, the urge of action, the urge to lash out either verbally or physically if we are physically or emotionally in danger. However, in those situations when we restrict this self-expression, it locks us in and feels like the body is shutting down. An example of this is someone being shouted at by a manager when they are threatening the job that is needed for their income. The initial urge to run or attack is that of 'fear' (the manager is actually attacking), but the choice to stay (because leaving the room may cause the person to lose the job) restricts the expression of 'fear', causing a backlash of adrenaline, and it is repressed inside the body.

"The best way to escape from your problem is to solve it."
Robert Anthony

The body's fear

The body itself has natural defences relating to this. If we sit with our legs over the side of a high seat (feet off the floor) and gently tap our knee in a soft place just above the kneecap, the natural reaction is for the lower leg to jump (which is known as the knee jerk reaction).

This reaction is in place because pressure builds up on tendons (from the tap) which attach the muscle of the thigh (quadriceps) to the kneecap (patella tendon). The body's mind (neural connection) starts to assume that if the pressure builds up too much on the tendon that it may become damaged and therefore inoperable. The nervous centre of the body then tells the leg muscle to contract (by making the lower leg jump) and has the effect of loosening the stretched tendon (releasing the pressure).

The above reaction, for the purpose of this chapter, can be likened to fear; it is the body's natural reaction to defend itself against a threat that can cause physical or emotional damage. The knee jerk reaction above however is an "automated" reaction and therefore beyond our conscious control. In many situations where we become confused and frozen it is simply because we disengage our thoughts (the conscious mind) and worry about the situation (or again, this loop could be a belief pattern).

Fear is therefore a reaction to avoid 'real' threats!

Anxiety

Anxiety is the phrase that will be the keystone to the rest of the book. Anxiety in essence is the source of pain and suffering in its most potent form.

The key to the fight, flight or freeze reaction in relation to anxiety is therefore directly connected with the mind's association to current situations based on previous experiences (the videos).

An example of this would be as follows:

A young child is playing in the park and feels the urge to sing a song; the child feels that it would be a nice gesture to do for a parent who is looking at them with a smile. When the child begins to sing, one of their young friends begins to laugh and make fun of the song, thereby intentionally humiliating the child as they sing. The child looks to the parent for support and the parent turns away due to being momentarily

distracted by another parent speaking to them. It is not that the parent is uncaring, but they have just not seen the situation as serious as the young child may.
The child who sang may record this situation as:

"I am totally vulnerable with no support"

and then log this experience as:

"If I want to express myself, I will be attacked and nobody will be there to support me if I am attacked"

If the above experience was too traumatic for the child to handle (feeling rejected and alone), it may be stored as a threat and other similar situations in the future will be avoided. The real pain however has been created from the child not knowing what to do or how to handle the situation (we will cover this in the self-esteem recovery model). So, it is their lack of understanding of what to do which has caused confusion.
Obviously it won't always be as straightforward as 'one' situation that causes major stored traumas unless it is a very serious incident, but the above is an overview and a guide.

In many cases, if a person experiences something which is a threat and they do not know how to handle it there is a high chance that they will attempt to avoid it in the future. This is unless the person has believes that challenges are exciting, but if the situation was potentially dangerous, the protector self always sits on the side of safety (again please refer to the pain-pleasure principle from the earlier chapter).

The above reaction for the protector self would seem a perfectly logical survival mechanism as it is a reaction to keep the child's body and wellbeing safe from harm. Yet if the memory is not updated in the future, the protector self will only have old beliefs and videos to relate future situations to. If the old beliefs and videos are from a time when the child was too small to deal effectively with the situation (which many children are), that is where the problems really begin to grow.

If we then look at the child's misaligned stored belief…

'Every time I want to express myself, I will be attacked and nobody will be there to support me"

…then project the child forward in time 20 years, it is more than possible that their protector self will reconnect to this same belief (which has probably amplified many times and associated to other situations) and avoid situations of self-expression. This is, provided the belief has not been updated or masked (we will be discussing masking in great detail soon). The reason this will happen is that the protector self will still be believe that they are as helpless today as they were back when they were young (re-associated memory). In today's reality they may be more than capable of handling the situation (if they have learned new skills), but if their protector self is trapped in time it will still assume that they have the same abilities as when it happened. In this reaction it may disregard all new learnings and override them in an anxiety trigger. Our anxiety is not driven by fear of the current situation, but more by our association to it (stored inside the subconscious / Pandora's Box then projected onto the internal cinema screen).

This 'loop' is why some highly skilled people who can easily handle daily challenges 'today' can feel completely perplexed and are unable to connect to their abilities when the pressure is overwhelming.

The addictive anxiety-stress loop

When in the grip of an anxious stress reaction the last thing anybody would actually want to attract is more anxiety or stress. It is vital to note that stress and especially anxiety can be in and of themselves very self-generating and addictive. The stress becomes self-generating when the sufferer of the stress reaction and anxiety become increasingly aware of their suffering when in the grip of stress. This then creates further anxiety and in turn creates a loop pattern. This loop then only serves to increase the worry and reactions to create further suffering, and thus the spiral grows.

An example of an anxiety-stress loop would be as follows...

1. A pedestrian who is walking across a road looks up to see a reckless driver who sees them but keeps driving, nearly hitting them with the car.

2. The pedestrian's body automatically releases adrenaline (and other hormones) into their bloodstream to prepare them for a direct threat and to protect their health.

3. The feeling of a stress reaction may now make their legs shake, their heart pound and cause other physical reactions. These reactions may also create emotional worry which then plays over and over in their mind.

4. If the pedestrian's protector self keeps replaying the image of the near accident, the body will keep releasing adrenaline (plus other hormones) into the bloodstream to protect from the 'now-imagined' threat.

5. The continually high levels of stress hormones in the body now speed up the neural connections and increase the thought patterns. The protector self now becomes increasingly bombarded with internal cinema screen thoughts of danger and releases yet more stress hormones even though the event has finished.

6. The cycle continues.

Again, from the naïve onlooker's point of view it may appear confusing as to why the person who was 'nearly' involved in the accident would keep replaying the scene over and over.

The naïve onlooker may say things like…

"Stop worrying all the time"
'Don't read too much into it"
'Just forget about it"
"Calm down"
'Put it to the back of your mind"

However, as we all know when a person is in the grip of stress, telling them to stop worrying will often have very little effect upon their state of mind.

Anxiety is a fear of what we perceive to be real rather than what is actually real. A dog biting us will cause fear, while worrying about a dog biting us is anxiety. To the mind, both are one and the same as the mind has no idea what is real and what is imagined (the internal cinema screen). This is where the phrase comes from that "perception is reality".

Anxiety is therefore a reaction to avoid 'imagined' threats.

Chapter summary

To conclude this chapter, it is essential to revisit the difference between fear and anxiety and study the body's reactions and responses. To understand the body and how it works is one of the main components of breaking free from the mask and the con.

As we discussed earlier, under extreme stress reactions (fight, flight or freeze) the body and mind can become 'hijacked', which is an overwhelming reaction from the adrenal hormones in which the body can shut down or the person can feel confused and trapped in time and old outdated memories. Becoming aware of these reactions can prepare the mind for when they do happen, as in the good Boy Scout saying "be prepared".
Awareness is the key!

Personal reflection exercises

1. List out any current unhelpful or limiting beliefs you may have about various different areas of your life. Remember, beliefs are perceptions and not always facts.

2. Go through each of these and then ask whether they are true or not. They can only be true if you can 'prove them'! This also means everybody would have to agree. This may contradict question 1, but do it anyway.

3. Ask yourself where you may have learned these beliefs from, e.g. other people or situations (you may not be aware of all of them, but do your best).

4. What supporting evidence do you have for each belief that feels real but is not actually valid? e.g. other people tell you it is true.

7

The Peer Idolisation Scale

Now that we have looked at some of the foundations of the mind and how it can put the world together, it is important to start to look at 'why' it has perceived it in such a way. Once we understand this it will be easier to see the mask and the con.
The peer idolisation scale is my own design created through a mix of Maslow's hierarchy of needs and my own research of social habits and patterns that I have observed in others. As with all my work I suggest that you view it through your own filter and take a reflective view as this will support your growth.

First though please take a moment to reflect on these two definitions before progressing

1: Manipulation
This term is to be used for a person projecting views or opinions onto another person for the manipulator's own interest in which the other person's feelings are not taken into consideration. An example here

would be if a person is afraid of their partner splitting up with them and they were to continually say 'I love you' or use a form of guilt to stop their partner from leaving.

2: Influence

This term is to be used for a person projecting views or opinions onto another person for the greater good of all people involved, where all parties' feelings are taken into consideration. An example here would be if a parent were to discipline a child for the child's best interest so they did not come to harm (such as restricting sugar for a sugar-addicted child). The child may not like the discipline and may get upset, but it is for their best interest and is an act of love.

NB: *The reason that both these definitions have been included is to explain that there is always one of two motives towards another person in regards to their actions. It is also important to note that through this chapter there will be some explanations that may appear to be sided towards the abuse and neglectful actions towards a child. All children will experience a range of emotional projections from those around them; the healthier and loving emotions will create pleasurable videos, though in this chapter that is not the main concern. The main area we will be covering in this chapter is when a child is subjected to disconnecting and painful emotional projections of their peers, which in turn create anxiety and will be recorded as a pain video for the protector self to react to when viewed on the internal cinema screen.*

The perception of pain

As previously discussed, the mind is focused on survival and moves away from that which is perceived to be painful (or threatening) and towards that which is perceived to be pleasurable (or non-threatening). This as mentioned is governed by the metaphorical protector self and that part of us which is continually observing all situations we encounter and creating the optimum environment for the promotion of health and wellbeing.

Each person's protector self will only concern itself with the person it is looking after and will make decisions based on what it thinks is the best option in regards to their safety and emotional well-being. This is as simple as to either remove the person from pain or move them towards pleasure. Young children and some adults can sometimes have a very strong connection to their protector self without conscious control, and in some cases this can be perceived by onlookers as self-infatuation or vanity.

It could become confusing however, when we observe people in society who take harmful drugs, get in fights, keep re-living the same harmful situations or people who take their own lives through depression, to think that their protector self is actually looking out for them. However, even in those circumstances their protector self is looking out for their best interests, although it may appear that nothing could be further from the truth.

If this is to make any sense, we first need to look at this from the protector self's point of view. There are two types of pain we can observe; the first is physical and the second is emotional. Although the physical pain may at first seem the most threatening of the two, in many situations (as we saw with the boxer in an earlier chapter) it can in fact be the pain that most people would prefer to endure rather than the emotional suffering. The protector self creates the logic from the statement in a previous chapter, which stated:

We can become anxious of that which we do not understand!

Physical pain is usually created from a source that we can observe, whether that's a physical collision, from an attacker or an accident. In many cases we can observe where the source of the pain is being derived from and either protect ourselves or remove ourselves as we saw in the last chapter. If we can observe the source we can gather other information such as how and why the pain is there and can assume from experience how long it will be there for, and even if we can't, in some cases we can learn to control it.

NB: *Although this is also not to insinuate that physical pain is always seen this way as in many long-term pain sufferers, the physical pain may take preference over everything else. It is also vital to note that for some long-term pain sufferers - especially* *for those who have medical conditions which may not be fully understood - it can be very difficult to know how long the pain will be there or where it is coming from. Pain of this nature could bring with it immense anxiety. In reality then, the pain that a person will avoid the most and feel most anxious about is the greater of whichever pain they are facing.*

For this example though, we will observe a person who is not experiencing any physical pain. In this situation their emotional pain will become the most apparent. This could also be classed as the assumed pain (internal cinema screen / anxiety) rather than actual physical pain of the body (physical damage). We can see this if somebody is upset over a relatively small debt (emotional) but then broke their arm (physical). If the pain in their arm was seen as the higher of the two their protector self would focus on the arm and not the debt. However, when the arm has healed the debt may take the protector self's attention again (anxiety).

In the absence of physical pain, emotional pain can be very destructive to the focus and balance of a person. There are many reasons for this as we will cover further along, but is a big area is that many people will unfortunately receive very little social, psychological or emotional education through their schooling years. This lack of understanding of how their mind and emotions put the world together can leave some people at a loss as to why they are feeling certain emotions and/or how to change their emotional state and beliefs in the long term. When some people experience a deep hurt emotionally, such as the loss of a loved one, an accident or a relationship breakup, some questions that arise in response to the pain could be:

"Why am I feeling this way?"
"Where is it coming from?"
"How long will it stay?
"Will it come back when it goes?"
"Will it get any worse?"

Leading to a very common anxiety…

"What if it doesn't go and I can't cope?"

Looking at it from this angle it is easier to make sense of why a person may take harmful drugs, undertake actions that reject people and in some cases even take their own lives. For some people who may be suffering the seemingly endless wrath of the emotional pain that swirls around in their mind and lashes them with voices of suffering, any option of stopping it will be considered. In their mind if the pain can be decreased, if not temporarily removed (or so it would appear), by the drugs and alcohol then the strain will lighten, and if the pain has been removed from perception (even if by the taking of harmful substances), the result is pleasure.

This last statement may sound confusing, as we may wonder how could taking a harmful drug or alcohol creates pleasure, but if pain is reduced from say a 9/10 to a 6/10, even though they are still in pain it is now lower than it was before due to the drug; therefore, as it feels less intense it will by comparison feel like a level of pleasure. At its most severe stage of pain, even death to some people may feel like a relief as it can prevent the mind from having to listen to a constant loop of emotional suffering caused by the internal cinema screen and Pandora's Box.

Again, in the absence of physical pain, the emotional pain (anxiety) becomes the protector self's main concern. As we will see though, it is the protector self's coping mechanisms (fight, flight and freeze) plus a lack of education in how to understand the mind and the emotions that are the main cause of self-damaging behaviour - which in turn leave the mind wide open to the mask and the con.

The peer idolisation scale

The peer idolisation scale is a metaphorical design which has been created to help define a clearer understanding of how the mind may create misaligned beliefs (videos) in younger years in regards to the environment of which a child is dependent on for food, water and security. If physical or emotional challenges were to arise to the virtually defenceless child, these can then be stored and could later amplify to create low self-esteem, shame, guilt or various forms of anxiety. Within this model my aim is to offer a possible option and define a potentially logical reason as to why a person may create and hold these limiting beliefs, which in turn continually project potentially threatening images on the internal cinema screen. Which then create perceived threats for the protector self to defend against (anxiety).

Important note!

To emphasise the point of the model I will be using quite amplified examples of situations which a child may face. These amplified examples may not be relevant to 'everybody' and different people will have had varying different experiences as they were growing up. So with this chapter please take the information and view it through your own perception and adapt it to your own personal experiences.

Emotional loop programmes can be learned at any age depending upon the person's emotional vulnerability. The reason I have used the perspective of a child in this model is that we will often be at our most vulnerable when we are a child.

The two environments for a child

Environment 1: A child is in a healthy and safe environment

The child's peers display good self-esteem and are connected to themselves and the child. They will have stress in their lives as that is natural to all people, but they can handle their daily challenges. They can also accommodate for the extra energy required to support the child. The peers feel comfortable with the child pushing their boundaries to grow and even going into slight defiance by screaming or throwing things, but all is done with healthy enforced boundaries. This can usually give a child a sense of connection and understanding that it is ok to express themselves and still be accepted. In turn, this can lead to healthy growth and a confidence to test more of their current reality knowing that their survival (food, shelter) will still be supplied. This does not mean that the parent/peer is totally without control; if no control is exercised a child would have no guidance or boundaries, which could cause confusion. However, the control in the security section is comfortable without excessive force.

Environment 2: A child is in an unhealthy and unsafe environment

The child's peers display low self-esteem and feel an overwhelming or erratic sense of stress to the daily challenges of life. Their fight, flight or freeze reactions are in regular use and the peers struggle to cope with the extra energy required to support a child/children.

If the peer begins to act in a controlling or rejecting manner, the child's protector self will naturally trigger to protect the child's health and wellbeing. It will do this as the child is dependent upon the peers for survival and security.

If the child's survival (food, water or support) is threatened or restricted the child will develop coping mechanisms to regain balance (discussed in this chapter). Sometimes this even means allowing themselves to be degraded, beaten or ignored and all because the child needs the peers to survive and is in effect powerless to change their environment. The child may not fight back in the initial stages as if the peer shows aggression, abandonment or other emotional manipulations the child's protector self may be anxious of physical or emotional harm.

It is in this environment that the foundations of low self-esteem and shame can be created. Beliefs such as "I am dependant on others for my survival and I have to act to their desires or I could be harmed or suffer loss" and "I am not good enough to take care of myself" may start to manifest.

The two main sections of the peer idolisation scale – Connection and disconnection

Dividing the scale into these two sections can help you understand the range of emotions that can be felt during the course of daily life, both in the positive times of the day but more importantly in stressful situations too. Being aware of the emotions in these two separate sections can help the mind gain clarity in potentially overwhelming situations.

The benefit of being able to understand the emotions can bring with it focus and energy with the potential of being able to reduce the anxiety that may arise from the confusion of not knowing the structure of the emotional self.

The theory of the peer idolisation scale is that the more aware the mind can become in regards to the emotional reaction to a given situation, the more power the conscious mind can exercise over any potential challenges. If the conscious mind can bring the attention back to the present moment in challenging situations, the internal cinema screen will not be as active and therefore not trigger the protector self into action (fight, flight or freeze).

However, it is important to note that just being aware and using mindfulness is not the ultimate solution. Pandora's Box reactions are rooted into a deeper part of the psyche and have access to more emotions than the conscious mind as we covered earlier. Therefore, the complete solution is to cleanse Pandora's Box of limiting beliefs.
With that said though, gaining awareness of how the emotions are creating reactions and then being able to see the path they take is the first step to gaining control over your reactions. This will inevitably require practice and discipline.

Understanding the scale
The list of emotions on the peer idolisation scale below is by no means exhaustive but will give an outline as to the different emotions which can be felt in each section.

The scale is as follows.

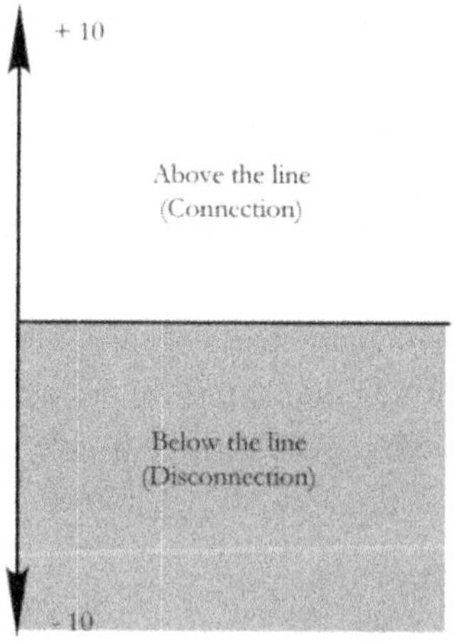

On the scale we can observe 3 main points of reference:

1. 0 up to +10 (Pleasure)
2. 0 (Neutral)
3. 0 down to -10 (Pain)

1. The pleasure / connection section (0 up to +10)

From the point of 0 (in the middle of the scale) rising to the point of +10 (the highest point on the scale) refers to when a person feels in a secure place in life emotionally.

This is the section where a person would feel a range of positive emotions such as creativity, joy and love (plus many others). This section can be classed as a connective environment with a feeling of trust of others and of the self. There will also be a feeling of being safe and secure in relation to the self and others. This section is what will be classed as "above the line".

The more pleasurable a belief feels in a particular area of life, the higher on the scale it will be placed. These could be in areas such as business, finance, relationships and home. This section is also described as the connection area as when the mind is in a state of pleasure it will move towards that which it sees as the source of the pleasure i.e. another person.

If we take Joe Bloggs for example (from earlier), he may feel that walking along the road in his hometown could register on the scale as +1. At this stage he is comfortable but not elated. Whereas visiting his family (on the same street) after his challenging situation in London may register as a +10, which for him may feel like the emotion of pure joy or love. The higher up the scale the emotion registers, the higher the emotion will feel.

Emotions that may be felt here could be:

- Joy
- Appreciation
- Empowered
- Freedom
- Love
- Passion
- Enthusiasm
- Eagerness
- Happiness
- Positive expectation
- Self-belief
- Optimism
- Confidence
- Creativity
- Fun

2. **The neutral zone (Point 0)**

Point '0' refers to when a person is feeling ambivalent in their views. Ambivalence is a state of mind where a person has not yet made a decision on what something is or what something means to them. At this stage a person experiencing a stressful situation could be at a risk of the survival drive going either way. An example of this would be when a person is called into the office and their manager or manageress is unemotional. With little to no feedback it can be a challenge for the mind to make a decision on how to feel (and for any videos to be replayed) so may be feeling confused and intensely scanning the situation for more information on what to do or think.

3. **The pain / disconnection section (0 down to -10)**

The stage of 0 down to -10 is in essence the polar opposite of section 1. It is in this section where the disconnecting emotions will start to be created in the mind. These emotions are triggered when the protector self observes a video on the internal cinema screen that is related to pain; the more intense or painful the video association, the further down the scale it will be placed. However, as we recall, it is the person's perception that will decide where they place the experience on the scale. This is why different people can have different perceptions.

This section has also been described as the disconnection section. When the mind observes discomfort it will move away from the source of the pain i.e. another person.

Again if we take Joe Bloggs he may feel that going into a social gathering is a -1 if he is feeling a little unsure of himself with new people. At this level the protector self will be on guard but not too involved. Yet due to his challenging experience in his last job role, he may place going for a job interview as -8 or -9 on the scale, in which the protector self will be heavily involved and ready to move him away from the situation to keep him safe.

Emotions that may be felt here could be:

- Boredom
- Frustration
- Guilt
- Powerlessness
- Disappointment
- Irritation
- Impatience
- Overwhelming
- Anger
- Revenge
- Hatred/Rage
- Jealousy
- Doubt
- Worry
- Blame

A quick review of beliefs

If we recall, a belief is comprised of two parts:

Part 1: The physiological memory of the stimulus (the sensory image = brain)
Part 2: The emotional association of that image (on the above scale = mind)

Using the peer idolisation scale we can start to see that current situations in life which are associated to pleasurable past experiences (or videos) are connected to emotions at the top of the scale and be moved towards. Whereas current situations in life which are associated to past experiences (or videos) that are connected to emotions at the bottom of the scale will be seen as pain and be moved away from.

How it all works

As mentioned the peer idolisation scale is a theory and is therefore, like all psychological models, unable to be proven scientifically as there are simply too many variables in human psychology. However, using the peer idolisation scale as a base structure, we can use conscious logic to gain a sense of structure as to how the mind constructs a person's world in their mind using the comparison of pain and pleasure. We will now cover two main stages that progressively compound to create belief structures or how a person sees their own worth/value internally (on the internal cinema screen), which then creates shame and guilt beliefs.

Shame and guilt will be formed when the child is actually (or perceives that they are) in an unhealthy or unsafe environment and compares themselves in a negative manner. The environment that we are discussing here has the angle of the child and peer in the home environment which would insinuate a parent or a guardian. It is true a parent or guardian can have a tremendous power over a child. However, it is also important to note that a child can gain their perceptions of the world from other environments too, such as school, neighbours, other children or very intense one-off experiences of trauma. Please bear in mind that this chapter is also to be cross-referenced with the next chapter on shame and guilt.

NB: *Also, a point to note in this chapter is that I will be mainly using the example of food, water and shelter as a child's primary anxiety in life. However, emotional abuse such as anxiety of rejection or neglect can be just as traumatic to a child's perception.*

The Peer Idolisation Model: Stage 1 - Birth

The basic fact of life is that a child is born into the world and presented with a body that they do not know how to use, a language from the parents that they do not understand and a total lack of power in every way, shape and form. This leaves the child completely dependent on the adults and peers who surround them in their environment. The child's (or child's protector self's) primary goal is survival (food, water and shelter) and given that they are totally dependent upon those around them for these needs (thereby having no independence) it can leave the new-born at the mercy of others' decisions for survival.

If we are to fully understand why the child's protector self is so fundamentally aware of their surroundings it is helpful to first observe Maslow's hierarchy of needs (Abraham Maslow 1943). In this model we can see that the mind's protector self needs to fulfil certain needs in a particular order of validity from the lower levels of the pyramid before it can move on to fulfil the higher levels.

Maslow's hierarchy

Abraham Maslow, born 1st April 1908, developed the theory of human motivation now known as Maslow's Hierarchy of Needs. A psychologist, Maslow noted that some human needs were more essential to physical and emotional health than others. Through careful research Maslow divided each of those needs into five general categories, ranging from the most urgent to the most desired. The five levels are physiological, safety, belonging/love, esteem, and self-actualization.

Maslow first published his theory in the 1940s, and it soon became widely accepted in the fields of psychology and anthropology. Maslow was a professor at Brandeis University from 1951 until 1969; his major papers included *Toward a Psychology of Being* (1962) and *Motivation and Personality* (1954).

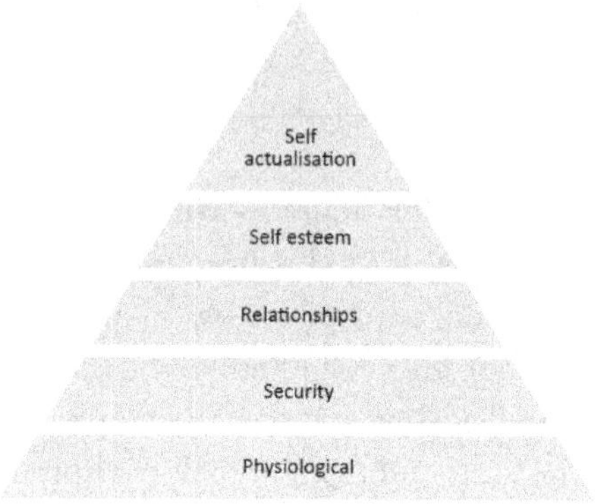

Maslows hierarchy of needs

Level one - Basic needs

This is the level at which a person requires food, water and shelter. Without food and water, life would not be possible. It is possible to survive without shelter for a certain amount of time, but again a severe threat to the health would be imminent. This then is more important to life than any other area, as without it the physical body will die.

Level two - Security needs

Once a person has the ability to eat and stay alive, the next fundamental need is that of security. This security covers two main areas, which are the external an internal security needs. This area will need to be observed from two angles.

1. External security

This is the security of the actual environment such as financial wealth, nutrition, physical harm and potential social environmental risks. Any loss to this area is classed as fear or an actual threat.

2. *Internal security*

This is the perceived security reflections within the mind which may or may not be real but can still be perceived as real. For example, if a person is worried about losing money then financial debt to them could create an anxiety around losing their home or the like. This area is classed as anxiety or imagined threat.

Level three - Relationship needs

Once the physiological needs and security needs are fulfilled, a person may feel secure enough to 'truly' connect with other people and form connected relationships with those people like and different from him or herself. It is possible for a person to connect to others without fulfilling the security needs, but the connection will be hampered as the protector self will always be on guard. In this state it will be looking out for threats to the emotional and physical self, and therefore never connecting 100%. Obviously though, a person can feel more secure with certain people over others, which can lead a person to feel more comfortable in being vulnerable with those they trust as opposed to those they do not trust.

The degree of satisfaction derived from this area can be directly related to how secure a person feels in their life in relation to each person in their life. When a person feels completely secure, they can choose to be emotionally open and loving to accept other people and their differences. Love and acceptance are about being emotionally open, which the protector self will not allow unless the person feels secure around the other people. In the protector self's view, total giving of one's self when they feel at risk of harm could lead to potential threat and therefore pain.

Level four - Self-esteem needs

When a person feels comfortable in connecting with other people and can form effective relationships (people skills), they can then progress to attain high self-esteem. Self-esteem is an ability to see the true inner self, self-worth and know of the inherent value. Only when a person is in a highly secure place are they able to truly look within without self-doubt or anxiety. This may seem very similar to level 2, but where a person at level 2 knows they can just about defend themselves, a person at level 4 is comfortable enough to feel vulnerable, which is the opposite of defending the self. However in different fields, some may challenge this saying that if perception is reality then surely self-esteem can be attained before relationship needs, which is a valid point and is one of those areas where psychological models can only ever be classed as theories rather than facts.

Level five - Self-actualisation

This is the highest level and has many differing views in society. However, for the purpose of the Life Beyond the Mask book I will be describing it as a discovering of one's purpose in life. This can be classed as the giving of oneself to the higher ideal and becoming all that one is truly capable of. It can also be in regards to making a difference in the world without the need to receive anything in return as true abundance has already been attained.

The Peer Idolisation Model: Stage 2 - The pecking order

Understanding that the child is completely dependent upon their peers for their food (it does not always have to be the birth parents) the child will now start to learn that they ideally have to work together with the peers in order to get food (i.e. survival). The food and water however is a physical need, but the child will also have another need - 'the emotional self', which also requires attention. However, although the physical body cannot survive without food and water, the body can physically survive without connection and emotional attention (though this can also be debated).

However it has been recorded that situations of emotional neglect can create a level of pain and emotional dysfunction. Some theorists have even hypothesised that emotional neglect can cause physiological damage and/or illness. However, the need for food and water will still be a higher priority of the two needs.

Naturally each child is usually born with a desire to explore, grow and learn, and their emotional drive can usually start very high on the peer idolisation scale. Unless for some other reason, a child will usually have a drive to connect to other people and to their surroundings as this is the most logical method for growth and survival. Here we can class the child's emotional level as "above the line" (0 – plus 10) as they may not have been exposed to any major challenges or traumas. Yet if the child is above the line they may not have had an experience in defending themselves as they will be too preoccupied with food, water and emotional gratification. Therefore, if they come into contact with parents or peers who do display personality behaviours in the lower section (0 down to - 10); this will naturally cause the child confusion and anxiety. If their food, water or emotional connection are at threat this will immediately engage the protector self and may create a need to adapt to their surroundings to ensure their needs are met.

The skill of rapport

Rapport is the ability to create close and harmonious relationships with people in the environment. In this state the members of the group will understand each other's feelings or ideas and communicate in a connected fashion. Rapport for a child or anybody who associates around other people is an essential trait of survival and is driven from the logic that similar people connect and support each other. It is in this stage that the child can then begin to adapt their personality to their environment by creating rapport with the parents or peers (or the main influences) in their life of the different environments.

Given that the child has not yet learned about how to act and conduct themselves in their environment, they may in this stage begin to create a rapport by copying the mannerisms of their peers or acting in the same way.

For the purpose of understanding this level of rapport in regards to the mask and the con, we will look at how the mind can trap itself in a pattern of low self-esteem or unhelpful behaviour. In this case then, rapport can be created for two main reasons:

1. To connect to the others of the group, thus leading to acceptance. If they are accepted and wanted their chance of survival and connection will dramatically increase.

2. Usually unbeknown to the child at the time they can learn "This is the way I should behave in life to avoid pain". As mentioned, a child is completely dependent upon the adults around them so survival (physical and emotional) will rate very highly on their list of needs. If the child is unsure of their world through lack of knowledge, they may copy the behaviours of those around them assuming that they are the correct template for the best options of survival. The mind of a child is very impressionable and is always finding new ways to understand how to act, which again leads to survival.

Dropping down the scale

Given that every person alive is on their own journey of emotional growth, it can obviously be an option where a child can be born to parents or peers who have low self-esteem and low confidence. This does not have to be in all areas of their life; in some areas a parent or peer may be very self aware, but in others they may struggle immensely. Yet as mentioned a child will also be learning about the world from all of the environments in which they find themselves.

Sometimes they may be exposed to very loving and connecting environments, which can create healthy and connecting videos of association. However, other situations in life can become a battleground with competition everywhere. If the child and the child's protector self do not have sufficient skills to deal with these challenging experiences they can be stored as painful beliefs and association and placed in the lower section of the scale. To see potentially painful environmental messages that a child could be exposed to we simply need to look in the papers or watch the news on TV, which in its majority is usually negative information of crime, suffering and loss.

If a child was to be born into a negative environment they will be subconsciously picking up behaviours and habits of how to act and react in their environment without even realising it. If left unchecked, this can lead to an inability to control their emotions due to the protector self continually taking control by engaging the fight, flight or freeze reaction - all of which is directly related to the con.

The 3 emotional wounds – A creation of shame

The Emotional Wound Part 1: My environment is not safe!

Going on the assumption that a child is naturally born with a mindset drawn to connection, it can thus be understood why it can be a common trait for them to adopt and learn their parents'/peers' personality and mannerisms. This, as mentioned earlier, is to gain rapport and therefore increase the connection, security and to learn how to act in life. A child will learn from those around them as that is the only template they have for reflection and discovering how to act in the world.

However (and this is where the mind can learn misaligned beliefs), if the child is in an environment that is in any way threatening or perceived as threatening to their protector self, potentially dangerous situations will start to be recorded as videos and stored within either the subconscious or Pandora's Box for future reference in other situation.

With the child having so much dependency upon their peers, if the environment is in any way threatening, the child can start to feel insecure about their own abilities of self-protection. This can be amplified if there is a lack of support or an environment of potential disconnection (aloofness). This, bound with the mindset that we may naturally become anxious of that which we do not understand, can cause the first cataclysmic backlash of emotions. The reason for this is that the child is attempting to create a secure environment but will at the same time feel anxious that they are insecure. They feel insecure because they are too young to understand the negative actions of the parents or peers.

For example, one parent shouting at another parent in front of the child (which can be a common and normal life experience) may be seen to the child that their whole environment could collapse at any given moment (if they feel vulnerable). Again, as the child is dependent on the environment, the argument could (in their eyes) have a direct impact on their security. In reality the argument may be because the adults have a disagreement, but the child may not see it that way because they are in total dependency and helplessness. Although a simple one-off argument may only have very little impact, continual occurrences may compound to create a trauma for that individual.

A point to note here is that although a parent or peer does not have to be outwardly aggressive or angry for a child to feel insecure. Any 'below the line' emotions intensely projected onto a vulnerable child can cause upset or anxiety. It can also be assumed that all parents and peers will at some point display emotions that are below the line. This is only human as the emotional scale for any person will rise and fall throughout the day.

Situations such as drug abuse or perceived continual rejection patterns (a peer's need to be alone through continual exhaustion or anxiety) can in some situations have a dramatic effect on a young mind. This can create such beliefs as shame and guilt in the child from the peer appearing as one personality one minute and a different one the next. The child will have no experience of how to handle this situation if they have not been taught any knowledge of how to cope or how to ensure their safety and survival. The child therefore cannot understand why this is happening and can become unsure if the parent or peer will leave or become disconnected forever.

Although this may seem extremely dramatic to an adult reading this, it is suggested that it is viewed through the eyes of a small dependent child. Through these eyes it is easier to understand why a child can become anxious. Also, we only need to look around in today's society at how many people have a desperate need for approval from their peers. The need for approval is usually driven by an anxiety of abandonment created from shame.

The Emotional Wound Part 2: It is not safe to be me!

One main survival mechanism that the child may adopt in order to cope in an insecure environment will be to 'fit in' or not cause any upset or disturbance. The purpose of doing this is to reduce any form of anxiety for the parent/guardian. The purpose of doing this is to ideally restore any disturbed security

.

Although with this 'fitting in' conformity, the child will have to become what is known as the **conditioned self** (a behaviour designed to fit in to the erratic surroundings) rather than their **true self** (a following of the desires to do new things/ autonomy). However, becoming the conditioned self through anxiety of not having any food, shelter or security causes the second cataclysmic backlash of emotions as they are in effect giving up 'their desires' (in essence who they are) in order to gain food or acceptance. When a child gives up on their true self to become their conditioned self (to resolve trauma) it can in many ways feel like an emotional death. Again if we look at this from a child's perspective 'who they are' is all they have.

Although it is true that we all need to adapt to our surrounding to some degree as we cannot simply walk around doing what we want without considering others' feelings, the adaption in 'this' stage is completely forced due to there being a fear or anxiety towards survival or security.

It is also important to note that some children will appear to go the opposite way and fight back in pure frustration and anger. Yet as anger is created through anxiety (the fight part of fight, flight or freeze), behind the anger there will always be vulnerability.

Some children can also create a conditioned self in the form of groups whom are different than their immediate peers to feel as though they fit in and are valued. We can see this when frustrated children join gangs or clubs that they may not want to join, but feel it is their best option of safety and connection.

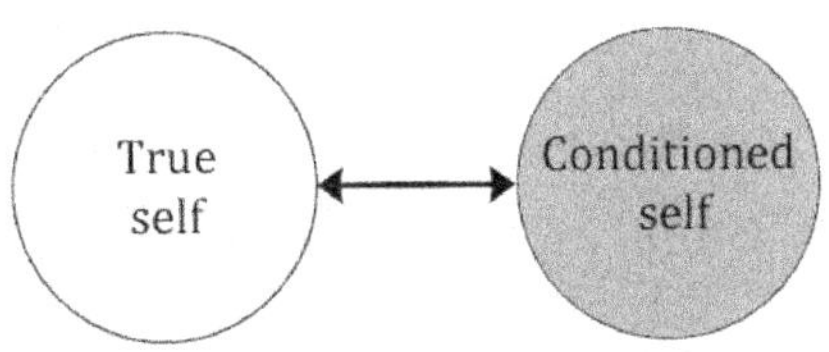

Although the conditioned self is not the ideal emotional place to be in, it is still the best option of survival in the environment that the child sees (real or imagined). So, for the child to stay in the role of the conditioned self and 'fit in', the protector self must place certain safety measures in their mind to prevent the child from overriding the desire to be their true self again. This pattern can be learned through reward and punishment:

Belief 1: If you are your conditioned self and do as others expect - you are safe!

Belief 2: If you act as your true self and act different than the 'house rules' - you are not safe!

Indeed, if the house rules are created by overly controlling peers, the child's protector self will look for survival first and self-expression second. This means that even if the child wants to scream and shout from the sheer frustration of the confusion they feel in their environment, the protector self will override this drive and attempt to create submissiveness by initiating stage 3 of the peer idolisation model (see below).

NB: *The only active self-expression a child really has when feeling frustrated is to make noise and move objects about (throwing toys, food etc.). However, if doing this creates a potential risk of perceived rejection, the "protector self" will override self-expression and create submissiveness. All of this will be going on behind the scenes unbeknown to the conscious mind.*

This, however, is not always the case as many parents will agree; sometimes the child will display characteristics of the exact opposite personality and become extremely vocal or destructive (for more information on this, please refer to the section on the mask in the self-esteem recovery model). Also these actions could simply be a learned programme that the protector self has created "I shout = people give me attention" (get needs met = pleasure).

The Emotional Wound Part 3: They are right, I am wrong!

Here it is important to note that if the child is immensely anxious or in a very toxic and threatening environment, they may make even extreme abuse acceptable in their mind as they do not see any other options of survival or protection. It is in this stage when abusive peers can project extremely negative emotions onto a child and the child will appear as if it's acceptable by not fighting back. In reality though, the child's protector self is supressing their emotional expression in order to survive.

In order to keep the child in the conditioned self, thereby preserving security, the protector self must create a sense of rationality to the conscious mind to justify the suppressed behaviour and self expression. However, as we have seen so far, what the mind perceives as rational and what is actually rational can be very different and easily distorted. It is in this state that a sense of shame and guilt can be created.

Shame: The feeling that 'I am' something wrong – who 'I' am is flawed and worth-less

Guilt: The feeling that 'I have done' something wrong – my actions are incorrect

Although we will cover different paths of these two areas in more depth in the next chapter, for this chapter we will look at how the protector self may twist potential reality to ensure emotional suppression and therefore increase potential safety. So, in a potentially threatening environment, the child's protector self (or learned habits / projections) may say to the child:

Shame phrases
"You are useless"
"You are being told off because you are not good enough"
"You have no value"

Guilt phrases
"It's because you get in the way people are mad with you'
"You are so selfish and should do more for others"
"You are making too much noise and that's why your Mum/Dad/Peer is mad at you"

Although this sounds like the child's own protector self is being immensely abusive to the child, if the protector self feels that stopping the child from being themselves will ensure safety and reward, then suppression becomes the lesser of two evils and is therefore deemed as pleasure or a benefit.
Another way to look at this is, rather than reject the source of survival (parents/peers) it is safer to reject the self emotionally. Although at the time this causes a severe internal pain (shame), if we look at this rationally it is safer than cutting off food and shelter and emotional safety.

In essence to the child this can be likened to an 'emotional death' and can be so traumatic to the child that this very memory (video) can become deeply suppressed within Pandora's Box. As we recall, although memories and beliefs which become suppressed in Pandora's Box are hidden away from the consciousness, it does not stop the video from projecting itself onto the internal cinema screen in the future years.

It is this stage, however, which I feel causes the most painful cataclysmic backlash of all, which is…

'I believe that they are right and I am fundamentally flawed' (shame – 'I' am wrong)

If we then mix this belief with a potentially negative environment where peers may be projecting their own insecurities onto the child, it is logical to understand how confusing and traumatised the child can feel whilst trying to balance the environment.

For the child, the act of giving up on 'who I am' (i.e. the suppression of the true self or self-expression to become the conditioned self) can create one of the most painful emotional backlashes of emotions the human psyche can face. This backlash can be one of the main causes of self-hatred, self-loathing, guilt, shame and low self-esteem.

The act of preserving the peer's integrity, which thereby keeps the security of food, shelter and other needs, is the title of this section. We in effect 'idolise' the very people that keep us alive; we protect our providers at all cost! Remember this point for the con and the mask.

The 3 emotional wounds – The creation of shame

1. **The Emotional Wound Part 1: My environment is not safe!**

2. **The Emotional Wound Part 2: It is not safe to be me!**

3. **The Emotional Wound Part 3: They are right I am wrong!**

An example projected future

For this example we will take a person in their 30's who has now been employed for a while and their manager starts to be rude, ignorant or even aggressive towards them.

If the employee had created a shame-based self-image from a challenging childhood environment and then suppressed that video in Pandora's Box it is possible that they would immediately give all their power to the manager. A shame-based belief is an internal representation of 'who I am is not good enough'. If they believe that they are not good enough this belief will then be used as the template for the protector self. Also, if the employee viewed their manager in a "pseudo-peer role" their mind may still act and react in the same manner it did when they were a child.

It is by looking at life in this way that we can start to understand why highly intelligent, creative and skilled adults can become trapped in workplace bullying and abuse. Even though as an adult they have the power to defend themselves competently.

The loop pattern

At this point I will again repeat myself (as I will do often throughout this book) on the topic that the subconscious mind cannot analyse its own beliefs. If the above pattern (of the employee) is buried deep in their Pandora's Box, the conscious mind may not be able to see the pattern and will therefore be unable to update it. This is how people can appear to be unable to break free from unhealthy environments such as negative job roles or abusive relationships (self fulfilling prophecy).

In an example of person becoming trapped in a job role with a negative manager it may be that they believe that if they move on from their current career or manager, nobody else would ever want to employ them as they are so fundamentally wrong. This however would cause immense confusion for the conscious mind, which cannot see into Pandora's Box. This confusion would appear because the conscious mind cannot see the logic of why the protector self and subconscious would allow this to continue. It is through this confusion that people can often claim they have 'irrational behaviour'.
The protector self will carry on protecting its beliefs and keep on protecting the mind today just as it did when the person was very young (state recall), and it will do this until the subconscious and especially Pandora's Box is updated. Again, just to emphasize, this is why simple mindfulness and positive thinking techniques will only ever be a temporary solution as these level of techniques are conscious based strategies.

The peer idolisation scale is a theory to observe possible actions and reactions of children who then carry those beliefs into adulthood. Understanding how the mind processes information is essential if we are to understand how it becomes vulnerable to the mask and the con.

As it is plain to see from the above analogy, a trapped emotion may continue to be replayed upon the inner cinema screen for the protector self to react (re-act) to until it is updated. In some cases of trauma or limiting belief further professional support may be required in order to release the trapped emotion. A trapped emotion within the subconscious mind will cause the protector to continually react to the videos replaying on the internal cinema screen. The continual videos replaying will then lead to continual stress reactions when similar events are experienced. This loop will then not only lead to an increase in stress, but also greater vulnerability to the mask and the con.

Chapter summary

See through your protector self's eyes, not yours

In all my years teaching emotional development, the main reason I see people face a challenges with this level of information is that they are seeing the world through their conscious mind only. The main part of the mind is subconscious and therefore will act and react more readily to what is stored within (videos) rather than today's reality.

Take a moment and ask yourself which situations in life you feel you act 'irrationally' in. Once you have this list look at it through the conscious mind and then review it through your protector self's eyes (and past videos tricking the mind), and look for the 'logic' in the apparent 'irrational' actions.

The vulnerable child / adult

As mentioned the protector self will engage when it thinks you are in danger. The reason I refer so much to the adult to child is because when a child is so young they have very little power and therefore may feel that challenging situations are much more of a threat than an adult would. However, it is possible to create limiting belief loops at any age if the mind is in a particularly vulnerable place. In all the years I have been coaching (from my personal viewpoint), 90% of peoples' anxieties 'today' have been created from a childhood era.

Take a moment to reflect on anything that your protector self may have seen as a trauma when you were younger. Remember that your protector self will see through the eyes of when you were that age if it has been supressed or running a limiting belief.

Connection and disconnection

Binary code is a language a computer will use and is basically 0 or 1. Zero is no action and 1 is action, and although this sounds black and white this also is how the subconscious mind will act. If a child or adult feels vulnerable around another person their protector self will naturally engage to disconnect them from the potential threat. This threat may either be coming from the person's own paranoia (internal cinema screen) distorting the current situation, or the other person is actually a threat.

Reflect upon all the experiences that you have had with other people and recall all of the people in your life whom you felt 1: Particularly connected to and 2: Those you felt disconnected from. Once you have this list, make some notes as to why you feel this may be.

The emotional wounds

Here we discussed the 3 main emotional wounds 1: My environment is not safe, 2: It is not safe to be me and 3: They are right, I am wrong. A child may be placed in an unhealthy environment and then convince themselves that it is 'they' who are wrong. This can then lead to major confusion as their natural instinct is to connect, but the protector self may assume that the world is a threat. This in my view is the leading cause of challenges in relationships.

Reflect upon your past experiences and ask yourself if you may have felt any of these three emotional wounds through your life. If you can relate to these emotional wounds then list them out and ask yourself whether any of these memories are still in the forefront of your mind today.

Adapt to survive

Situations do not have to be extremely violent to be traumatic! Any emotions from below the line which is continually projected upon a child (or the mind at any age) can lead to identity confusion. Adults around a child will not always be doing these actions on purpose and many will be completely unaware that they are doing them at all. However, the protector self may override the desire to be the 'true self' (thereby becoming the conditioned self) in order to create the best option of survival.

Take a moment and ask yourself if (or when) you have created any coping patterns (being your conditioned self) to win other peoples' approval or to stay safe (emotionally or physically). A way to check if these actions are coming from the 3 emotional wounds will be if you feel compelled to do these rather than choosing to (e.g. I have to listen to 'everybody' or I have to do more / be the best I can be).

8

Shame and Guilt

As we have already started to discover, shame and guilt are by far two of the most destructive emotions to the emotional psyche. The reason for this is that they are the deepest wounds that a person can create in regards to their internal self-image. Here, please note that I said 'the person creates', as the truth is that shame, guilt and other painful emotions are created from the mind either misinterpreting the situation or not having sufficient emotional ability / skills to defend themselves against the challenge or trauma.

The self-image (or residual self-image as I sometimes refer to) is who we 'think' we are. The best way I could describe this is if a person were to look into a mirror (metaphorically) to which the mirror would show them who they 'assume' they were. This image is based upon the perceptions of how competent 'they feel' they are derived from their interpretation of all of their experiences in their life. It could also be said that they would see who they 'think' they are, rather than who they actually are.

An example of this would be as follows:

Person A compliments Person B on how nice they look
Person B rejects the comment saying they look a mess

Here we have two conflicting opinions, which is always a possibility as how good another person looks is always in the perception of the other person's opinion.

However, in this case if Person B was dressed smartly and of a good appearance but their internal residual self-image was low, then they would see 'themselves' as sub-standard and will reject the compliment.

In this example, Person B's internal mirror is obviously not reflecting actual reality as that 'is' good enough (dressed smartly), but it would be reflecting the self-image that they have created on their internal cinema screen. Here we can revisit the phrase…

We do not see reality; we see what 'we think' is reality!

Or,

Perception is reality.

Yet the reason that shame and guilt can be so destructive is that they are not only the source of all other negative emotions, but they are both an attack on the self or the 'I' which is created from the belief that…

Who 'I' am is inadequate! (Shame)
Let's look deeper into this.

The twins of destruction!
To understand the concept of shame and guilt we need to clearly define the separation between a person and their actions. These may sound the same, but they are not.

If we look at the diagram below it is noticeable that there is a centre circle that leads out to several other circles. The two parts are:

1. The centre circle: is 'who I am'
2. The outer circles: are 'what I do'

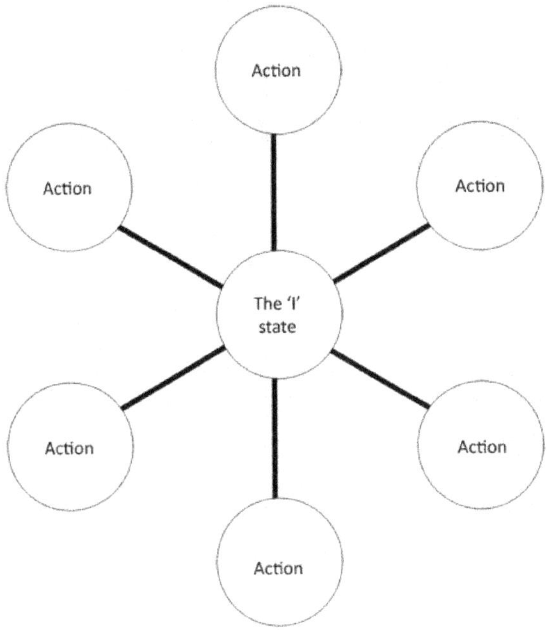

A deeper look

1. **The centre circle: is 'who I am'**

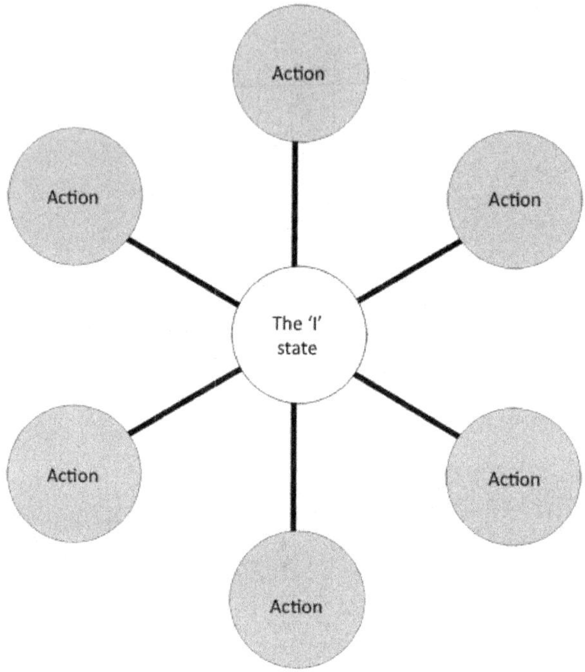

Although the term 'I' self can sometimes become very esoteric and complex leading to an explanation requiring an entire book on the spiritual self or the soul, for this definition I will keep it very clean cut. The 'I' for this chapter is basically a person in a state of free will. This can also be known as an autonomous, true self or independent mindset that makes decisions free from external approval or an anxiety of rejection.

When a person's psyche is free from overwhelming stress reactions, their mind will be able to see current situations clearly and be present tense. This 'being present' is an ability to see reality as it actually is rather than what the mind 'thinks' it is (conscious awareness of the mind without hijacks).

In other words, we can say that the 'who I am' state is a person at peace. They are able to cope with or rationalise any internal or external stress experiences. This then will create a state of 'being present' and the ability to make choices consciously.
Another way of looking at this is that the 'who I am' is like a computer that has tremendous power and ability and is running smoothly without any contradictive viruses causing disruption to the processor.

2. The outer circles: is 'what I do'

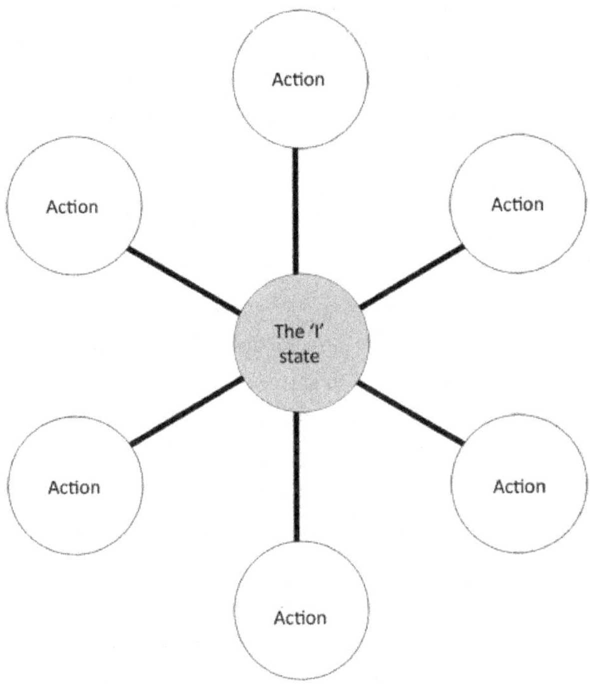

If the centre circle is a person being present and connected to their true potential, then the outer circles are the actions that they take (or anything separate from the 'I' self). Actions will cover things such as painting a picture, talking with friends, cooking food, learning new skills and so on.

As described in 'who I am', if the centre is a computer with all the potential, then the outer circles are the computer programmes taking action in the physical world.

As we go through this chapter it is important to keep these two definitions clearly in your mind as to understand the mask and the con, we also need to understand that 'who I am' is NOT 'what I do'. The reason for this will become more apparent as we progress through the chapters.

The 'who I am' is your true self (and yourself at peace) and the 'what I do' is the actions which are taken and are learned, processed and stored within the cognitive brain. Therefore, 'what you do' can be changed when you learn new skills and adapt to situations. Also actions can be driven from the true self (the 'I' state) OR the conditioned self (to seek approval).

The thought virus

As very few people in society are given a comprehensive education on social psychology, it leaves many people copying and pasting learned actions from their peers (as we saw in the peer idolisation scale).

So it is with this copying and pasting that if one person learns an incorrect mannerism and then projects it onto another person, unless that person was to alter the projection, the mannerism will again be projected upon a third person and thus the loop expands.

This copying and pasting could also be seen to act in a similar pattern to a virus. A virus will spread from person to person and continue to copy and paste itself as long as its host and subsequent hosts have a weaker immune system than the virus's ability to grow.

The metaphor for a weak immune system in an emotional virus can be a lack of education. This can then leave the mind unable to rationalise and harmonise the thought pattern or mannerism.

It is with this in mind that our peers could have unknowingly picked up thought patterns and mannerisms from others around them when they were young or when they were simply unaware. Unless resolved, the mannerism will grow within their mind and then be projected onto other people around them. If the other people are susceptible then they will also contract the mannerism virus to then pass on.

Take the example:

1. Joe's grandfather was born into a family that could not cope with their own stress. He watched them argue with each other and learned that if a person shouts and acts aggressively, people attacked them less. When people attacked Joe's grandfather he acted aggressively, and then he noticed that they started to attack him less too. Joe's grandfather's stress reduced by controlling the situation.

2. Joe's grandfather feels uncomfortable in social situations due to low self-esteem and then controls his group of friends by acting aggressively if they ever become too loud. This aggression virus passes to Joe's grandfather's friend Mike, who then projects it onto his wife who also starts to let the virus take over. Both Mike and his wife are extremely stressed. They now both use the aggression control virus to control other people in their social group, which works as the other people feel intimidated.
3. Some of the people in Mike and his wife's social group take on the virus and start acting aggressively and some do not and either speak to them or leave the group.

4. The aggression virus is now projected onto Peter, who is Mike's child. Peter unknowingly contracts the virus and also starts acting aggressively (to be like his dad). Peter is deemed a trouble child and Mike punishes him with aggression to try and control him.

5. The aggressive punishment causes Peter to act with very low self-esteem and he becomes shy. At this stage we can see the virus mutate from 'fight' to 'flight' and Peter now alternates between aggression and shyness.

6. Peter now has a daughter (Sarah) and projects his confused emotional mannerisms virus onto her. Due to Sarah's lack of emotional education she becomes confused and also contracts the virus.

7. Sarah, now in her early 20's, struggles to understand why her relationships never last more than 3 months and she is described as being 'high maintenance' in relationships.

8. The virus continues to spread.

The reason that I shared that last example is to explain that when we encounter people who are outwardly aggressive or manipulative, it is not that they are purposely out to hurt anybody. As we have already covered, the mind will move away from pain and towards pleasure. To attack another person is a disconnection and therefore will always be viewed as a pain association. For a person to attack another person it simply means that they have contracted a thought virus that is causing them pain, and they are unable to cope with it through a lack of education and stress.
In the reverse though, if they perceive that attacking another person will result in their friends valuing them more (peer expectation reward), then attacking another person will create a pleasure response (the aim of approval from peers).

With that aside, if we are vulnerable to attack, encountering people who manipulate emotions will then be a threat to our health and wellbeing. This described virus loop is the same structure as to how shame and guilt can be created and then go on to create further loops within Pandora's Box.

The definition of shame

Of the two destructive emotions (shame and guilt), shame is by far the most destructive of all given that it is a projection of 'who I am' is inadequate. If the 'who I am' is seen as flawed then it naturally goes to say that 'what I do' will also be seen as flawed, as 'what I do' is an action which is created from 'who I am'. However, some people with shame can appear very confident in 'what they do', but there will be more about why that happens when we cover the mask.

The emotion of shame can also only ever be self-generated. Shame is a person's evaluation of their own worth based upon experiences which they have interpreted. Even if many peers have projected abuse onto another person it is still and can only be their self-reflection which creates the shame in their own eyes.

"No one can make you feel inferior without your consent."
- Eleanor Roosevelt, This is My Story

As we saw with the above thought virus explanation, a person can only contract a virus if their psychological immune system is weak or vulnerable.

When a person displays shame, they may display any form of fight, flight or freeze reactions to protect themselves. When a person sees themselves as shame based, it creates a reflection that they have little or no inherent value or worth regardless of what they do or achieve. We can see this when some people buy new items of clothing or achieve great success, but may feel unworthy of the achievement or being celebrated by other people.

Shame is born when we create a misaligned self-image of low worth in comparison to our peer group. This is based on other people's projections of disconnection or telling us that we are not good enough. We then believe their views and directly or indirectly internalise them, running them as our own interpretation.

The definition of guilt

As shame is a perception of 'who I am' being inadequate, then guilt is a perception that 'what I do' is inadequate. Usually if a person has shame in their emotional psyche, guilt will also be present. The reason for this is that if shame says 'who I am' is inadequate, then this virus will naturally spread to 'what I do', which creates further viruses. This can happen because it is the 'I' (reflected self-worth by comparison to those around us) that creates the action (what I do).

For a person carrying the emotion of guilt, underneath (behind any masks they may create) they will have a feeling that they are wrong in the actions they take or they could have done it better. We can see guilt arising when a person says a particular word on an extremely regular basis, and that word is 'sorry'.

The word 'sorry' is an apology a person is making to another person for a perceived wrong or error that they have made. 'Sorry' is unnecessarily used far too often today in many parts of the world, although it can be dependent upon culture too.

Also, if a person feels guilty they can often apologise for everything they do so they can say to the other that they have seen their error and are making the other person aware before they possibly attack (paranoia or actual toxic environment).

As with shame, guilt is another self-generated emotional virus. If a person is carrying a belief of 'what I do' is inadequate, then they may start to perceive the things that they do as being seen by other people as inadequate, whether they are or not.

In some cases this can also become a self-fulfilling prophecy as they may make actions subconsciously which are out of character but end up being incorrect. They may do this because they may become anxious that they do everything wrong, which will cause them to continually think about the incorrect action rather than the correct one.

An example of this could be - Don't drop your keys!

A person walking down the road late at night may think over and over "Don't drop your keys". They think about it all the way home and then find that they have dropped them. The reason for this is that the mind won't reject a negative statement. The active words in the above statement were 'drop your keys'. This then creates an internal image on the internal cinema screen and the mind assumes that it is a request and takes action e.g. dropping the keys. The mind is not attacking the person, it is simply following orders. The human subconscious mind is quite 'think and do' - it doesn't question, it just takes action. It is only the conscious mind that can understand that 'don't drop your keys' actually means the opposite.

Chapter summary

Who you are

Without looking as this term in a spiritual sense, the term 'I' is classed as a person in a state of confident free will (true self). In this state you will have direct access to your inner drives and desires and feel connected with other people, understanding that many different types of personalities will create a community.
Take a moment and list all of the times you can remember when you were/are your true self (in the 'I' state). This will be when you have felt true inspiration and desires from within, with or without another's input. An example of this would be if you wanted to paint or play a musical instrument and even if everybody else disagreed with you…you still felt the drive to do it.
Be aware that some people have become so used to thinking about other people's opinions that they can barely remember a time when they were in their 'I' state.

What you do

The actions you take are not who you are, but what you do! Your 'I' state is the potential and your actions are the creation of the thoughts. Your actions can be driven 'from' two sources, 1: Your natural drive for the highest ideal (the 'I' state) or 2: A need to gain approval or control (the conditioned self).
Reflect upon all of the main actions that you have taken in the last month and ask yourself which of these two states your motivation was driven from.

Shame and guilt

Shame and guilt are two of the most destructive emotions that a human being can face. Recall…guilt is a belief that you have 'done' something wrong and shame is a belief that you 'are' something wrong. This can be an extremely sensitive area for many people to reflect upon, so please be aware of your emotional state when reviewing this area.

Reflect upon the last few months of your life and recall any experiences in which you may have felt either of these two emotions. For example, a guilt reaction may be that you feel you did not stay long enough or were not entertaining enough when you visited a friend and a shame reaction may be that you feel unworthy of a friend's compliment.

Remember that there are no requirements for you to answer these questions if this feels a little too sensitive.

The thought virus

It is very easy for a person to pick up a habit from another person if they are not aware of their emotions in that moment. In essence, if we were to let our guards down in an erratic environment a thought virus could easily transfer.

Take a moment and list out all of the beliefs, reactions and expectations that you currently act and react upon and do your best to trace back where they may have come from. For example, if you are a worrier and describe yourself as a worrier, upon reflection you may realise that one of your parents describes themselves in the exact same way.

The obedient mind

Although the conscious mind can make its own decisions, the subconscious mind is quite robotic in its function. The subconscious mind is quite autonomous and will follow the programmes which have been stored. This can cause confusion if we look at this through the conscious mind only as it may appear that the subconscious is not functioning correctly.

Take a moment and reflect upon all of the actions and reactions which you don't want to do but automatically act out anyway. For example, if a person held a belief that they 'are clumsy' but doesn't want to be this way, yet upon reflection they often tell themselves not to be 'so clumsy' (the subconscious acts out what it think the words mean… 'so clumsy').

9

Self Esteem Recovery Model

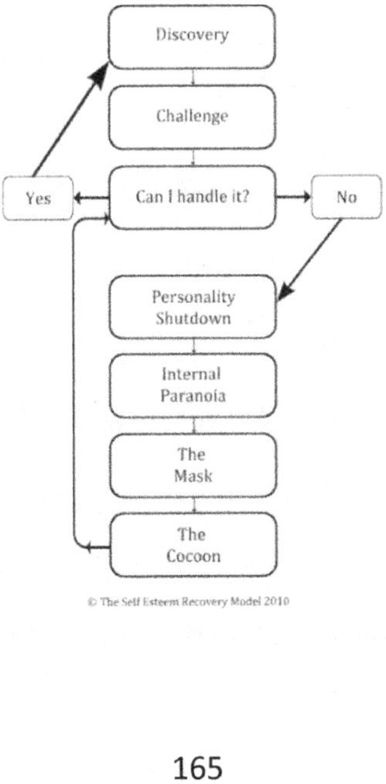

If a sense of power and control is to be gained over the mask and the con, it is essential to put all the information into step-by-step structures and diagrams. The benefit of this is that it allows the conscious mind to understand complex information. When the conscious mind has more awareness it can start to understand the structure that the protector self is functioning from and a harmony between the two minds can begin to grow.

The self-esteem recovery model is another of my own designs to map the path that the mind can take during two alternative states of experience. These two pathways can be likened to the connected and disconnected states from the peer idolisation scale.

The self-esteem recovery model, as with all others models, has been designed to give a structure and further understanding to how the subconscious mind and protector self respond or react to with traumatic or challenging experiences.

NB: *Through this chapter we will be using the example of a parent to a child. Again though, it is very important to see this only as an example of a situation and not as one experience that can cause major trauma to a child. It is impossible for a parent to cater to every need a child has and therefore it is not to insinuate that it is only the parents responsibility or that it is all the parents' fault as that is simply not true. Yes, if a child is neglected then changes need to be made, but too often the parents will get the blame for a challenged child when there are so many other variables to consider. The situations which can drive a child to path two rather than path one are any situations in which a child becomes overwhelmed.*

Please refer to the diagram when working through each stage.

The two paths on the self-esteem recovery model are:

1. Learning, growth and self-discovery (connection)
2. Coping with and recovering from trauma (disconnection)

Path one – Learning, growth and self-discovery

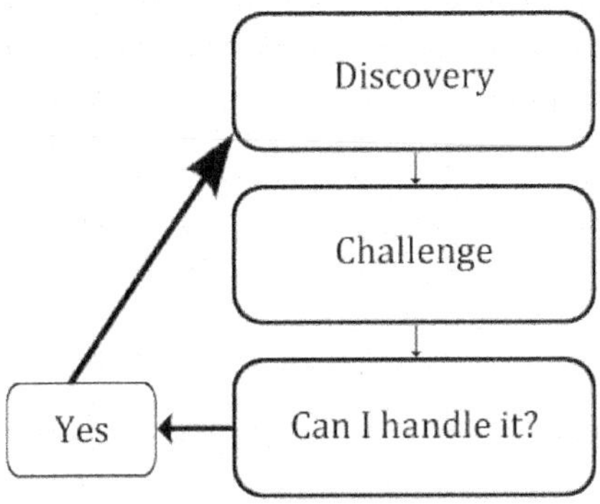

© The Self Esteem Recovery Model - Path 1 - 2010

Path one in detail:

Path one of the self-esteem recovery model is related to the 'connection' stage in the peer idolisation model and is therefore seen as pleasure or a healthy growth of an individual.

For a child to gain the healthiest learning opportunity, the environment must be relatively challenging (to induce growth) but still within their capabilities. An example of this would be stacking bricks; at first the bricks may fall, but the environment is safe. So the child attempts to stack them again, this time realising that a steadier hand is needed. They take extra care and the next time the bricks balance. The child feels like they have grown and new learning has taken place.

Path one: Stage 1 – Discovery

The discovery stage is the part of each person that has the deep-seated urge to grow. We are born with a natural instinct to learn, to discover a sense of meaning and a sense of purpose. The more a person can grow, the more independent they become, leading to a greater awareness for survival and creative expression.

The mind in its natural state drives a person forward through a sense of desire or an instinct to observe new things. The mind is naturally inquisitive; it wants to pick things up, look under things, (and as our abilities grow) to ask questions, travel and meet new people. For most people this sense of hunger and curiosity is not something that they choose to have, it is simply a natural drive.

This drive can be subdued though through low self-esteem, shame or anxiety or pain as we will see in path two. Even though it can be subdued, it does not disappear entirely. For the millions of people who assume that they may have lost their spirit of adventure, the truth is that it has not gone, it has just been suppressed by the protector self deeming there to be a pain associated to self-expression. This can be likened to putting a blindfold over our eyes so we cannot see the sun - the sun is always there, but it is just that we cannot see it at that moment.

Path one: Stage 1 - Discovery

An example of this would be a child climbing on a chair to get cookies (pleasure) from a jar on top on the kitchen unit. The chair is unstable and the child is unsure, but the discovery drive pushes the child to achieve their goal (no pain is associated to this action yet because no painful videos have been recorded). The child does not know the outcome of their ventures though, they just try to attain it anyway.

Path one: Stage 2 – Challenge

If the discovery stage can be likened to a child moving along a path in a straight line, then the aim is simply to get from point A to point B. However, a challenge in this model is simply an object or a challenge (pain) that gets in the way of the child moving forward on that line, thereby causing a hindrance or resistance.

Life however is full of challenges and things which get in the way are natural. To understand this in a clearer manner, we can use a metaphorical description that life is similar to that of a bumper car at the fairground. Sometimes people and situations will clash, sometimes one car will win and sometimes the other car will win. Sometimes it will be equal and one or both cars have to reverse to get out of the situation. Life is full of challenges and those challenges can either help us grow or cause us pain.

At this stage though it is only important to recognise that life will naturally bring us challenges which we may store (videos) as pain or pleasure. As in the diagram, our discovery stage is attempting to move forward toward a chosen goal (i.e. to discover) and a challenge is something that stops (or stands in the way of) us reaching the goal from the discovery stage

A metaphor of a challenge on path one

A challenge to the child attempting to get cookies from the top of the kitchen unit would be a parent walking in the kitchen, picking up the child and carrying them off into another room, then smiling at them explaining that their lunch is nearly ready. The child has now encountered a challenge to attaining their goal.

Path one: Stage 3 – Question, does this challenge mean pain or pleasure?

Surprisingly, it is not actually the challenge itself that causes emotional pain or pleasure (although it may not seem that way). The challenge itself is simply a situation and is an experience that happens to us i.e. being picked up by a parent and carried out of the room (the challenge to the child getting the cookies).

The pain or pleasure association (the video) therefore doesn't come from the challenge or the experience, but rather from the **person's perception**

of the challenge and whether the current challenge (experience) means pain (disconnection) or pleasure (connection) to their environment.
This perception will be driven from one of two sources:

Source one – We have never experienced this before and it presents itself as a pain or pleasure to our senses. We then store this as a new learning experience (create a new belief).

Source two – We have experienced this before and we assume that the same result will happen again (a belief has been previously formed in association with the experience).

Stage 3 of the self-esteem recovery model is where we assign 'meaning' to the challenge (or our perception of the situation) that we face. We assign whether that challenge means pain or pleasure to our environment. In the description for path one (a connection state) the threat or challenge is minimal (the parent picking up the child and carrying them to another room whilst smiling at them). The protector self has not been triggered and a new learning has occurred. The creative mind which wants to grow will now go back to the discovery stage (stage one) and either aim for another pleasure or will try again for the original aim (the cookies).

Metaphor
The child is carried off into another room away from the cookies, but looks up to see a smiling parent full of love. The child associates pleasure to the experience and feels safe in growing. They can store this challenge as 'connected' and either change their desire to the cookies or try a new strategy to get the cookies next time.

Path one has now been completed and the loop will cycle until a challenge brings too much pain association to the child and they move to path two.
Path one is a harmonious loop of growth and self-discovery and brings with it a feeling of fulfilment for the individual as it causes the mind and inner creativity to grow.

Path two in detail:

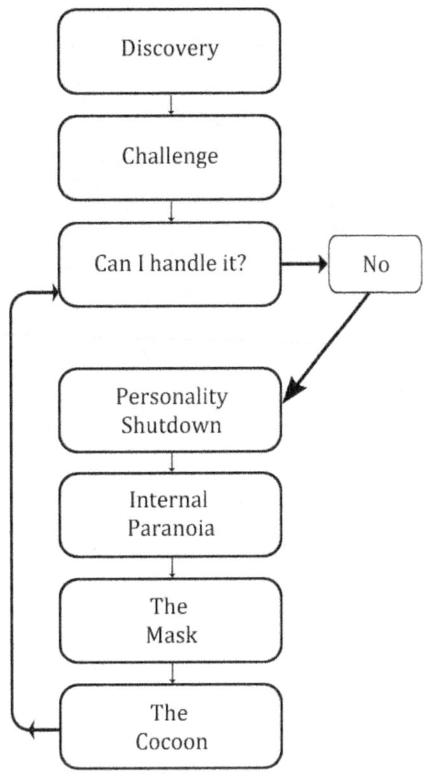

© The Self Esteem Recovery Model - Path 2 - 2010

In many ways, path two is the opposing side of path one and is the path that the mind walks after making an entirely different decision at the questioning stage. From the model we see of path two, it appears as a looming and heavy journey that many would rather avoid. This path seems as if it could spiral into torment and unfortunately for those who walk it this is how it can feel on a daily basis. In many senses it is true that this path can cause suffering and emotional pain, because in these stages (or some of them) they breed depression, shame, guilt, loss of feelings, low self-esteem and apathy, and more importantly a breeding ground for the con.

The above path (path two) may not sound as appetising as the first, but rest assured there is a happy ending (should the walker of path two choose to take it). Although there can be suffering in certain stages, it does not necessarily mean that that is how it will be forever. At this point we need to remember that the protector self part of the mind is always within, looking for new and creative ways to avoid pain and take each person's situation back up into the connect section. We also need to remember that there is a door that can be walked through to reach path one again as long as we see it (or choose to). This is what I aim to share in path two.

On path two, we can observe the step-by-step approach as how the mind initially copes with trauma and then continually attempts to restore harmony.

NB: *It is possible for any of the stages on path two to be reversed and not continue to the next stage, but only if the protector self has sufficient information to update the original association of pain within Pandora's Box which caused the decision to go along the route of path two.*

Path two: Stage 1 – Discovery

At this stage, as the aim is to show the different choices we can make in overwhelming challenging situations, we will assume that the child is in the same situation as path one but the only difference is that the 'challenge' they face - which this time is traumatic and disconnecting.

Metaphor

The child is climbing on a chair to get cookies from a jar on top on the kitchen unit; the chair is unstable and the child is unsure but the drive pushes them to achieve their goal (no pain is associated with this action).

Path two: Stage 2 – Challenge Metaphor

This time the parent walks into the kitchen in anger and although they have never scolded the child for climbing on a chair to get cookies before, this scene causes the parent distress (the parent's inability to cope with the situation) and they pick up the child and shout at them whilst carrying them into another room. The parent sits the child on the sofa and tells them to stop being naughty, then leaves the room and slams the door.

Path two: Stage 3 – Question, does this challenge mean pain or pleasure?

With such a distressing reaction from the parent (guardian or provider in the child's eyes), the protector self of the child is immediately alerted and starts to relate the situation to the potential rejection of the guardian and/or loss of security (pain). Unknowingly, the child can mistakenly internalise this as:

"I have taken an action that could potentially threaten my security and connection"

The child could also then believe that the responsibility of the whole situation rests on 'their' shoulders. Though really the trauma happened due to the peer not being able to cope with the child taking an action on a situation and the parent's fight or flight stress reaction had triggered. For the child's protector self, which is recording all potential threats as videos, if there is not a sufficient amount of resources to draw on (knowledge and experience) the protector self will not know how to handle the situation or regain security and connection. In the confusion the child's protector self will associate the pain (disconnection) to the action they took, linking that to which the discovery drive (their true self) has been trying to achieve.

Metaphor

The child does not know what to do and feels afraid and anxious, but is unsure as to why (the protector self's hidden reaction, I am not good enough) and the child now has pain associated with their discovery drive (i.e. getting cookies / self-expression).

Path two: Stage 4 – Personality shutdown

As the association of pain (and disconnection) is now connected to the initial drive of discovery (stage one) and the challenge (stage two/parents reaction), the protector self will now assume command of the child's decisions and begin the process of disconnection from the 'true self' and adopts the 'conditioned self' persona. This is where the "I must fit in" reaction occurs and as discussed before this happens in order to preserve the provider of food, water, shelter and social acceptance. The personality shutdown stage behaviour is distinguishable to the outside world through emotions such apathy, demotivation, sadness and a general loss of drive. At this stage the lack of drive may only be related to the action of 'getting cookies'.

Signs and symptoms of personality shutdown

When a person is in the initial stages of personality shutdown, there will be a general air of frustration twinned with a reluctance to take action. This if left will slowly grow into apathy and an avoidance of taking actions related to their original trauma.

Metaphor

The child has now become anxious as their protector self starts to display images of pain associated to the cookies on the inner cinema screen. So the child is not even seeing reality, but what they are told is reality on the internal cinema screen. The internal cinema screen is the memory of the rejection and pain of the parent shouting. This image will be played over and over again until the child submits to the desire to get more cookies or the image is changed.

Path two: Stage 5 – Internal paranoia

The stage of internal paranoia is actually in many ways a self-generation of worry and anxiety. If we take into account that now the protector self has switched on personality shutdown (Stage 4) and a sense of apathy begins to manifest in the mind. In many cases, this 'shutting down' brings with it a reluctance to socialise or connect with others. Being alone or restricting outside influences after perceiving trauma (stage 3) is a lethal cocktail which will breed paranoia because new information and experiences are not being created in the outside world or physical reality to compare with the memories of trauma (the inner cinema screen projections).

The loop of the mind in this stage is that if we associate pain to a situation and the protector self keeps playing the memory over and over (to try and keep us safe from harm), the mind is left continually focused upon the image of pain and suffering. The pain and suffering is painful in and of itself, but there is also a secondary pain that comes with this. The mind also associates similar memories together as a way of learning, and if enough memories connect together they created a generalised belief. The internal cinema screen can then become an inferno of pain association, creating a downward spiral effect on the emotions. This pain loop compounds, sending the protector self into a panic, which then creates even more protection mechanisms.

Signs and symptoms

A person in the internal paranoia stage will begin to manifest anxiety towards other areas in life rather than just the original trauma. For example, a person believing they are not good enough at singing (through a previous criticism or insult) could develop a generalised sense of anxiety in social situations. In the paranoia stage the memories will warp into a generalised "I am not good enough as a person" (shame) as opposed to just feeling self-conscious about being a singer.

At the paranoid stage adrenal hormones (caused by anxiety from the internal cinema screen) would usually be released into the body so often that the body becomes overwhelmed and drained (which can be temporarily reduced by exercise, rest and nutrition). Alternatively they may display a look of worry or distance (facially/physically) (flight) from having to continually endure the internal images of distress.

NB: *It is at this stage that the person's face and body language may start to display anxiety or a look of worry. Other members of society who feel insecure about themselves and who want to control other people to regain security in themselves will observe the look of worry on their target's face/ body and may begin to manipulate their target's weakness/ anxiety in a power game.*

Metaphor

The child now begins to get an internal feeling of anxiety about taking new challenges in general. To them (through lack of knowledge and Pandora's Box suppression) they are unsure as to why. They start to notice a heavier feeling of uneasiness when new challenges present themselves either at home or at school. The original anxiety of "I get hurt if I try to get cookies" has grown into "I may get hurt if I do new things" (generalised).

Path 2: Stage 6 – The mask

The mask stage is classed as a coping mechanism in which the protector self begins to use a different strategy to attempt to cope with the warped reaction of the internal cinema screen in relation to the original trauma.

This in many ways would seem a very contorted reaction for the mind to undertake because looking at it from an observer's point of view, it was the protector self forcing the initial withdrawal that created stages 4 and 5. So, in effect the mask is a secondary coping mechanism to cope with the primary coping mechanism. However, the protector self is doing its best to cope with the situations it faces in daily life with the experiences and information it has been exposed to, which then clashes with the internal cinema screen.

NB: *A physical representation of the above would be in the physical condition known as kyphosis lordosis. This condition causes a person to develop an arched lower back and hunched shoulders (giving an 'S' shape to the spine from a side point of view).*

This condition can sometimes be caused by a weak pelvis structure (or other joint issues), which unable to support itself begins to arch the lower back (leaning backwards). If this were to continue to arch backwards it would give the person a feeling of 'leaning back too far' and would eventually become off balance (this can be likened to stages 4 and 5 in the self-esteem recovery model). So, to cope with the imbalance of the lower back the upper body (shoulders) begin to hunch forward. This then brings the body's centre of gravity back to a form of stability (stage 6, the mask). The body will physiologically be out of line through the condition, but at least it is stable for the time being.

To serve and protect

The mask coping mechanism is very powerful on many levels and can be very complex to not only the wearer but to society at large. The mask in its makeup is an outward disguise or a front a person creates. The reason for this is that the person suffering from the continual images on the internal cinema screen from the paranoia stage will be so overwhelmed that they want to protect themselves from the stress overload.

A mask will usually be an action, personality or material gain which reflects the opposite of what the person is trying to hide from in their paranoia.

We will cover types of masks further along in this chapter, but a quick example would be:

- **Internal paranoia**

Continually showing images on the inner cinema screen of memories/ feelings that they are not valuable enough in society (worth 'less' to others).

- **Anxiety reaction**

Continual worry that the paranoia image will become true and people will reject them.

- **Mask reaction**

The person works hard and strategically in the corporate world and amasses a great financial wealth. With that wealth, they set up a company and hire lots of employees. With so many people now 'needing' the person (for money, opportunity and other gains) the person can now easily distract themselves from the internal pain by looking at what they have achieved and how many people do 'need' them. However, we also need to remember that the original memory of worthlessness / fear of rejection has not been resolved and is still trapped in time (inside the persons subconscious or Pandora's Box.

The mask is a trick, a con (but not 'the' con), not only to society, but to the person wearing the mask. As the mask is very powerful and elusive it can be very difficult to decipher what is a genuine desire from the heart (true self) and what is the mask that has been created to disguise the internal paranoia (conditioned self).

The protector self creates the mask for two reasons, and the wearer of the mask can use it for either or both:

Reason 1: To hide from the paranoia of the internal cinema screen (distraction)

Reason 2: To prove to others that the person opposite of what is being hidden in the paranoia (protection)

Reason 1: To hide from paranoia

There is a phrase which is apt here which says "What you are doing is so loud I can't hear what you say." A mask can sometimes be very action orientated (as we will see in the following examples), however, on path two it is still a distraction from the internal paranoia. A classic mask here is the stereotypical workaholic who is so busy all the time they haven't got time to stop (or stop and listen to their internal paranoia).

Reason 2: To prove to others

One of the most potent emotional pains a human being can suffer is that of rejection of those they love, leading to loneliness and isolation. It is an anxiety that is so powerful it can even lead people to take their own lives. Some people may disagree, claiming they do not need other people 'ever', but this is a mask of denial. Connection to others is a survival mechanism and although people can be comfortable being alone and like their own company, to disconnect from others goes against our natural flow.

If the person who has an internal paranoia believes that they are not good enough and people will reject them for who they are, the mask can then drive the person to take actions in the physical world which give the impression to the outside world that they are the opposite of who they wrongly believe they are. They will do this because inside they are anxious that others in society/peers will see them as not good enough/rejectable (as in the above example).

If we go back to the introduction of this book and recall the story of sugar and salt, it is easier to see how well hidden a mask can become. What appears to the outside world to be a successful exterior (and in many ways can be, if other people's lives are enriched) could in fact be being driven by a feeling of inadequacy, worthlessness or rejection.
But how do you tell the difference? (We shall soon find out.)

Types of masks
There can be literally thousands of types of masks and they can become anything and anyone. Remember, any external motivation driven by a sense of anxiety or paranoia is a mask. With it being possible that anybody taking any action could be wearing a mask, how do you tell the salt from the sugar? As mentioned there is a way to find out which action is a mask and which action is genuine choice. To look deeper at the mask stage though, here are some more possibilities.

Example 1
A person works 80 hours per week and hardly spends any time at home with their children and partner.

Mask's possible emotional driver
I can prove to people that I am a hard worker and get respect from my peers.

What the mask may be disguising
I am not good enough as who I am, so I have to impress people with my skills.
I can't face my partner and children as I do not feel worthy of their love or affection.

Example 2

A person goes out and has many sexual relationships and never commits to anybody claiming to be free and single.

Mask's possible emotional driver

I can have lots of attention and I'm desired. I also feel in control that others can't reject me.

What the mask may be disguising

An anxiety of not being good enough as a person and if anybody was to get too close they may see how unworthy I am.
There is not enough in life and it will run out eventually so I must get it while it is here (scarcity mindset).

Example 3

A person who speaks in an authoritarian tone almost continually, claiming it to be 'just the way they are'.

Mask's possible emotional driver

If I am seen as an authority and borderline confrontational, then people will respect me and listen to me.

What the mask may be disguising

I am too weak in comparison to other people and I am ashamed that I feel anxious about life's challenges and confrontations.

Metaphor (path 2 - stage 6)

The child (cookies) now becomes so frustrated from the continual feelings of stress and constantly hiding from their anxiety that they reverse their behaviour and start to become loud and boisterous, sometimes causing disruption at school and at home.
The parents and teacher are confused as to why and punish the child, which starts the cycle all over again.

Path 2: Stage 7 – The cocoon
Although the mask in stage 6 may seem an entangled maze in which the wearer of the mask would be forever imprisoned, the protector self has a very clever trick hiding up its sleeve and this is what is known as the cocoon stage. Remember the story of Pandora's Box where after all the suffering has been let out the spirit of hope appears?

If we take the example of the caterpillar that crawls along and one day starts to spin a cocoon around itself, at first it would seem as though the caterpillar is becoming trapped and is unable to escape, and in many ways that is true. The caterpillar will just sit there, but underneath the shell something very powerful is going on - the caterpillar is changing into a butterfly.
As a caterpillar its life is restricted and movement is slow, but as a butterfly the world is its garden and free to move about.

The cocoon stage is literally the phoenix from the flames stage, in which the person who is suffering the internal torment of paranoia and living behind the mask now has the chance to walk free and let go of the past trauma.

Just as with the caterpillar **the mask now 'can' actually becomes a cocoon** (a safe place and protection) for the person to hide within themselves. This protection bubble (if used correctly) can bring with it a feeling of security around others in society as everybody else will usually only be able to see the person's mask (again, if used correctly). This allows the person to go to the quiet place within and have time to question the original trauma back at stage 3. Though if the trauma is deeply embedded in Pandora's Box then usually a form of therapy or an intervention from an experience therapist may be required.

The cocoon stage is an essential part of growth, but also one of becoming totally vulnerable and open to the original trauma. Anybody who wears a mask can usually only move into this stage under three conditions:

Condition 1: They trust their mask's ability to give the appearance that they are the opposite of what they are scared people will see them as. This appearance will be to trick prying eyes or people who may want to emotionally manipulate them.

Condition 2: They have knowledge of their mind/psychology and how to move forward. They also have the ability to realise that their original trauma (stage 3) is just a past memory trapped in time and is not real anymore (or they have other options today).

Condition 3: They are in a safe and healthy environment that will not aggressively override their ability to defend themselves.

These three conditions are vital if a person is going to leave the comfort of their mask (which in some cases can be extremely comfortable) and release their original trauma.
Remember, the protector self will never move towards what it thinks is pain; pain (or anxiety) is a perception and therefore malleable. However, if the physical environment is challenging or threatening the change can only happen if the physical environment is able to be controlled or adapted, thereby lowering the threat the protector self sees.

Knowledge is power at this stage and knowledge gives the person an ability to question the original trauma (which will then stop the replay upon the internal cinema screen). It is the stage 3 trauma that was originally trapped inside and has just grown and grown. If the original trauma is released and come to terms with (which can in many cases be relatively easy to cope with when seen through today's eyes), the mask will have no power over the person anymore and they can choose to wear it or not. The mask though is sometimes very useful to wear (even once the trauma has been released) as it can give the appearance of what people want to see and can support them (optional conditioned self). This is extremely powerful in the world of business, **but we are only free if we can choose to wear the mask rather than being forced to by the protector self.**

Metaphor

The child (cookies) (who has now a grown to become a teenager) has now become the captain of every ball sport in school and is regarded as a true leader (mask). Although it has helped other pupils gain confidence and self-esteem (by the child/teenager taking this role), as the original trauma (stage 3) has not been updated, it is still the child's mask that is driving the teenager to be this leader.

The inner reflection…

The teenager is feeling more confident and secure in his environment and knows that he has control. With this confidence, one day the teenager sits quietly and remembers how humiliated and small he felt that he was carried off and shouted at for trying to get the cookies. He also remembers how angry and resentful he felt not only at the parent for stopping him, but more so at himself for backing down and feeling scared (resentment towards the protector self reaction), and although it is a bitter pill to swallow he realises that he is not that helpless child anymore and he is growing to be a man. From here, he sees the mask as a valuable part of who he is and realises that he does not always have to be a leader if he does not want to be. A sense of relief flows through him as he now sees he has a choice and does not have to fight all the time to prove his worth. The anxiety reduces as the old belief updates itself, his stress reactions slow from releasing as much adrenal hormones and he feels a new sense of energy and freedom.

NB: *Although the last example presented the teenager as sitting and letting go, in many cases it is not so simple. The protector self must trust the new thoughts and unlock old ones. Also, the belief may be buried under many compounded limiting beliefs stemming from the original trauma. A release of trauma can sometimes take a few hours and sometimes as long as a year to eighteen months if the person has a particularly complex protector self. That being said, should the person resist change or the therapist/coach is of a poor standard, the change may not happen at all. It has been known for a person who is scared to change to continue being treated with a poor quality therapist in order to hinder the change.*

Ignorance is bliss?

Many people are trapped in their world and in their mind. Also, many people are unaware of how to be free, mainly through a lack of education. Thus, they accept to live their life in pain, hoping to cope. This is no one's fault but just the way life is!

Take a moment as you walk around in your daily life and look around at how many people cling to their masks and refuse to let go. Or, if you feel that if they lose their mask or upon having their mask taken away, they become a shell of their former power.

Any house built on sand will surely fall.

"A house must be built on solid foundations if it is to last. The same principle applies to man, otherwise he too will sink back into the soft ground and becomes swallowed up by the world of illusion."

Sai Baba

Giving up on the security of what feels safe is not easy and can sometimes be near impossible if there is nothing more secure to replace it with. Many cultures in society today unfortunately live this way. They place great pressure on themselves to be more confident or go for their dreams, but they don't release the deeper trauma nor do they have anything to replace their mask with. With this strategy their protector self will hold them firmly in place, helping them to avoid pain. Looking at it this way, is it any wonder why millions of people all over the world take prescription medication for nerves, or alcohol or illegal drugs? In a world where there seems to be no other escape from the suffering, a source of avoidance becomes imminent and if drugs and alcohol suppress their pain, they become a pleasure enhancer as we have previously discussed.

However, taking the time to learn psychological concepts and understanding the ideas and strategies set out in this book (as you are doing) and understanding other authors' points of view are the first steps to letting go of the mask and the con, but freedom comes step by step.

Chapter summary

Path 1 – Growth

The healthiest path that we can face in life is one where we will receive a challenge which will push us to grow, and then we learn to adapt around that challenge and create a new skill set.

Take a moment and reflect upon all of the times that you can remember where you faced a challenge that was quite taxing but you eventually figured out a way in which to successfully negotiate the challenge and then grew as a result.

Path 2 – Shutdown

For many people who walk path 2 it can often become an unpleasant experience. This can be especially more challenging if part of their mind is locked within Pandora's Box.

Optional: Take a moment and reflect upon quite challenging times which you have faced but became too overwhelming for you to cope with. Then, do your best to trace your reactions and actions at each stage of path 2 on the self-esteem recovery model.

The creation of the mask

When the mind feels that it cannot cope with situation (either in reality or projected) it will seek to protect. One way of doing this is to create a mask which projects one image to the outside world whilst concealing their assumed self-image. The mask can be many different things in life, healthy or unhealthy.

Take a moment and ask yourself if you currently have any masks which you depend upon to make you feel more secure. Once you have this list…mark them out of 10 as to how dependant you are on each one.

The creation of the cocoon

The cocoon is an internal space in which the mind can feel that there is a wall of protection from the outside world. When the mind is under pressure this is an extremely useful ability. The walls of the cocoon will be created from a variety of masks. Ideally the masks will be healthy projections rather than the unhealthy ones (more on this is in upcoming chapters).

Take a moment and reflect upon any masks you currently have in your life that are helping you feel more secure. When you have these in your mind be aware that this can be healthy and is your mind doing the very best it can to keep you safe. Before you can change something you first have to become aware.

No judgement – I should have done…

Through the years of my coaching practice I have heard many people viscously berate themselves for being on path 2 and how they should have 'done better' or 'been stronger'. If this happens it is the mind attempting to live up to the unobtainable high expectations of other people.

Take a look at your current life and ask yourself how often you criticise yourself for not being good enough in some way. This can also be in a 'joking' type fashion for many people. Remember, a criticism is still a criticism!

10

The Dependency Cycle

The dependency cycle is a model of my own creation which aims to explain how a person can be taught dependency to another person by another person through a system of pain and pleasure.

As an overview there are three states to take into account...

1. **Dependence**
This is a state in which a person is unable to cope on their own through daily life or a particular situation. In this state they will require another person's support to help them complete actions they could not otherwise complete themselves or with their own abilities.

2. Independence

This is a state in which a person has acquired sufficient skills to cope with life's challenges and becomes autonomous and can take action by themselves.

3. Interdependence

This is a state in which a person realises that each and every other person has different skills. They then choose to work in harmony with other people whom have other skills complementary to their own. This is the ideal state where we can depend upon others whom we can trust whilst they support us in temporary times of need.

The dependency cycle

The dependency cycle refers to a person who is continually relying on other people to complete actions when is not required. Obviously this is essential when we are young as children are completely dependent upon adults, as we saw in the peer idolisation chapter. This could also be noted if a person is working in a job and is dependent upon the company to pay their wages. However, the dependency I will cover here is a much more complicated and elusive one regarding shame and guilt.

Whilst going through the stages of the dependency cycle it is possible to see that the cycle could be used from an influencer role (there to help and support the other) or a manipulator role (there to control the other for the manipulator's best interest). For this description we will look at a controlling manipulation. For a review on the influencer and manipulator please revisit the earlier chapter on the peer idolisation scale.

The dependency cycle is as follows…

Stage one: Person A and Person B are free thinking

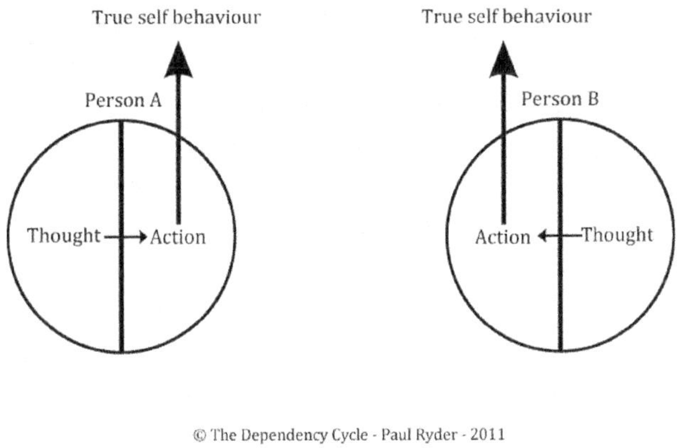

As we can see on the circle that represents Person A, there are two halves: thought (independent thinking) and action (Person A's physical movements, behaviours etc.).

If we look just below the circle we can see the line going from thought to action. This line is to represent that Person A thinks about taking an action (picking up a glass of milk for example) and then takes action on that thought. This is classed as autonomous as they thought about it and then took action. There is no protector self activity as there is no threat in regards to picking up the glass of milk (discovery – stage 1 of the self esteem recovery model).

Stage two: Person B projects control and Person A stops

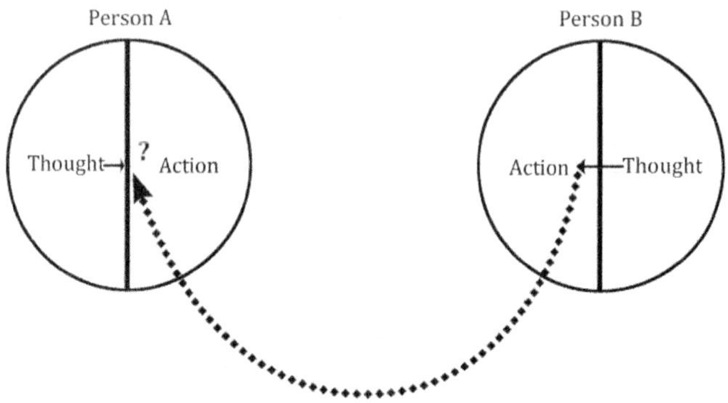

© The Dependency Cycle - Paul Ryder - 2011

Person B now comes into the room and notices Person A taking an action (e.g. picking up a glass of milk) and then shouts aggressively (or another form of threat) at Person A, giving them a shock. Person B's reaction was aimed at gaining the attention of Person A (gaining control of their focus by overwhelming them). As we can see Person B stops Person A in mid action (this reaction only happens if Person A feels overwhelmed by the attack from Person B).

Stage three: Person A feels pain from stage two

Person A was not expecting this reaction from Person B and is attempting to process the situation. Whilst Person A is processing, Person B is still shouting aggressively. Person A now goes into fight, flight or inertia (can take any of the three reactions). In this state it is difficult for Person A to think clearly and their body starts to release stress hormones into their bloodstream, which create physical discomfort and emotional confusion (pain).

It is to be noted that this will only happen if Person A feels a sense of threat from Person B. This could be an intimidation (if you pick that up you will be in trouble), rejection (if you pick that up I will not like you anymore) or a guilt trip (why do you try to pick that up, you know it hurts my feelings). Although we are using a glass of milk as the example this could be any number of actions from Person B.

Stage four: Person A defers to Person B for a decision on their action

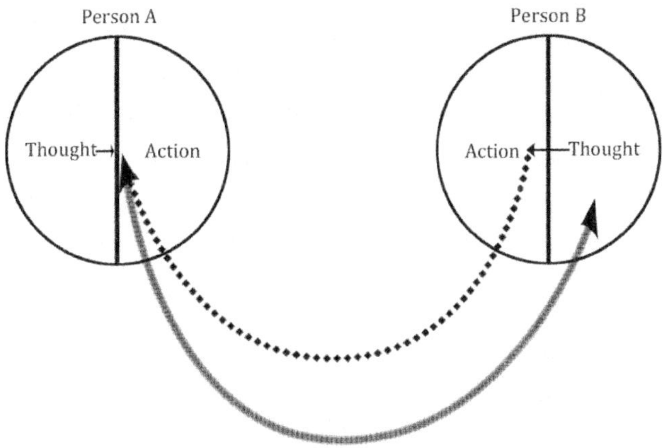

© The Dependency Cycle - Paul Ryder - 2011

Due to the aggression/intimidation or potential rejection from Person B, Person A now becomes reluctant to take action on their desired choice (to pick up the glass of milk) as they believe that taking action = pain.

So Person A makes a choice to defer all the control of the situation to Person B. This can come in the form of a question "What would you like me to do" or crying and lowering body language (signifying that Person A is subliminally saying that Person B is more powerful). Or it could be phrases such as "I am sorry for going against your wishes."

What is really happening subliminally is that Person B (if being manipulative and not influencing) is insinuating that Person A is causing them pain by their actions. Another way of viewing this is that Person B is saying that it's Person A's fault that Person B is upset and feeling pain (which then leads to their aggression or shouting). Person B could also insinuate that Person A is not capable and should ask for support.

The actual truth though is that Person B is refusing to take responsibility for their own emotional reactions (internal cinema screen / protector self reaction) and blaming Person A for how they feel.
Person A, not being aware of what is actually happening, subliminally defers control to Person B in an attempt to stop them from attacking further.

Stage five: Person B feels more in control and stops the attack to Person A

Due to Person B refusing to take responsibility for how they feel in their environment, when Person A gives control completely, Person B now feels more secure and their stress reactions calm down and they stop the attack. This is due to their protector self feeling more in control.

Stage six: (Option 1) Person B 'gives' Person A permission to continue the action under Person B's guidelines. Person A is now following orders from Person B to lessen the anxiety and future attacks

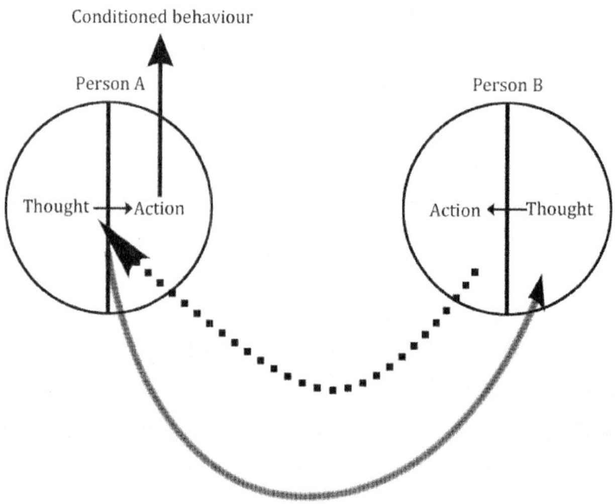

Now Person B feels secure again they tell Person A that they can continue (to pick up the glass of milk), or they tell them 'how' to do the action, which Person A abides by in an attempt to keep the peace. Person A then completes their chosen action.

Stage six: (Option 2) Person B 'does NOT' give permission to continue or any feedback on how to continue the action. Person A feels anxious and confused.

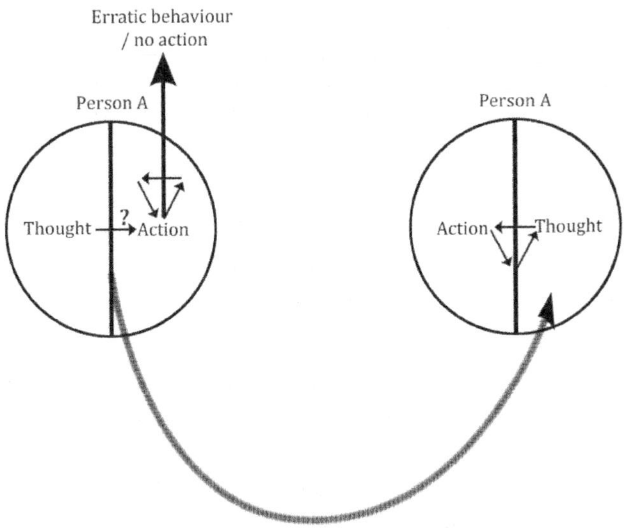

© The Dependency Cycle - Paul Ryder - 2011

In option 2, this time Person B 'does not' give permission for Person A to continue the action, which leaves Person A wanting to take an action but waiting for permission, resulting in confusion and stress.

As long as Person A refuses to take action based upon their anxiety of Person B's attack, the stress reaction in Person A will continue to grow in association to taking action.
If this situation is left long enough the continual stress reactions for Person A can drain their energy. They can also become trapped in a loop

of wanting to take action but also become extremely anxious of taking action. This type of behaviour is also known as learned helplessness.

Stage seven: Person A creates a dependency loop belief pattern to Person B.

As stress grows for Person A, their protector self may create a belief that in order to keep the peace or avoid pain, they should consult Person B before making a decision or taking action. If left unchecked or unresolved, this thought virus can multiply and Person A may continually ask other people in their life for permission before taking action.

Shame and guilt are two peas in a pod

As we can see through the above description it is extremely easy for a frustrated peer or adult to create a dependency cycle to a child or person who is unsure of the situation.

We can see that it is Person B who is blaming their pain on Person A (when you pick up that glass of milk it hurts my feelings) and then controlling Person A to make Person B's environment seem more secure. However, this is a major error on Person B's behalf as if a person tries to control other people all the time, each time they control it only strengthens their own anxiety (as we will see in upcoming chapters).

Though for Person A, not only is Person B insinuating that Person A's actions are inadequate (guilt), they are also insinuating that their choices and decisions are inadequate (shame) and if Person A chooses to accept the dependency cycle that is projected on them, then they may ALSO accept that Person B's view of them is correct (that they are inadequate).

Sometime though if Person A is a small child and has no other options (as we saw in the peer idolisation scale), the child will accept the programme not knowing any other way.

A review of the term dependency

So let's just re-review the definition we looked at earlier on the area of dependency:

1. **Dependence**

   This is a state in which a person is unable to cope on their own through daily life. In this state they will require another person's support to help them complete actions they could not otherwise complete themselves.

Looking at this term whilst taking the above loop into account we can now adjust the definition accordingly (for the conditioned self anyway):

1. **Dependence**

   This is a state in which a person **thinks** they are unable to take actions upon their own free will due to the expectation of a painful result of rejection or other emotional discomfort. To reduce the potential conflict they defer their decision-making to other people to be granted permission for their actions. A person in this state will be anxious of the other person attacking their choices and prejudges the actions of others through their paranoia.

Reversal

However, in reversal of this situation sometimes people will just follow a manipulator's demands as it keeps the peace. They may not have anxiety around the manipulator, but they realise that asking for permission is the easiest option in a difficult situation. They will not respect or value the manipulator, but deferring the choice to the other is the lesser of two evils. We can see this in the workplace when a member of staff who is calm and confident will ask the permission of a manager that they do not like or value for permission to take an action as they realise that not doing this will result in the manager bullying other members of the team.

The confusion

When a person is in a shame or guilt based dependency loop it can be very confusing for the conscious mind to understand why they take the actions they do. Again though, please look at this through the protectors self's eyes, which may be reaction from memories and beliefs which are suppressed and loop within Pandora's Box.

Also, it can be very confusing for other people around a person carrying shame or guilt based dependency as it can appear as if they are needy or weak. This inferiority complex can become especially confusing to others if that person is a manager, a figure of authority or a parent. However, the mind is very clever and has found a VERY unique way to cover up an inferiority complex whilst it is trapped in the mind.
Welcome to Life Beyond the Mask.

Chapter summary

The 3 states!

In life we will go through 3 different states depending upon the situation we are in.
1. Dependence (we completely rely on another person as we are unable to support ourselves).
2. Independence (we are free to make our own decisions and act autonomously).
3. Interdependence (we work together, merging our skills with other people to create a greater outcome).
Take a reflective look at all of the current situations in your life and ask yourself which state you are mainly in during each one. Once you have done this reflect upon this even deeper. For example, if you feel you are 'dependant' upon your job, take another view in the fact that your company hires you for your skills, therefore your job is in fact state 3 (interdependence).

When do you give your power away?

If there has been a dependency loop instilled in you from when you were very young you may not even be aware that you give power away. However, there will often be subtle emotional cues when you are in the loop, such as a feeling of guilt or helplessness.

Take a reflective observation of all of the people in your life and ask yourself if you feel you may be in the dependency cycle with them. Do you feel the need to ask for their opinion or approval before making a decision? Do you feel like you may 'offend' them if you do not ask for their permission? Take this question slowly as the answers may feel quite elusive.

Other people who attempt to control!

As mentioned (earlier in this book), the loud and controlling people are relatively easy to recognise! However, there are many different types of control mannerisms that another person can use which need to be taken into account.

Again, take a reflective look at all of the people in your life and ask yourself if you feel that they knowingly or unknowingly attempt to trigger a dependency reaction within you. Your feelings are the best indicator for this. If you are being triggered into a dependency loop you may feel distaste towards the other person or also a needy helplessness or 'I have to' when around them.

Trust yourself?

As we saw in the dependency cycle, one person either knowingly or unknowingly manipulates the other person into feeling guilty about not asking for approval before taking action. Although there will be times in life where asking for approval is healthy, in this loop the purpose is to emotionally control the other to doubt their own opinion, thereby the other person will gain control.

Take a moment and ask yourself how much you truly trust your own opinion and abilities and in which areas. Also, ask yourself if you can recall any times in life where other people insinuated that your opinion was not of value and you believed them, even though they were wrong.

The anxiety of letting go / saying no!

Many times in life people become so anxious of what 'may' happen that they don't take action at all. Many times it can feel easier to just go along with the flow rather than face the what 'may' happen.

If you have found yourself in any form of dependency cycle with another person but find it quite challenging to break, ask yourself what images are being created upon your internal cinema screen if you do not do as they request. For example, if you did not go to an 'expected event' because you did not want to, is there an anxiety that they may not speak to you for a long time?

11

Discover the Con!

Before we begin this chapter it is essential that you have read all of the previous chapters and fully understand them. Keep refreshing your mind on the information and models so they are clear and make sense to you. It is also important that you have taken the time to relate them to your own life and to cross-reference the information to your past experiences. Now this is not to insinuate that you have had any major trauma or that I know what you have personally experienced. The reason that it is vital to cover all these areas is that if there are any memories or beliefs hidden from your conscious mind, then the more information of anxiety associations you are aware of the stronger your abilities will be.

If the techniques or models are hazy or unclear in any way, 'the con' can also appear hazy and unclear and therefore potentially remain invisible to your awareness. If the con is able to hide from your awareness, any coping mechanisms or masks that have been created to protect you from old habit patterns can remain unchanged and will continue. In life it is

sometimes the smallest of unchecked points which place huge blocks in the path to the solution you seek.
Remember, the key to unlocking your mind is to allow the conscious mind (your awareness and present day focus) to connect to past trapped memories and old beliefs and update them. To do this we need to allow both minds to communicate through your protector self. Once your **protector self** realises that holding onto old suppressed habits is causing you more pain than pleasure it will move to a new reference. The old beliefs will then automatically be updated, allowing you to move forward and reach your aims.

Gut Feeling?

"How do you feel?"

If we recall, some of the situations you have experienced may be suppressed within Pandora's Box and therefore hidden from your conscious mind. This obviously poses a challenge, but is not without hope. Although we sometimes may not be able to understand the reasons for emotional triggers in everyday life, there is still a tracker chip attached to the suppressed memories and beliefs - this tracker chip is... YOUR FEELINGS!

When going through this chapter it is vital that you do the following:

TRUST YOUR FEELINGS!

A gut feeling of pain or anxiety (that you may not be able to logically understand or relate to any memory) is your subconscious communicating to you that something has been picked up on its radar, but the subconscious is having difficulty putting the information into conscious terms (usually from lack of communication ability or suppressed stress reactions).

For example you may meet somebody at a party and although they may appear to be kind and respectful, something within you says they are suspicious and should be avoided.
This person offers you a 'business deal' that sounds amazing, but your gut feeling says to avoid it. You go against your gut feeling and invest and then lose money when you find out the business liquidates the next day.

So in regards to this chapter if you read something and you 'think' that it is not relevant to you, but you notice that you 'feel' irritated, upset or any disconnection emotions then that is your gut feeling by-passing the analytical mind. In a sense it is saying that although it cannot tell you why the information is relevant, it is actually VERY relevant and you should take note.

If you always do what you have always done, you will always get what you have always got
Albert Einstein

Going forward
So let me ask you a question:

What is it that you want in life?

As an emotional development coach and trainer, I ask that question to many people and I hear many answers. For some it may be in the area of relationships. To others it may be in the area of career, and yet to others it could be something else that they want to achieve. In all conversations though I hear the same thing…
A person who wants to reach a certain state in their life but something is stopping them!

By the time somebody contacts me for coaching, they have usually realised that the very thing that is stopping them is not something 'outside' of them, but something 'inside' of them. Their gut feeling has communicated to them that something within them is holding them back and although their subconscious mind cannot explain 'what' it is (through the disconnection of the two minds), it is saying that something needs to change. A great description I heard in the film The Matrix was the metaphor of the 'splinter in your mind'. You can feel that something is there, but you may not know what it is.

So let me ask you again… what is it that you really want?

Is it the relationship or the self-awareness to get a relationship?

Is it the financial return from business or the self-awareness to release the blockage that stops you?

Or is it to connect to a loved one who disconnected from you in a family feud or the self-awareness to realise why the disconnection is happening?

I have always liked this excerpt from the book The Vision of Buddhism:

"We make ourselves miserable by first closing ourselves off from reality and then collecting this and that in an attempt to make ourselves happy by possessing happiness. But happiness is not something I have; it is something I myself want to be. Trying to be happy by accumulating possessions is like trying to satisfy hunger by taping sandwiches all over my body."
Roger J. Corless, Vision of Buddhism: The Space Under the Tree

Awareness is the key
This can be a very delicate chapter and one that should be read two or more times until full understanding can be comprehended. This is in no way intended to question your intelligence, far from it. Remember, your protector self may be trying to inhibit an understanding of the lessons in this programme because it may require a change in consciousness to understand the solution.
If your protector self is anxious of the change, it may be through one of these six reasons…

1. If your protector self is anxious about change due to lack of skills to cope with the change.

2. If your protector self feels that if you become aware of the mask and the con it will cause you emotional pain or loss (remembering the stored memories that have not been updated).

3. If the protector self feels that the new information could pose a threat to current beliefs and require too much effort to change.

4. If there is a distraction anxiety programme. For example, if your mind created a phobia of spiders, but really that phobia was to distract you from a deeper anxiety that your protector self could not cope with (e.g. keeping your mind busy).

5. A self-fulfilling prophecy (e.g. "I can't be happy as I am too damaged") coming from learned helplessness or low self-esteem. The mind will try to screen out new learnings or give you a temporary blindness. This 'blindness' is similar to when we lose our keys and they are right in front of us. We have this because the mind is thinking "I can't find my keys" so it obeys and appears to make them vanish even though they are right there in front of us.

6. If gaining power over the self could lead to the anxiety of more pain. For example, the anxiety that "If I can stand up for myself the bully at work will see me as a threat and attack so it's easier to stay small".

Take notes!

When I coach a client one to one, I will always ask them to make notes of their findings in a journal. For many clients this assumed 'easy task' can be more challenging than they anticipated and they often 'accidentally forget' to make notes. However, this is not a simple case of forgetting; it is usually the protector self working from one of the six points above.

Making notes will help you bring to your consciousness the information that can enable change to happen. It can also create the awareness to make changes if they need to be made (if they actually do). Therefore it is advisable to keep notes on your thoughts at all times as you read through each part of this chapter (as you will have ideally been doing already).

If for example you find that reading parts of this chapter brings back memories or distracts you to do other things whilst reading (checking emails and texts etc.), then this is a sign that your mind is trying to distract your attention, thereby stopping conscious awareness from understanding the con. If this happens your conscious mind may become confused and not take in the information that could be the key to the lock on the chain that you want to break free from.

With one to one client sessions I always notice a distinct difference in the success rate of those clients who make notes compared to those who do not. Even if a client says they have made notes (when it is obvious they have not) the results are the same. It is much more challenging to bring awareness to the conscious mind from the subconscious mind (and especially Pandora's Box) if thoughts are analysed in your head alone.

From this point on, please be aware that some people will be more vulnerable to the con than others. Also note that the con will not be in all areas of your life all the time. The con will be more potent where there are weaknesses in your self-esteem, confidence and self-image.
Being blunt, I will say that the con trickster can manipulate you more easily at the points in your life where you have lower self-esteem and confidence.

Pre-emptive strike

Through the years of research leading up to the fruition of this programme, it has been interesting to hear people's reactions in relation to the mask and the con. Some people have been very open to listening about the con and have accepted their situation, allowing them to move to where they want to be.

However some other people have felt so uncomfortable in realising their situation that they have taken offence and felt erratic reactions (fight, flight or freeze). This is due to having to realise or admit to themselves that they were manipulated by others or have anxiety in their life today.

As you read through the chapter please be aware of your reactions. They may be one of the following…

"That was an interesting read" (as you put the programme on the shelf to gather dust)

"Yes I can see that happens in other people" (not me though)

"The con is interesting; it doesn't apply to me though"

"This programme is stupid" (an anxiety reaction)

"It is not a con it's just how life is"

"I'm fine as I am; yes I have my challenges, but who doesn't?"

"I don't need any of that mind control rubbish"

All of the above are obviously rejection statements, but if when you read this chapter you find that you do feel a negative reaction arising within, it is more important that you become aware of what has caused that re-action. Keep in your mind at all times the earlier statement to trust your feelings as it is the subconscious letting you know something that it can't articulate to you at the moment in time.

The truth is that in physical reality all you are doing when you are reading this book is… reading this book! They are simply words on a page and therefore that means any emotional reaction you have to reading them is 'the meaning' that you associate to them. So, unless you (or your subconscious mind) give the words meaning they would not be able to cause a reaction.

"The man who never alters his opinion is like standing water, and breeds reptiles of the mind."
William Blake

Stepping through the mirror

This chapter may not be something you would like to hear! This chapter may not be something you want to accept… but this chapter is the truth of how millions of people live their lives each and every day. The more this chapter stirs any dark feelings within such as anger, resentment, shame or guilt, which then causes you to want to avoid absorbing this information… the greater power the 'con' has over you. Whether you choose to let it remain in control or not is entirely up to you.

As we looked at earlier in this programme, a con is something which is undetectable to the person being conned. If it was observable by the victim, it would no longer be a con and the game would end.

Remember, you may not like what you are about to read, but be open minded as it is the only way to overcome any feelings of insecurity that reside within you.

How the con trick hides itself

The con in itself is powerful because of the following…

"A person forms a self-protection mask that they are too intelligent to fall for the con!"

Let us look at this statement more closely…

The one main part we need to look at here is in the realm of beliefs. A belief, as we have discussed, is an internal map of reality stored inside the subconscious mind. Once stored, the mind will start to base all future actions and behaviours from this map of reality (the internal cinema screen). The mind (or protector self part of it) will preserve these beliefs and be reluctant to change them. This is because the protector self assumes that this is the most efficient method of keeping us safe. In essence what is stored inside the mind as a belief will be protected by the protector self until more convincing information appears.

Like millions of people across the world the following thought loop could happen:

1. There is an anxiety or worry about rejection from other people held within the subconscious and to create a safety mechanism it will trigger the protector self.

2. Once the protector self becomes involved if it only has limited knowledge (a lack of psychological education) to be able to deal with the challenge it will protect by forming a mask (coping mechanism – stage 6 of the self-esteem recovery model).

3. The mask may come in the form of feeling like it is important to always be good enough and never get things wrong. This can also be a conviction that we know what we are doing or have high intelligence.

4. The mind would do this if it is anxious of rejection from looking stupid (social anxiety).

5. However, if the person was to be conned, admitting that the con trick was overwhelming, it would then question the protector self's mask and whether it is as intelligent as it assumed.
6. This could then be perceived as a possibility that we are of a lesser intelligence (other people able to see the perceived suppressed self image) and therefore possibly be open to scrutiny.

7. This could then lead to a perception that others will reject us or think less of us, leading towards pain.

In healthy social connections it is very unlikely that a person would get rejected by their peer group for simply 'not knowing' things or getting something wrong. Though if a person finds themselves in a particularly erratic social environment where their peers are emotionally below the line, getting rejected for 'not being perfect' may be commonplace. This rejection may come in the form of public humiliation, light humour, a slight change in tone of voice or direct interrogation. So, the reaction a person's protector self may display will be dependent upon two factors:

1. **Their own perception of the world (internal reality)**
2. **Their 'actual' social environment (external reality)**

However, to the protector self either one of the above will still lead to the same pain association if stored as such. Therefore, a potential threat will automatically trigger a coping strategy (mask) to keep the person safe from threat.

It is this (self-trapping mask) that the 'con' relies on. As we saw earlier in this book, many people who have been conned would rather take the loss and not admit to it (anxious of rejection) rather than admit to it and trigger their anxiety (the internal cinema screen of them 'looking stupid' and 'being rejected'). Therefore the con relies upon the victim's unwillingness to accept that they have been conned, or have been overpowered by somebody with a greater knowledge or ability. At the baseline of all of this though is that the con is actually a direct threat to one of the 'deadly sins'... **their pride!**

The seven deadly sins –
Wrath, greed, sloth, pride, lust, envy, and gluttony!

Pride comes before a fall – (external validation)
No matter how the words are spun, pride is a rigid emotion that leaves people powerless! Pride is different from simply admiring one's own achievements in a process of assessing growth of skills. Although the term 'pride' may appear to be a good thing - e.g. having pride in one's work etc. - it is actually a dependency loop. This dependency loop as we

saw in an earlier chapter is an external validation which traps a person in their limited belief patterns through relying on other people's approval.

Pride is a pattern where a person relies upon their actions (the 'what I do' state) rather than their own self-worth (the 'I' state) for validation to their peers. An example of this is the person who will stand at the side of their shiny new car with their chest sticking out as people admire 'their' car, but if the car was not there they may just feel worth 'less'.

If this pride in the external is then used as a mask the protector self is reluctant to let this pattern go until it sees another alternative. If no alternative is available then the protector self will use the only option it has. This then leaves the person trapped and vulnerable to the con trickster to take what they want or to manipulate the victim into giving them what they ask for.

Breaking point

It is also important to note that the con trickster will only have power over another person (via manipulation) as long as their 'breaking point' is not triggered. Everybody has a breaking point and this is where a person is so frustrated that they override their anxiety of looking stupid or the threat. Here the pain of being conned would outweigh the pain of the anxiety of potential rejection. In some of my workshops I will call this section 'the theory of 6.8'.

The theory of 6.8

The theory of 6.8 is to assume that your emotional scale is on a scale of 1 – 10. At the bottom of the scale (number 1) your emotions are calm and relaxed. This would be like a relaxed sunny picnic with friends. At the top of the scale (number 10) your emotions are at an absolute maximum of fight to protect yourself (as in a psychotic rage). Level 10 would be likened to your reaction to somebody attacking the person you love the most in the world (or whatever would trigger you to become enraged).

The example I use in class is that if a person is pushed (or attacked) then the theory is that their breaking point is number 7 out of 10. 7 out of 10 is where they have had enough and begin to fight back (though some may fight back sooner). Therefore the con trickster will push or manipulate a person at the level of 6.8 which engages their frustration and stress levels, but is not so intense that they will fight back. Thus, the victim will stay in a confused state and continue to protect themselves through their mask and remain vulnerable to the con.

When in this loop, the manipulation is performed during the con while the victim is distracted in a vain attempt to preserve their mask's integrity. It is a person's pride or the need to prove to others that they are good enough that allows them to be conned. Threaten a person's pride mask (or threaten to expose their inner insecurities) and they will become a sitting duck and totally vulnerable to the con (in an environment where they feel vulnerable). As we see over and over again through this book all of this is going on behind the scenes in our lives in subconscious communication, leaving the conscious mind (our awareness) completely oblivious to what is happening.

In an attempt to protect their mask (which is really protecting their self-worth) the con is therefore dismissed by the victim. If we look at this logically, admitting that they have been conned also means that they have to admit that they have perceived low self-worth (inner insecurity) as the two are emotionally bound together in the victim's mind, so to deny one they have to automatically deny the other.
In many cases, the more obvious and blatant the con, the more it will easily be dismissed by the general population as there is seemingly nothing to be suspicious of.

And now I present to you.... THE CON!

The term 'con' is a cold word and I have named it as such to give that impression – cold! If I described it with a nice fluffy description tied up with pink ribbons and glitter it may not appear as something that you need take notice of. So, the way I will share it with you is blunt and cold to emphasise that this IS something you need to be aware of.

The con itself is rampant throughout the human race and people are knowingly and unknowingly conning each other and being conned at different points throughout their day. However, the con trick can appear one minute and vanish the next, only to appear again when a person drops into lower self-esteem and needs to reassure themselves with external validation.

Very few people are aware of the con when it is happening and it is because of the above. To unlock the con means to face the pain of why it is there in the first place (stage 3 of the self-esteem recovery model). As mentioned though, if the protector self has no alternative it will hide the mask in plain sight.

The con is as follows…

1. Person A creates insecurity (shame/guilt) through any of the threats previously discussed (stage 3 of the self-esteem recovery model).

2. Person A's protector self is unable to handle the stress reaction due to lack of knowledge so creates a mask (stage 6 of the self-esteem recovery model).

3. Person A is now deriving their self-worth from the mask, which forces the person into external validation for self-worth. (I am not valuable for who I am, I am only valuable and accepted for my actions or what I do/have/look like) (shame).

4. Person A's protector self is now anxious of letting go of the mask as it is assuming that it will lead to some form of rejection. Low self-image.

5. Person B enters the scene.

6. Person B now knowingly or unknowingly offers Person A a 'solution' to keep their insecurities (low self-worth/shame/guilt) hidden from the views of others who they perceive may reject them.

7. This solution is insinuated that it will keep Person A's mask secure and powerful (often Person B is unaware that they are doing this).

8. Person A's protector self accepts the 'solution', which results in a feeling that their mask is secure and powerful, thereby protecting them from any form of rejection.

9. When Person A's protector self feels that the mask is secure, the protector self can relax and it stops triggering stress reactions (fight, flight or freeze).

10. Person A's physiology calms down due to the lowered stress hormone release.

11. Person A feels happier and relaxes.

12. Person B (or Person C, D or others) now insinuates that the 'solution' that Person A took last time is not as secure as they thought it was and that to be completely secure Person A now needs to invest more time, effort or energy into a new or current 'solution'.

13. Person A's protector self goes into a panic, assuming that if it does not acquire the new and updated 'solution' that the mask will collapse and they will have to face rejection through others being able to 'see' their low self-worth.

14. Person A's protector self now desperately grabs at this new and updated 'solution' and immediately feels secure once again.

15. If Person A does not update their own Pandora's Box belief (stage 3 of the self esteem recovery model) their protector self will become dependent upon the next 'new solution' for security.

16. Person A is now dependent upon the 'external solution' (and future solutions) to ensure that they feel secure.

Put in other terms...

1. Some people (in society) either consciously or subconsciously realise that some people wear a mask in certain parts of their lives which protects their insecurities in that area.

2. The insecure person's mask which has been created in that particular area of their insecurities will aim to gain control in the external world to distract from the perceived internal inadequacy.

3. The control aims to gain power or external acquirements to create a feeling of presence or validity in society.

4. Their protector self does this so it can create validation as to why they are valuable (I am important because of my looks/status/skills) to other people allowing them to connect. Whereas the underlying worry is an anxiety that they as an individual are not valuable in and of themselves (low self-esteem/shame).

5. The truth is that the 'self' is always good enough. However, if the subconscious has been tricked into thinking that it is worth 'less' (by peer projections) then the protector self will assume this is reality and act accordingly (an opinion posing as a fact or truth).

6. The protector self will then look to attract the highest ranking acquirement to impress others based upon what they perceive as their peer group's desired value (money/power/intelligence etc.).

7. The insecure persons protector self assumes that once they attain this acquirement their peer group will accept them. They may have seen this pattern from other people in their life (a thought virus or rapport).

8. Other people in society, now consciously or sub consciously realising a person's 'need' to attain these acquirements, will offer or sell what their protector self so desperately wants.

9. All the 'salesperson' needs to do is convince the person who is wearing the mask that what they invested in a while ago is now not good enough and their protector self will start to panic.

10. The 'salesperson' now offers the insecure person a 'new' option to which their protector self overrides their logical and conscious mind and they buy.

NB: *It is more than possible that both people in the above loop can be living through their masks. The insecure person buying from the salesperson, but also the salesperson themselves. The salesperson may be selling their product to gain approval from work colleagues. Therefore, both people are now in what is known as a 'co-dependency' loop.*

The greatest illusion

The overwhelming perception of low self-esteem/shame in an insecure person creates an anxiety that they may be rejected by peers for their perceived inner worthlessness. However, this perception of inner worthlessness can ONLY EVER BE an illusion. The actual 'self' is merely the human mind at rest and therefore can never be worthless. The term worth 'less' is an opinion or a judgement from another person or social group. As we have discussed, the only people who would 'judge' are people in fight, flight or freeze and therefore taking the action to reduce their own emotional pain. Therefore, judgement or criticism is not personal but the other person's inability to cope with their own pain and insecurities.

To add more power to this we need to look at the state of a person's mind who would criticise or judge a child (the onset of shame for a child if they believe the judgement). A person in a stress reaction will react in fight, flight or freeze. For a peer to attack an innocent child, it is not the child who is wrong; rather, it's the peer's inability to cope with their own reality. Therefore, if they can control the child they assume that their stress levels will reduce. Unfortunately though, a very potent action to ensure a child's compliance is to threaten the child's safety so they are too afraid to challenge their peer's opinion. In effect this turns the child against themselves (to create a belief that they think they are not good enough).

The futile search

A child or an adult in a state of shame will never be able to find the cause of what they should feel ashamed of. This leads to an endless loop of self-destruction thoughts. The reason they will never be able to find an answer is simply because it doesn't exist. What has happened is that the child was blamed for something they 'did' (an action) and then told that 'they' were not good enough (an attack on the self). The child then becomes confused and forms shame..

As mentioned the con may not apply to all areas of your life; it may only be a few or it may be many. For example, a person feeling confident with running their own company/business may not feel anxious at work, but may feel very anxious in a relationship (through feeling unlovable). This person will then be most vulnerable to the con in their relationships. In a situation where the person is vulnerable in their relationships, they may be conned into doing everything for their partner or being taken advantage of. Or, if they are not yet in a relationship they may be conned into dating somebody they do not want to date or sold expensive dating agency fees 'to find their soul mate'. As we saw above they will do this in order to conceal their insecurities that they feel unwanted by a partner. Yet, it is essential to note that it may not be as straightforward as it appears.

For example; a person may appear to be desperate to get into a relationship, claiming it to be what they want. If it is a 'desperate need' rather than just desire, it is a possibility that their desired relationship is a mask. However, the entire relationships drive could be covering up a need to impress their parents as they feel that they are not good enough in their eyes. They may feel that getting into a relationship would stop their parents feeling disappointed that they are single.
So although it may appear that their mask is to get into a relationship to feel valued from a partner, it could actually be coming from a different source - their parents' validity. If on top of this they decide to work 80 hours a week to make themselves too busy because they have stress around a relationship (creating a valid excuse), we then have a third mask in the mix and it is easy to see how compounded masks can confuse and disorientate.

Logically speaking, in this example the drive for a relationship is not built from love but from anxiety, then if they did manage to get into a relationship it may struggle or end up co-dependent.

Life Beyond the Mask – an overview
The con is very powerful in its construct and many levels deep. If your protector self has realised that you are caught up in what you have just read, there may be a chance that it creates a reaction of denial. So, let's go deeper.

The entire programme and all its models will now come together to show you the structure of the con. As suggested, please make notes while reading this chapter.

Stage 1:
A child is born and is craving for security (food, shelter, water and love), but also has a thirst for growth, so begins to explore the world to discover more about it.

Stage 2:
The child is open and quickly learning from their surrounding environment. The healthy lessons which are learned are not of concern here. What is of concern is how the child can learn low self-esteem/shame, which will primarily be learned from 3 sources of input:

Source A: The peer idolisation model in which the child will copy mannerisms and behaviours from the parent or peer of low self-esteem. They then begin to act them out, not realising what they are doing. They also may create a conditioned self in the aim of pleasing their peers.

Source B: Stage 3 of the self-esteem recovery model where their protector self stores an experience of pain and then buries it in denial (Pandora's Box) only for it to be used in reference on the internal cinema screen until it is changed.

Source C: The dependency loop in which (through a pain and pleasure cycle) a person can be taught to defer all of their decision making to another person whilst simultaneously creating a shame/guilt based loop.

Stage 3:
The child has now started believing that they are somehow inadequate, which causes emotional pain and an anxiety of perceived disconnection. They also assume an incorrect view of their environment and of their peers from a lack of psychological knowledge (however their environment may also be toxic).
The child's protector self is now frantically trying to find an option in which they can restore a connection to their peer group to reconnect to safety and love.
The child's protector self realises that if they perform certain actions or achieve a certain standard then their peer group will reward them with acceptance and connection (a conditional peer group attitude).
The child's protector self then forms the belief that attention and connection is rewarded from achieving certain levels or standards. This is also known as 'I am valued for what I do or what I have' (the 'what I do' state) rather than 'who I am' (the 'I' state).

We can see this in the example of when a child (or usually an adult) feels the need to give gifts or do things for others as opposed to just connecting as an equal in their social group. This could be a 'If I do something nice for you, hopefully you will accept me' loop.

Stage 4:

The child, now feeling ashamed or 'rejectable' because of their perceived belief that 'who they are is of lesser value', builds a mask and hides behind it (external acquirements). They do this as they are anxious that not doing this will create social rejection.

This perception of social rejection is being driven from the internal paranoia of 'I am of lesser value' and the belief that people would not want to associate with somebody of lesser value. This will also be driven from previous memories when they were a child or helplessly dependant. A child who is criticised for 'getting in the way' or being 'a burden' when they are dependant on others for survival can form this belief very quickly.

Stage 5:

The child (now an adult and if not updated their belief) will have been feeling extreme conflict within their mind from the conscious and the subconscious having opposing views.

1. Their protector self, which is reacting from suppressed memories trapped in Pandora's Box replaying on the internal cinema screen, will be releasing stress hormones into the bloodstream to protect against a potential threat.

2. The conscious mind, which sees today and is confused as to why the subconscious mind is reacting.

To the adult this will give a feeling of wanting to embrace life (conscious reality) but also feeling extreme anxiety about taking action (subconscious reality).

This conflict will create a fight, flight or freeze reaction for the adult as they want to move forward but if feels as though an invisible force is holding them back. This can feel very confusing as to why as there may appear no logical reason for the invisible force to be there. The reactions could be anger, rage, confusion, self-criticism, demotivation, sadness, guilt, shame or many other disconnecting emotions.

Stage 6:
Rather than risking social rejection (for who they wrongly assume they are inside), the adult's protector self will now desperately cling to the mask. It will also dedicate as much energy as it can to ensure it disguises what they are trying to hide from society (that they are lesser in value – the invisible force).
In many cases this is usually hidden from the person's conscious mind, which is denial created by the protector self to help stop any further suffering (a mask within a mask).
This is where a stage of generalisation may appear such as 'I may as well keep doing what I am doing as it is always going to be the same with everybody I meet' (social paranoia).

Stage 7:
Certain people in society (consciously or subconsciously) can see the adult's desperation to keep their mask secure in whichever area they feel vulnerable in. They may then start to offer the adult (at a price) acquirements which can aid their mask's power. The adult feels compelled to accept and in many cases will pay whatever it takes to get these acquirements (the con).

Stage 8:
The adult now feels that these acquirements ease their suffering (of being seen as lesser value and emotions such as guilt and shame) behind their now-perceived secure mask which is reliant upon these external acquirements.

However, this stage is much deeper than it may seem, because if the person relies upon another acquirement to feel valuable, it is in fact a disconnection from their self-esteem. Every time a person relies upon anything external to feel valuable, they are in fact making their self-esteem weaker and weaker. In reality they are saying "I am only valuable if I have my mask" (or an external acquirement). Every time they strengthen their mask, they also drain their self-worth and self-esteem, making them even more vulnerable to the con.

As we saw in earlier chapters, the mask is a coping mechanism and is created to ease emotional pain. If a person is so used to living in the shadow of their mask, it is possible for a habit pattern to build up and all realisation of their addiction to the mask to fade into the background. Additionally, every time a person strengthens their mask it causes yet more internal pain which can be pushed into denial by the protector self.

Stage 9:
The adult, who has been conned into gaining these external acquirements not only by their protector self, but also by others in society, has developed the habit of knowing that they can ease the pain of shame and guilt. Each time they connect to an external acquirement they feel better about themselves and gain a small sense of perceived self-worth. However, as we can see, their self-worth is now chained to the external acquirements. If the external acquirements are not accessible their protector self becomes anxious of the rejection and creates pain. The adult is now addicted to the need for external acquirement and continues to gain more in order to ease their suffering (low self-esteem).

Stage 10:
The very people who con the adult will appear to the adult as their saviour or 'solution provider' because the more acquirements their 'pain easer' provides, the more secure the adult will feel. This is the most fatal of all the stages because the adult will now protect the very person who is conning them, because they see them as the one who stops their pain. Yet the truth is that it actually locks them into the addiction. If then the person consciously tries to give up the addiction (using will power and positive self-talk only) their protector self (subconscious) will fight them, assuming that they are going to feel pain. The more they consciously try and escape the more trapped they become, and the more trapped they become the easier it is for others to con them.

This is why will power, such as giving up smoking and New Year's resolutions, only last a short duration or fail time and time again. A person's conscious decision will be attacked by their own protector self's delusion, believing its actions will keep them safe.

A very blunt metaphor

As you can plainly see from this, it is similar to a drug dealer and their buyers (metaphorically speaking). The user takes the drug to end some form of pain or suffering. The user gets high, and the pain goes away. The user comes back down and wants the high back again to stop the pain or discomfort. The user then goes back to the supplier and buys more. In the case of dangerous narcotics, the drug is actually causing the user physical harm, but the user doesn't care anymore as the addiction is now too strong (pleasure outweighs the pain re: the boxer). In reference to the legal implications of drugs, even if the police ask the user who the dealer is, the user may in some cases refuse to co-operate because it puts acquiring their 'high' at risk. The cycle then starts again, leaving the victim trapped.

"That's all very well, but it doesn't apply to me!"

Did that thought just cross your mind as you read the above stages? If it did you will join the millions of other people who think the same way, but trust me, the con is hiding in many people! Also, what is more unnerving is that if you are caught in your own cycle, the above thought will be coming directly from your protector self to get you to avoid unlocking your mask as it is anxious that doing so can lead to a greater pain.
So how do you tell the difference if you're in the con or not?
Keep reading!

Take into account what was just mentioned about the above scenario. A person's protector self will reject any threat to the very thing that allows them to hide from their emotional pain (i.e. any threat to their mask). If the pain association is strong enough they won't even realise that it is being hidden, because a person's protector self already knows what they are going to think even before they think it. That is the role of the protector self! Unfortunately, in the con, it is unknowingly hiding the key to the door that can set you free. Don't ever lose hope though as there are many other options that can be taken.

Going deeper down the rabbit hole – the mask in full view

In order to really see this chapter in its entirety, we need to go back a step and look at what **the mask** actually is. Yes, it is an 'external acquirement', but exactly how deep does this go?

The answer is, extremely deep!

As discussed, a mask is an external acquirement, which literally means ANYTHING which is created from and hidden within (sugar and salt) anything which is external to your 'true self' (the mind at peace). To see this in detail we will divide your life into several areas and see all the different places in which a mask could actually live.

Area 1: Your material possessions
Area 2: Your skills/ personality
Area 3: Your social connections

Now we will expand each of these 3 areas.

Area 1: Your material possessions

(These not only include what you can purchase, but also your physical body)

Car
House(s)
Money
Clothes
Boat
Land
Equipment
Physical Shape

Facial Appearance
Hair/skin/eyes
Drugs/alcohol
Add any others…

Area 2: Your skills/personality

Comedian
Leader
Intellectual
Knowledgeable
Entertainer
Caring
Supporter
Listener
Dedicated
Achiever
Role Model
Mentor
Teacher
Fun
Advisor
Bully
Manipulator
Seducer
Alpha Male/Female
Victim
Add any others…

Area 3: Your social connections

Friends
Lovers
Partner

Career Status
Acquaintances
Role Model
Socially Desired
Popularity
Staff

As you can see, each of the above areas are ALSO all a part of natural life and are acquirements that are useful in a person's healthy growth in life, but it is within this very illusion that makes the con that much harder to see.

Because the truth is…

A person can be conned only to the level to which they are addicted to the mask and anxious of letting it go! If a person feels that they can't let go of any of the above without feeling intense pain, then it is a mask and they can be conned!

The more a person is addicted to their mask (and the less they want to let go of it) for feeling they will be rejected for their low self-worth, the more vulnerable they are to the con. It is not WHAT the mask is that is the real issue, but the fact that the person is addicted to it.

In reality anything you are addicted to and makes you feel that can avoid your own inner insecurities is a mask, and therefore makes you vulnerable to the con.

Let's see some real life scenarios of clients whom I have worked with and how they could be and have been conned.

Scenario 1

A person who has a powerful career which makes them feel that they are important in society. To the outside world, they look like a leader and a provider of support for the community (which is actually true), but inside they are scared of losing their employment in case society sees them as worthless. Their career is then their addicted mask.

The con they endured

Their manager walks up to them one day and asks them to work 60 hours this week (extra time) for the company at the same pay (taking one for the team). Their manager says that although they have areas they can improve upon (subliminally saying they are not good enough), they will be very proud of them if they work the extra time for no money as it proves to the company that they are a 'team player' (the pain reliever / con)!

Working the extra hours while believing in the recognition triggers a feeling of self-worth in the employee. Unfortunately though, this means that the employee will barely see their family that week. The employee's protector self forces the employee to say yes, believing it will keep them safe as it can't cope with the anxiety of what people would think of them if they were to be fired for lack of dedication. The employee is now mad at themselves for agreeing (the conscious mind) and the inner conflict and stress heightens in their daily life.

Scenario 2

A young person is shopping to go on a night out with their friends. Their social group is very judgemental and all wear masks of 'I am good enough if I look very attractive'. The young person who is shopping is always complimented by their social group for looking 'very attractive'; their clothes, their hair and even their walk is admired. They have assumed that their looks are what is valuable about them and is why people like them. Their mask is their appearance, which for this client was formed at home through parents who lived through their children defining them as a 'pretty child'. The mask is also compounded and strengthened by their chosen social environment, which is very judgemental.

The con they endured

They walk into a shop and are approached by a very charismatic salesperson. The salesperson, wanting to achieve their 'sales target' to impress their manager (the salesperson's mask at a guess), subconsciously notices a look in the person's eye who is shopping that their looks are vitally important to them (usually both people are unaware of this). The salesperson takes them to the most expensive section of the shop and then shows them a new coat costing £800.

The salesperson now convinces them that unless they spend the £800 on the coat, they will look like yesterday's fashion and not 'be cool'. The person's protector self starts to panic upon hearing the salesperson's threat and becomes unable to think clearly, so takes the only option which it can see (the very convincing salesperson's view).

They buy the coat only after their protector self has shown them an internal cinema screen image of being rejected for not being 'cool'. Even though they do not have the money to afford the coat as they are a student on minimum wage, they take out a loan and are now in financial debt.

Although the person goes home with a nice new coat, they also go home with a feeling of confusion as to why they bought it, a large dose of stress hormones and a feeling of resentment towards themselves for buying something just so they look 'cool'.

Scenario 3

A person who is overly nice and accommodating to everybody is seen by society and their social group as a good person. They start to gain the attention of a certain other person in their social group since they have recently become single. Although the accommodating person is nice to everybody they meet, the reason for their actions is that they are harbouring a sense of guilt about letting people down, so their mask has adapted into what is known as a people pleaser.

The con they endured

A member of their social group would like to date them. When they ask for a date the nice person politely tries to refuse. Although they never explain why, it is actually because they do not find them desirable. The member of the social group then insinuates that they have been leading them on by giving them attention and now they feel very hurt and let down. This then intensely triggers the nice person's sense of guilt and they change their answer and say yes to a date. The driver is through guilt of seeing the other's hurt feelings and the perception that they have 'let them down'.

Scenario 4

A person who is seen to be a 'fitness freak' by their social group as they exercise regularly feels a sense of significance from their 'title' in the social group (a mask of identity). They always put up a good challenge to their fitness opponents and this gets people talking about them and their reputation grows.

The underlying reason they train so hard is because even though they are now slim and toned, they still view themselves as overweight as they were years before. They feel anxious about social rejection because that image is playing on their internal cinema screen and therefore feel anxious about rejection by their peers in the real world. They formed this belief as they were bullied for their shape when they were younger and have not come to terms with it.

The con they endured

They are sat watching TV and notice an advert for a new exercise nutrition supplement that 'GUARANTEES' more weight loss than any other supplement on the market. Their protector self now sees this opportunity to get an even better physique and therefore even more admiration from their peer group. However, the 'full' course of the supplement (small print) costs over £1,000 and they really do not have the money. However, the next advert 'just happens to be' a zero-percent interest credit card with flashy words like 'no risk' and 'easy payments', and so they sign up immediately without reading the credit card's small print either and in a year end up heavily in debt.

Let's take another view on society…
How many people do you know who…

- Only ever define themselves by which job they have?
- Will talk about their partner continually?

- Always steer a conversation to their level of knowledge?
- Always tell you about new things they have bought?

Yet we can also notice that when these things are removed or not included in their conversation they may start to become quiet and uncomfortable in the social setting.
People who talk about their status (or mask) continually to the detriment of all else are subliminally addicted to their mask and will defend their mask with all they have. Again though, most times these very same people, who can be the nicest, kindest and loving people you have ever met, may not even be aware of what is driving them.

A person will be defending their mask (and therefore open to being conned) any time they…

- Are scared to leave a job but don't know why
- Can't leave a relationship but can't explain why
- Feels they 'have' to do something to get approval
- Allow another person to abuse them and never stand up for themselves
- Cheat on their lover
- Buy things they do not need when they feel anxious
- Spend money they don't have on things they don't need
- Is loud or overbearing when it is not required
- Bully or manipulate other people
- Refuse to change who they even though they hurt their loved ones
- Take drugs/alcohol excessively
- 'Have' to be the best at everything they do
- Can never say no
- Become everything to everyone and in the process lose their own identity
- Are people pleasers - 'the yes person'
- Are obsessive or compulsive (a difference from just motivation)
- Check emails and texts continually when not required

- Ring their partner or friends repeatedly when not required
- Are never still or can't sit quietly
- Work too much at the office when not required
- Feel unable to leave the house without the right clothes/makeup
- Weigh themselves 10 times a day
- Plus many more…

The list of reactions in relation to the con is endless and therefore a person's vulnerability to the con is endless. However, as mentioned they are only vulnerable in the areas in which they feel vulnerable from low self-esteem or shame. If there is no vulnerability it cannot be exploited.

"It did not feel like something that was going to take over my life and destroy it. It felt like a subtle flower instead of a manipulative demon. That's the mystery of heroin."
Corey Feldman

So there we have it, the con is unveiled and how you are now seeing your world after reading this chapter is for you to decide. However, there is still much more to look at behind the scenes. Simply just 'knowing' the con is not the full picture. As I mentioned there are many levels to this and if for some people this chapter still does not feel as relevant as it could be, the next chapters will open up much more.

That said, what we have looked at so far, although it can sound quite intense, it is not the real risk to your life and happiness! Underneath the surface of all of this is something much more painful. Not dealing with this deeper potential threat could have a seriously damaging effect on you, your health, your family and your social life. This is not meant to pose any intimidation, far from it, but is written to help you realise and let go of the con and live a life which you are in control of and live in peace with the people you love.

"Your task is not to seek for love,
but merely to seek and find all the barriers within
yourself that you have built against it."
Rumi

"There is a life-force within your soul, seek that life.
There is a gem in the mountain of your body, seek that mine.
O traveller, if you are in search of that
Don't look outside, look inside yourself and seek that."
Rumi

In the next chapter we will take a deep look into the effect of ignoring the mask and the con. Again though, remember that it is important to be aware that although anybody is vulnerable to the con and anybody can be a con trickster, many people in the game are not aware of it. Most of the people who manipulate others are not malicious in their intent; in many cases they have just learned behaviour and are using it without even knowing it.

So shall we just BLAME everybody else?
As you can see the con is where one person can convince another person to do something they don't always want to do. However, they do the action because the emotional pain of not protecting themselves is something they feel they cannot cope with, so the mask is the lesser of two evils.

So does this mean we should blame the people who sell their products or want us to do the things we don't want to do? NO!
The truth is that it is not other people who are the main con tricksters! The main con trickster is your very own protector self in its complete confusion trying to keep you safe.

With this in mind, if you are aware that another person is manipulating you, do not become angry at them as this will accomplish nothing except conflict. The only true way to end a manipulation is to become aware of why it is happening and why you have attracted them into your life. Then and only then can you learn to move forward through it. However, we shall cover much more on this in the next chapter.

Chapter summary

Trust your gut!

One of the best quotes I have ever heard is that 'intuition is recognition'! When you have a 'gut feeling' it is simply that your very powerful subconscious mind has observed something within the current situation that it recognises as either pain or pleasure. However, the reason you just 'feel' it rather than 'consciously' know it is because there is too much information to consciously process in the moment. This could be a slight moment of somebody's mouth, eyes or head which you subconsciously have learned in the past is either trustworthy or suspicious.

Take a moment and note all of the times when you have had a gut feeling to do something or to avoid a situation and then ask yourself what your mind had subconsciously become aware of but your conscious mind could not process in the moment. What was it about a particular person or situation that you felt drawn to or repelled from?

The awareness of denial

Although there is a great deal of information I could cover on the area of denial, for this summary I will cover one of the main ones which is in relation to the gut feeling. In the dependency cycle we saw how other people can knowingly or unknowingly convince a person to doubt themselves and their own opinions. When this happens a person may also start to doubt their 'gut feeling', which can lead to a process of denial. For example, a person who gets a gut feeling may then create a dependency loop and assume that as the thought is coming from their 'own opinion' and their views are not valid, their gut feeling is also not valid, so they then deny the gut feeling.

Take a moment to revisit the list from the last example of all the times when you have had a gut feeling and then doubted and ignored what you felt. The main situations that you are looking for here is when you have denied your own true gut feeling and it had a disastrous effect.

An example here would be a person who had a gut feeling to avoid a particular social event, but then peers put pressure on them to attend. Indeed, when they attended it turned out to be an unpleasant atmosphere due to another attendee. The person had subconsciously realised the attendance of the abusive person but ignored it due to peer pressure.

The con trick

When we hear the phrase 'con trick' it would be easy to understand if our mind wandered to an image of one person manipulating another to deceive money or possessions, but the con in this book is much more severe! The con trick that we play on ourselves is simply to create external realities to distract us from the internal anxiety. However, this is a futile task and is unable to create inner peace as no matter how many external coping mechanisms are put in place, they will never alter the stored belief looping in time as the two are in separate realities.

Take a moment and reflect upon any areas of your past that still haunt you or any self-esteem issues which cause you to feel unsure of yourself. Once you have this then ask yourself if you are taking any actions to disprove these internal anxieties. Also, ask yourself how long you have been doing them and how much of a difference they really make. You will know you have an anxiety mask (a con) if you become anxious of not having it one day or it being taken away from you.

The good and bad masks of deception

Be aware that in life we all wear masks and sometime it is essential to create a persona in order to complete a certain task. An example of this is if a school teacher was having a hard day but needed to maintain a balanced emotional posture in order to inspire the children. However, the main area I am talking of here is when a person creates a mask through anxiety and is therefore covering up an emotional wound. It is important to note that there are both healthy and unhealthy anxiety masks. The healthy mask can promote growth at the same time as covering up a hidden insecurity, and the unhealthy mask can damage the health or other people / possessions.

Take a moment to reflect on any masks you may have and ask yourself which category they fit into. Again, please exercise caution with this, and this question does not have to be answered if it is too challenging. Do not judge yourself on the answer, just be aware!

Be responsible and give players a wide berth

If you are looped in an external con trick and feel compelled to buy the latest fashion or 'have to' do what others tell you to do, just be aware that this does not have to be forever. By understanding the lessons in this book and going on a journey of personal development it is possible to create an exit from the guilt and or shame beliefs.

By this I do not mean to insinuate cutting off those people in your life who love you and are accidentally projecting their expectations, rather to just be very aware of those who are open to 'playing the game'! The types I am referring to here are those pushy sales people or the guilt-tripping co-worker.

Take a moment and reflect upon all of the people in your life currently and ask yourself which of these can trigger an anxiety reaction in you. When you have this list look at what exactly it is that triggers the reaction - is it that they talk down to you, force you on to a pedestal or tell you endless stories of doom? **Awareness is the key!**

12

Ignorance is Bliss?

Over the years there have been many sayings that have become habits in modern day cultures. These habits are insinuating that if a person cannot 'see' a challenging situation or suppressed emotion then they automatically acquire some strange immunity towards it. It is as if some members of society are completely convinced that if they are not able to see something, there is nothing to worry about.

Hide and seek?

When I was a child myself, my neighbour had a boy who was five years younger than me. One day we decided to play hide and seek, a game which he had never played before. As it was his first game, being his friend I let him hide first as he wanted to, and I counted to ten and then went to find him. So I faced the wall and counted. However, when I turned round to go and look for him I saw something that confused me.

Although I had counted and given him time to hide, when I turned around he was stood in the middle of the garden with his hands over his eyes. At first I couldn't figure it out so I pretended to not see him and then played along, eventually tapping him on his shoulder and saying "Found you!", to which he squealed and giggled and said that now he would find me.

Being completely confused as the nine-year-old that I was, I asked 'the oracle' - my Mum :) - and she explained that very young children get confused with seeing things as separate from themselves (egocentric – seeing themselves as part of everything else) and in his world if he couldn't 'see me' then (in his world) I couldn't see him!

NB: *There is a distinct difference between egocentric and narcissism, although sometimes the two are confused in conversation. The egocentric will just see themselves as part of everything (or the centre of it) as they do not know any different, but will not be doing this for attention. Whereas the narcissist will place themselves at the centre of everything for attention and connection, which is a mask covering up the anxiety that they 'are not' involved in society.*

Now if we take the first part of this chapter…

"It is as if some members of society are completely convinced that if they are not able to see something, then there is nothing to worry about."

We can see how similar this is to a small child covering their eyes, believing that because they cannot see their game partner, their game partner cannot see them, when in reality the child covering their eyes is like a sitting duck. However, if we swap the two people playing a game of hide and seek to a grown adult having all of their power taken away by their own protector self, the whole scene grows quite dark.

When discussing the emotional self however, it is not a game. It is very real and although a person may cover their eyes to the unwanted feelings creating an emotional blindness, their protector self is sat inside their mind observing every move they make. Their protector self will also be ready to create a mask at the first sign of stress they deny.

Yet still some people choose the well-trodden path of avoidance and will use within their daily vocabulary phrases such as…

"Out of sight, out of mind"

"What the heart never knows the heart never grieves"

And the all-time favourite…

"Ignorance is bliss"

Ignorance is bliss is an ideal quote to begin this chapter with. The phrase implies that bliss (or a state of happiness) comes from the ignorance (lack of observation) of a current situation that causes upset or trauma. The statement in itself though is a paradox, because…

1. A person feels some sort of pain through an emotional reaction, but doesn't actually want to feel it.

2. The pain they feel is their reaction to the situation and their own perception and therefore self-created.

3. They have only two options to stop the reaction: they can either come to terms with it or suppress it.
4. If they do not know how to come to terms with it (lack of education) they can try to suppress it.

5. Again though, as their pain is coming from 'their own' reaction, suppressing it will not remove it so will continually cause pain on a subconscious level.

6. However, as we have seen the mind can create a mask to distract the conscious mind's attention.

7. The conscious mind is now tricked by the mask and the pain appears to vanish…

8. Yet the mask is only there because the protector self is trying to distract the conscious mind from the suppressed internal pain.

9. Although the person may not feel the pain, it hasn't gone away (just suppressed).

10. In reality the mind is continually focused on the pain and continually reacting to it. The mask is then created to distract the awareness. Therefore, the mask has been created from the pain. If the mask is there...so is the pain.

So is ignorance really bliss?

The mind cannot reject a thought

A test I do in my workshops is to ask the class the following question:

"DO NOT think of the colour blue!"

Try it yourself and notice what happens. Most people get the point and start to smile, but every now and then somebody will say that they can, to which the conversation goes…

Paul (me): What colour are you thinking of then?
Student: I'm thinking of orange.
Paul: Can I ask why you are thinking of orange?
Student: Because I don't want to think of…..

At that point they start to laugh as they realise that the only reason they thought of orange was to distract their mind from blue. So they did in fact think of blue first and then distract their mind by thinking of a different colour.

So try this:

DON'T think of your money worries
DON'T think of your appearance worries
DON'T think about your career worries
DON'T think about your rejection worries
DON'T think about .... (fill in the blank)

Put into another term – **the mind cannot reject a negative statement or thought.**

So in all reality, ignorance is not bliss, but far from it.

An example would be a scenario that has affected millions of people at some point in their life called the "bumping into the ex" (as in ex-partner/relationship).

In this scenario, if they were not deeply emotionally invested in their 'ex-partner when they separated then the stress reaction would be low.
However, imagine a person (Partner A) who was really attracted to their partner (Partner B), and then one day Partner B said the relationship was over. Partner A feels rejected and reacts with massive amounts of pain.
To feel pain when a person suddenly chooses to move on is quite a normal reaction, especially if we are not expecting it and are emotionally invested in the relationship. However, if this pain was to continue for a long period of time then this would be unhealthy and perhaps attached to a mask.

So in this example let us imagine that Partner A has attached themselves to the relationship as it makes them feel secure and that they are loved/wanted. Underneath though their attachment is driven by low self-esteem and they have abandonment issues.

1. At first, Partner A tries to move on with their life but has not come to terms with the rejection so still feels emotional pain.
   Although as mentioned this could be coming from their mind naturally trying to come to terms with what has happened, in this scenario it is that their protector self is feeling pain as they now

are anxious of being alone and abandoned (possibly a supressed belief from being young or another painful experience).

2. No matter how hard Partner A tries to put the loss of their relationship out of their mind it still continues to come back.
   This is the supressed belief 'I'm not wanted/not good enough' forcing its way through into their emotions from the internal cinema screen.

3. Their friends say 'don't worry' and 'there are plenty more fish in the sea', but this doesn't help stop the pain either.
   As mentioned, simply using conscious distraction to attempt to ignore the subconscious will have very little effect (so-called positive thinking).

4. So, Partner A, feeling very stressed and thinking about their relationship all the time, decides to join a health club and starts to exercise.
   In my years of working my way up the ladder I have worked in health clubs as a personal trainer for 15 years. During this time I have seen a great many people join the gym shortly after a relationship breakup.
   This is also a healthy option. Basically their protector self is releasing lots of stress hormones and the person wants to reduce them. Going to the gym burns off the excess adrenaline and cortisol, creating a calmer feeling.

5. Although the person now feels calmer, they notice that they still think about their relationship a great deal and want to get back together.
   This is where we introduce the sugar and salt metaphor. The salt in this situation is that Partner A wants to connect to another in a relationship, which is a perfectly healthy and natural drive. The sugar in this situation is that Person A wants to get back together with their partner to end the anxiety of being alone, and the internal confusion grows within their mind as it is difficult to decipher which from which.

6. This is where it can get complicated! As Partner A is now in the gym often, they start to get to know a few people. Subconsciously, they are giving off very subtle body language saying to other people that they are feeling insecure and lonely. This could be tone of voice, a lowering of the head etc.. However, in contrast they may actually look very confident. This is where their mask is saying to look confident, but their subconscious is feeling very insecure. We can see this in other people when we meet them and although they sound very confident, it triggers our gut feeling that they are not as confident as they say. To the observer it can be quite difficult to explain why they feel the other's incongruence.

7. Partner A's subtle projections of insecurity of being single are now noticed by another person (Person C) in the gym, who also feels insecure as they have recently become single. Both Partner A and Person C find themselves drawn to each other.
Looking at this from the outside we can now see that Partner A and Person C are drawn to each other as they are both looking to be in a relationship. The PRIMARY reason for this (in Person A and Person C) is to mask their emotional pain (being alone). However, as they both deny that they are feeling the pain, they also have to deny why they 'really' feel drawn to the other.

8. In their denial they justify their connection by saying that they have lots in common i.e. the gym, although this may be true it may also be a mask (conscious justification). They then decide to start a romantic relationship together based on their justification.

9. As we see, the drive for both of them is to avoid the pain of feeling alone and both people are actually using the other to feel secure (co-dependence). They then justify their attraction by conscious interests. However, the protector self of Person A and Person B feel insecure that the other will leave and they will be alone again. This will happen because although they are in a relationship now, neither of them has updated their anxiety of

feeling unwanted. They both start to depend upon each other more and more and begin to feel extremely anxious of the other one leaving. This anxiety is reflected to each other and both protector selves are now misassuming that the anxiety reactions they see in the other (nervousness etc...) is meaning that they want to leave (paranoia).

10. To combat this anxiety of being abandoned, both Partner A and Person C continually do more and more for each other and spend all their time together. The reason they do this is because they feel that if they continually spend time together then the other will not leave. The relationship now develops into a full co-dependency.

11. Both Partner A and Person C now start to feel overwhelmed by each other's dependency and feel supressed. Even though the relationship is now causing pain, neither of them will part company as the other person takes away their deeper pain of being alone.

12. The relationship continues to drag on and either becomes the norm or one person becomes so stressed that their protector self feels that being in the relationship is more painful than being alone.

Internal pain can project to all areas

Although the above example was a person in a romantic relationship, it is easy to see how this could also be a workplace or social reaction. Also, if we look at the above we can notice the following possibilities.

1. Partner A was assuming that it was their partner leaving them that caused the pain (stage 2 of the self-esteem recovery model), whereas in reality it was that Partner A was reminded of their anxiety of being alone when Partner B left (stage 3 of the self esteem recovery model).

Here we can see how Partner A made themselves powerless by in effect 'blaming' Partner B for their pain.

2. The driver of Partner A to get into a new relationship (with Person C) was to cover up their emotional pain. However, they could easily trick themselves into thinking that this connection could help them forget about Partner B (don't think of the colour BLUE). This is also known as a rebound and rarely lasts unless it's a genuine connection or becomes a co-dependency.

3. Partner A and Person C are now in a co-dependency and unless they face their deeper insecurity (the anxiety of being alone or abandoned), they will continue to use each other to cover up their pain. The con here is that both are being overly accommodating to each other to secure their approval, but also both Partner A's and Person C's protector selves are conning them into thinking 'If you get into a relationship then your pain will go away'.

Even though this may sound quite tangled, there are still other levels which are even deeper to consider such as compounded masks, coping mechanisms, their current environment and their state of health, to name a few.

When I coach a client one to one, it can often be quite easy to see the pattern of their mask (but this is only due to the 25 years of study and lots of trial and error in my own past). However, if I were to simply explain their mask (or con) to them as soon as I see it, in most cases their subconscious would ignore it as there are usually several masks all wrapped up in one.

For example, one client had this experience…

A young guy in his early 20's was running his own business and came to see me as he wanted help with getting into a relationship. In his childhood though his dad was extremely aloof, he had a very needy mother and also had two dominant sisters. Although there were very conflicting energies, he assumed that this was quite a normal family. To him it was, as he had no reference points and had become used to it from birth. He felt that he could not really claim that he'd had a difficult childhood.

The challenge was...

Although he wanted a relationship...

- He had abandonment issues around his dad to which he reacted in shame.
- He was emasculated by both of his sisters (his sisters saw him as weak and he believed them).
- He was anxious of letting go to women in case he was attacked emotionally.
- His mum was needy and his reaction was that he should do more to help people (guilt of feeling that he was never able to help his mum).
- In his business he was working 80 hours per week to prove his worth to his dad to win his approval (need).
- He also did too much for his clients, who took advantage of his need to help them.
- He became so physically drained that his sleep patterns and health suffered.
- His stress manifested as anger outbursts.

The result was that he would go on a date with a girl and project his belief that women are dominant or needy onto his date and then to control the situation he would appear aloof (a learned pattern from his dad).

Also he would usually be so tired from working so many hours that in conversation he would glaze over or become irritated easily. This would make his date feel uncomfortable and often cease all further contact.

Looking at it this way, I hope it is starting to help you see more and more clearly that a relationship / job change / losing weight etc. is not as straightforward as it appears. In life if a person has two or more masks all supporting each other, then changing one thing may lead to a major confusion, which increases the pain.

In the above example, my client's protector self was actually traumatised about getting into a relationship in case (in his eyes) he ended up with a very needy (his mum's energy) or a very dominant (his two sisters) woman. Although this may sound confusing, it is simply that his subconscious mind was basing all women on the main experiences of women he had met in his life (his mum and sisters).

His choice of working 80 hours a week were other masks; one mask to gain his dad's approval and another mask to make himself so exhausted that he didn't have time for a relationship (thereby keeping himself safe).

Remember, all of this is being driven by the supressed belief within his subconscious.

So I ask again… is ignorance really bliss?

In life there are many ways of avoiding what we do not want to see. However, simply avoiding an internal worry (stage 4 of the self-esteem recovery model) by covering it up with an avoidance strategy or mask (stage 6) is no different than putting a medical plaster over a poisonous splinter in the skin. As long as the splinter is in the skin it will continue to damage the tissue around it. The splinter has to be removed before the wound can fully heal (but to do that it needs to be faced).

Developing ignorance to a current anxiety is also classed as denial. To pretend it is not there in a blind hope that eventually it will simply go away is a recipe for disaster. Denial is yet another protector self behaviour pattern that we will cover further along, but for now we can revisit a previous story.

A review of the story of sugar and salt

As we saw in the earlier story on the sugar and salt, the cook was in denial that he had changed the king's meal and tried to cover it up. However, with all this new information we have now covered, we can see that there is much more to it.

Here we can ask questions such as,,,

Q: Was the cook really at peace with himself?
A: No, he was continually concerned that he would be found out and as the king's health became worse so did the cook's anxiety.

Q: Would the cook have felt safe?
A: Possibly not as if he told anybody it may have got back to the king (the onset of paranoia).

Q: What would the cook's physiology have been like?
A: We can assume that stress hormones were continually in his body wearing him down.

Q: Would the cook feel guilty or ashamed?
A: Again, more than likely as what he was doing was not admitting to hurting another person so he could not get caught (guilt = I have done something wrong).

We can see here that the longer the denial continues, not only does the mask get stronger, but the pressure can also increase exponentially for the cook!

If we have a guess at what the cook's internal cinema screen is showing it wouldn't be pleasant. It is likely that the stress in his physiology may be wearing him down from the inside. Although the body and mind are durable, there is only so much it can take before things take a turn for the worse.

So is ignorance really bliss?

The confusion of denial (stage 4 of the self-esteem recovery model)
A coping mechanism that the protector self can use during times of trauma and upset is that of denial. It is also highly recommended to review Elizabeth Kübler-Ross, who brought us the 'Grief cycle'. The grief cycle is a fantastic model which very eloquently explains how the mind copes with a trauma. The model also covers how the mind works through the stress to clear the trapped energy and trauma.

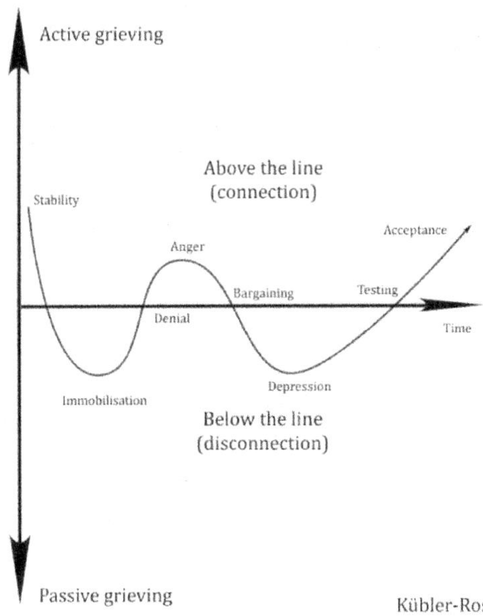

Kübler-Ross model

When a person is faced with a very traumatic situation which is beyond comprehension of their emotions at that time (such as the loss of a limb or the sudden death of a loved one), the protector self will usually create a mindset of denial. This can be classed as a buffer zone or in many respects a blindness to the situation. This is done to protect the conscious mind from the painful image. The reason for this is that if the conscious mind was allowed to observe the situation at that moment it could be too painful and possibly cause emotional overload or a nervous breakdown. This is similar to what an adult would do with a child if the adult saw an accident and then covered the child's eyes so they couldn't see it and subsequently feel upset.

Now if we imagine the challenge (stage 2 from the self-esteem recovery model), we see a child being rejected by a parent. The rejection may be so traumatic to the child (stage 3) that their protector self literally blinds their conscious mind from feeling the full feelings of the situation (stage 4). However, although the conscious may not see it, the subconscious mind is fully aware of the situation and will store this as a memory of danger (in Pandora's Box). If we recall, we see only through the conscious mind which is a mere 5%, but the subconscious stores experiences and creates beliefs which are then acted on and reacted to with what it thinks is a true map of the world.

NB and reminder: *Suppressed pain is not actually from our parents or anybody else's interaction in our life. The pain we feel is from 'our perception' of the situation (stage 3). Any painful experience can be stored as reference - rejection from friends, chased by a dog, watching a friend get bullied and a thousand other situations.*

Building the picture

If we revisit the chapter on the self-esteem recovery model with the child who is being carried off from trying to get the cookies and then told off by the parent, the child may find this so traumatic that their protector self literally blocks their emotions and feelings to this situation. Although the child may not fully feel traumatised, the memory of "I'm too weak" or "I'm wrong" has still been stored inside their subconscious mind. Yet because their conscious mind is not aware of it (through denial / Pandora's Box), the child may seemingly cope with the punishment quite well. Under the surface however, something much more painful may have been registered.

In reality (physical reality, rather than perceived reality), the child (at the time of taking the cookies) was actually physically and emotionally weaker than the parent. This is because the parent is fully grown and the child is physically smaller. However, if the child stores a belief in their mind that 'I am too weak' and then drops into denial, that belief could be stored in the Pandora's Box mind for years to come. Once in there it may start to attach itself to other memories. As the subconscious has no concept of time, their protector self may assume that 'I'm too weak' is a reality no matter what action is faced and no matter how old the person becomes (internal paranoia). That is of course 'unless' they change the stored belief.

It is essential that the process of denial is fully understood as this is one of the key components of the con.

A review of irrational beliefs

It is a widely-used term today to class anxiety that appears like it has no reason to be there as an irrational belief. This however is a limited observation of the person describing their reactions in relation to the human mind. The brain itself has been continually developing for thousands of years and although it may sometimes appear 'not' to function correctly, it is actually functioning perfectly normally (providing no disease, surgery or physical trauma has occurred). To describe something as irrational as this is likened to saying that the mind has no structure or purpose for it making the decision or the action it took (such as running off in tears after walking into a crowded room of friends). However, the mind is anything but irrational; in fact, it is perfectly logical. It is just that sometimes the conscious mind cannot understand why the subconscious mind has taken a certain action.

Supressed and painful memories (beliefs) create actions driven from the distorted reality of the past cross-referenced stimulus on the internal cinema's screen. These actions are created from the protector self assuming that the action (re-action) is the most effective way to avoid pain today. This is of course unless the 'current' situation **is** traumatic, as sometimes the environment can be hostile or violent.

If the memories and experiences of the past were painful and have been screened from the conscious mind in denial (i.e. our awareness of them), the subconscious will still act on them accordingly regardless of whether the person is consciously aware of them or not.

Just because a person is not aware of their inner anxieties does not mean that the subconscious mind will stop using them as a reference to guide itself around the world in which it lives. It is the protector self who is making the decisions under the surface and in many cases based on beliefs which were formed in the past and have not been updated to today's reality.

Believe it or not

In many ways the reactions from stored beliefs (if unchanged from when they were formed) can be as powerful in the current day as when they were originally created. We can see this happening for many people who have grown into an adult and their parent (who is now an equal adult) may criticize them and the adult child has an 'assumed' irrational reaction (such as shouting or storming off in a sulk). The reaction is not irrational but simply a looped belief pattern triggering off from the association (the parent).

Looking further into the term 'irrational beliefs' allows for a greater understanding of why there is so much confusion in relation to anxiety. The answer is that a person has two minds (conscious and subconscious mind), but they are only aware of their world through one (the conscious mind). As we saw in previous chapters, the conscious mind is aware of today and can see things as they really are, though the subconscious makes its judgement of the world by referring to past experiences and memories (the internal cinema screen). As long as there are unresolved painful experiences which have been suppressed in the subconscious then the protector self will keep reacting. This is the cause of the often quoted 'irrational behaviour'.

The challenge comes from the inability to update the beliefs because of the disconnection between the conscious and subconscious when in denial. The other reason for the inability to update the beliefs is through lack of adequate knowledge of how to update beliefs.

Let us revisit the child from the self-esteem recovery model (cookies) who received the painful experience, but this time we will create a different path that could happen.

1. The child is curious and climbs on a chair to get the cookies (stage 1 - discovery).

2. The child is picked up by an angry parent, carried off into another room and punished (a rejection and loss of love = pain) (stage 2 - challenge).

3. The child's protector self, in its confusion and panic (limited knowledge of the world), forms two beliefs: 1. "I am weak and can't succeed", 2. "My parent is correct to punish me as I am wrong for upsetting them" (peer idolisation / shame) (stage 3 - can I handle it = no).

4. The protector self is attempting to help the child survive but realises that these stored beliefs (1+2) are too traumatic for the child's thoughts to cope with. It then creates a denial programme in order to protect their conscious mind (stage 4 – personality shutdown).

5. The child now becomes shy and starts to lose interest in new things, but would usually have no idea why they are taking these actions (also stage 4).

6. The child grows to be a teenager and starts to get bullied for being shy. Teachers and other peers tell him to stop being soft and stand up for himself. The thought of fighting back fills him full of dread (again, he has no idea why). In reality his subconscious is still using the "I am weak and can't succeed" belief and carries on using it because no further education or situations have been introduced to remove the belief.

7. The child is eventually driven to the point of sheer frustration and continual internal paranoia (stage 5) from the "I am weak and can't succeed" belief being played over and over again. This is twinned with the continual release of painful stress hormones. Eventually he begins to fight back and starts to release his energy

by shouting and intimidating other peers (stage 6 - the mask and other coping mechanisms).

8. The teenager is classed as a trouble-causer, which further exasperates the feeling of rejection creating yet more beliefs of "I am taking the wrong actions" (guilt). These will then be put into denial inside the subconscious for self-esteem protection. Again, these denied beliefs will start to act as a reference system for the mind to assume as reality.

9. The teenager has now grown into a young man in college and begins to realise that people think highly of the captain of the football team. They see the captain as a leader and have high respect for him. The young man's protector self now sets a goal to become the captain of the football team in order to win the respect and admiration of his peers. This to the outside world looks like an admirable achievement, but in reality, the purpose of being captain is to be seen as a leader to hide from the fact that underneath there is a belief that states "I am weak and can't succeed".

10. The young man becomes the captain and as expected wins the attention and approval of many peers.

11. However, the young man's feeling of self-worth now relies on the fact that he is the captain of the football team. This is now classed as "external reliance" (the healthy mask). He feels worthy and can escape the internal paranoia (stage 5) as long as he can distract himself by looking at the fact that he is captain of the football team. This in itself is yet another form of denial as the original driving belief "I am weak and can't succeed" is still inside the subconscious mind. Although his conscious mind is seeing that he is successful because he is the captain of the football team, his subconscious belief will always be assessed by the protector self first. The protector self will still be using the two denied beliefs as reference and then reaction.

12. Over time the young man becomes a full-grown adult and begins to form a habit of being the best at everything he can. This again is driven from the original belief "I am weak and can't succeed". Through his achievements and high financial return in his job he is highly rewarded and admired by society as an achiever. However, in the other story where the teenager came to terms with his suppressed emotions, in this one he doesn't and continues to stay addicted to the mask.

13. Underneath all the perceived success (money, car and beautiful home) the man starts to become anxious about being found out that he is a fraud (the paranoia is now fighting against the mask). This is because the underlying beliefs are still buried and causing the protector self to react. He does not know why this is happening or where it is coming from (as it is a denied belief). The paranoia starts to build inside his mind as do the stress hormones in his body. This is from the original belief "I am weak and can't succeed" penetrating his life of perceived success (just like the sugar makes the king ill). So the man works even harder and achieves even more in an attempt to block the paranoia. This has an effect on his home life and his wife files for a divorce. No matter how much he achieves he is confused as to why he cannot escape the feelings. He has no idea why they are there, then classes this feeling as an irrational belief and continues to work even harder (whilst using alcohol as extra support).

14. One day his manager comes up to him and explains that due to cutbacks they will have to make him redundant. As his high-powered career has been his mask for so long he has become addicted to it. His protector self mind goes into a blind panic after losing his job and for a few days he turns to alcohol even more to block out his stress reactions. Again, he has no idea why he is panicking so much as logically he has no rational reason to act this way. Subconsciously though, his protector self is on red alert, believing that as he has lost his job (mask) the people that thought he was successful may now see him the way he was

perceived the day he was carried off by his parent - "I am weak and can't succeed". With his mask being taken away against his will he triggers the same helpless emotions as when he was a young child and feels powerless and vulnerable.

15. After losing his job he begins to grasp at other jobs in a panic to regain his mask. However, because he is now fighting with his insecurities his actions and mannerisms during the interviews appear desperate. This results in him failing the interviews and nobody employs him (self-fulfilling prophecy). To cope with his mask being taken away and suddenly seeing the full-blown anxiety that he has been hiding from all these years, he becomes shy and loses all drive for life (the protector self is once again in personality shutdown, stage 4). He then turns to alcohol or another drug (a different mask) to distract his pain.

The above situation (using different masks) is an all-too-familiar scenario for a great many of people each and every day. How many times do we hear the following…

- The 'nice guy' at work who is kind and respectful but one day he just started acting abusively to people at work?

- The often quoted 'midlife' crisis?

- The unfortunate situations where a person who seems to have everything to live for but one day, completely unexpectedly to those around them, takes their own life?

- The person who no matter how hard they try cannot seem to lose weight and yo-yo diets?

- The person who is calm and collected but once they drink alcohol turn aggressive or abusive?

These types of scenarios can happen in relationships, friendships, hobbies, health and anywhere. Any underlying belief of low self-esteem or low self-worth which is covered up by an external mask is always at risk as the protector self is still using the past denied belief as a map for today. Until that original belief is updated, the same pattern will happen over and over again as a mask can never change a belief; it can only protect the conscious mind.

It is possible for a person to live their whole life behind a mask and be fully unaware of doing so. The mask is such an advanced coping mechanism of denial (created by the protector self), that it is more than capable of tricking the conscious (thinking mind) of its existence.
One such way is known as 'habituation' (or accepting the situation as 'the norm'). We saw this in the sugar and salt story earlier where the king just became used to the illness. When a mask has been used for a certain period of time, the conscious mind eventually assumes that the mask is part of its reality through repeated exposure.

Points to note and perceived contradictions

In this chapter it may appear to state that people in life make decisions based on ignoring things that they do not want to see. Although this is true in some cases, it is not the case for all and only one side of the story.
The action of denial is only relevant if a person has experienced a situation before that they could not cope with and which is still supressed. Some people may choose actions in their daily lives based on the fact that they have not experienced the situation before. Therefore, they appear unaware.

Another area to note is that physiological health can affect the emotional drive in an inconsistent manner. Low blood sugar or tiredness for example can create brain fog which can create confusion.
Also, when it was stated before that ignorance is bliss, to some people this statement may be the truth. In reality, if there is no perceived threat there is nothing to become anxious about. Yet this area is a point worth

noting, as life can bring challenges whether we are ready or not. Take the following scenario…

Scenario

A young man moves to the city to live his dreams and discover new things in life. Before he moved to the city he lived in a pleasant village where people were nice to each other. Although there were quarrels every now and then, they never developed into anything too serious and challenges could be discussed to an amicable agreement.

At this stage the young man, even though he is an adult, has not stored any traumatic events. Even though he has lived what may be considered by many to be a 'good life', he actually has quite a blinkered view on the world. His awareness of life is limited as although his village was respectful to each other, in the city he has moved to there are many different types of people, some of which are unable to control their anger.

In his blinkered view (to his protector self) there has been no need to store any threats and create any anxieties towards potential situations, as there hasn't been any. To him, the world is a safe place and challenges in life can be easily worked through. This is the other side of ignorance! However, as stated, the young man's blinkered view is far from a real interpretation of the world as a whole and can lead to great risk (Be Prepared – chapter 2).

The young man naively walks through a dangerous part in the city late at night (without anxiety). He then comes across a gang of angry-looking men; they stop him and demand his money. He smiles and then starts to debate with them. His internal cinema screen is convinced that he can sort the challenge out (as he would in his home village). The angry men have no patience and become physically violent, and after knocking him to the floor they take his money and laugh in his face.

The young man lying there in pain asks a passer-by for help (expecting to be helped). The stranger walks past, telling him that he is stupid for not knowing the area and walks off. Thoughts swirl through the young man's head in confusion as to what has happened. Behind the scenes, the man's protector self is busy creating images and a new map of the world, which through ignorance and lack of psychological knowledge get buried in denial. As the young man lays there in a place he does not know, he starts to become aware of a strange feeling of anxiety. For the first time he feels the icy grip of a new thought of "I'm too weak to cope in the city" cloud his judgement and all he can think of is going home (removal of pain).

To stay in the comfort zone

Ignorance is bliss as long as life does not pose challenges that a person cannot cope with and which are below their pain threshold. Yet as we have already discussed life is not like that; life is full of unexpected challenges - some are achievable and some are not. It is impossible to expect to be able to handle all types of situations, but being able to handle the emotional reactions is something that is within a person's control.

Criminals and manipulators will prey on the ignorant minded (and those who are unaware) for an easy target. It is well known that many people who get mugged can act like a rabbit trapped in the car headlights and sometimes will stand there when attacked (freeze). In many cases the criminal does not even have to become violent, but simply to insinuate violence and the victim's protector self (going into overdrive through lack of knowledge) will follow orders, doing as the mugger or criminal tells them.

The above is why people can find themselves terrified to leave a job, leave a relationship or take on new challenges.

Remember, ignorance (or unawareness) will come from the following two areas:

1. The person has experienced the pain before and is suppressing it.

2. The person has never experienced it before and is cognitively unaware of it.

When actions are not driven from a mask

It is very important to note that not all success or actions are driven by a mask. The world would become a very challenging place if it was. If we go back to the starting stage of the peer idolisation scale and also to path one on the self-esteem recovery model, we can see that the natural drive of a person is to grow and connect with other people. These two drives are what make life enjoyable and give hope to those who are in a dark place. The heart is always 'searching for the light', as some would say. The reason for this is that when we are in a safe environment, the protector self can rest and energy output will be at its most efficient. In this state we will be calm and can genuinely give to others. This in turn allows others to feel more secure and harmonious. With this feeling of harmony, the mind will naturally begin to take more challenges in life and we can then grow as a human race. This is the ideal state to be in for optimum health, abundance and building a community.

Also, other drives such as hobbies and general interests are not driven from ignorance or denial. Usually when it is said that a person is 'in the zone' or 'doing their thing' they are connected to that part of themselves that wishes to self-express (the true self).

The difference between heaven and hell (a metaphor)

(This is not related to any religious orientation, it is just a story)

One day a man upon walking down the road began to wonder to himself what the difference was between heaven and hell. He went to sleep that night and had a dream.

In his dream the man was in a huge room and noticed two doors. On one door one he noticed a sign saying heaven and on the other he noticed a sign saying hell. As he stood next to one of the doors an omnipotent being of glowing light appeared, who gave the man the option to experience both realities so he could answer his question.

For his first choice the man decided to walk in to the door named 'hell', to which the omnipotent being joined him. Upon entering he saw an infinitely long table which was 1-meter wide. The man also noticed that there were millions of people stood all along both sides of the table waiting to be seated. On the table was the most exquisite banquet he had ever seen.

The omnipotent being now told everybody that they could eat. Before they sat down they all went to the wall and collected their knives and forks. However, the man then noticed that all the knives and forks were 1-meter long and when the people picked them up they glued themselves to the person's hands at the end of the piece of cutlery. All the people then went to the table to eat, but when they picked up food and tried to eat, the cutlery was so long that they could not get the food in their mouths. All the people sat there with the most amazing banquet but could not eat, but because they had already passed on in life they could not die. However, they could feel hunger and as the days passed the hunger became more and more painful and soon there was much suffering for them.

The omnipotent being turned to the man and explained…
"Hell is where there is abundance and you cannot get to it through selfish greed."

The man then asked to see heaven, and in a flash of light, he was taken there!
Upon opening his eyes, the man looked about and to his shock saw exactly the same scene as in hell, but 'before' the people had started to try to eat. They were all stood around the infinitely long table that was 1-meter wide and all the knives and forks were 1-meter long. It was again the same amazing banquet and with this the man started to feel uncomfortable. The omnipotent being once again said they could all eat. As before he watched all the people collect their knives and forks which then became glued to their hands.

However, upon watching all the people start to eat this time (in heaven), each time a person picked up some food they didn't feed themselves, but fed the person across from them on the other side of the table. The person who had just been fed returned the favour and soon all the people were happy and well fed.

The omnipotent being turned to the man and explained,,,
"Heaven is where everybody helps each other and reaches their aims by working together."

The reality of life
Before we begin to even look at breaking free of a mask and the con, it is essential to note that life is full of challenges. Some challenges will be difficult and workable, but some other challenges will be physically, mentally or emotionally impossible to overcome. This could be arguing with a parent or family member and they will not listen, all the way to an assault on the street in which the attacker has only one intention, which is to cause harm to the target/victim of their attack.

Although in many traumatic situations, especially where there is a loss of somebody close, the last thing on the mind is "that's just life". However in reality, life can be hard. Sometimes life will present situations where there is no way to reach the aim we had.

This is a reality that we have to face; sometimes we cannot win or succeed in the situation no matter what we do. This could be the loss of a house, career, physical health or any other area of our lives. Although something may have been able to be altered with hindsight, the result is the effect of a cause and now reality must be faced.

Yet even though sometimes we cannot control what is happening, we can control (with practice) how we emotionally deal with the situation. That is, providing we KNOW how to work the emotional self.
To emphasise this we can revisit the earlier example where a person can be left completely stranded in their car because they do not know how to fix mechanical faults. In just the same way we too can be left stranded if we do not know how to work or understand the emotions.

This does not mean that we have to be a genius with an IQ of 200+ - far from it in many cases. The key is about being aware that life is life and the only thing we really have any total control over is how we respond to situations as they arise. Firstly, how we control ourselves, then secondly how we take action to resolve the challenging situations.

Therefore it is essential to note that it is not the situation that has happened that causes repression and resentment. The thing that causes the pain is the person's protector self who hijacks their mind and refuses to accept the current reality. True resolution can only happen when we to come to terms with the situation by accepting that it is something beyond our control or level of ability to cope.

However, refusing to accept the reality of a challenging situation is what causes continual repression, leading to cause and effect in our emotions. This is then repeated on the internal cinema screen, causing the protector self to react in fight, flight or freeze. The pain could be a loved one being abusive, being rejected by a friend, not be able to reach a goal or an aim, being bullied in the workplace or a million other scenarios that daily life presents to people all across the world.

We shall cover much more about this area in the chapter on creating a cocoon.

"A grain of sand in the eye can obscure a mountain"
Chinese proverb

Chapter summary

Hiding in plain sight

It is my complete hope and intention that you are now fully aware of how elusive the con trick can be. Many of the things that people do each and every day may be intertwined in the very aim to cover up insecurity. However, it is also important to note that it is each person's free will to choose what they do with their own life and it is not for anybody else to tell them what to do.

Take a moment and reflect upon how many people are taking actions in their lives to cover up an insecurity and they have no idea of their actions.

This could be a neighbour's motivation to buy a new car 'every' year or the co-worker who proudly shows a photo of their lover just a little 'too often'. Remember, a mask is only a mask if a person is taking an action to cover up an internal anxiety. This is an extremely tricky area to decipher and will require a great deal of reflection.

Ignorance is not bliss

Life can be challenging - of that there is no doubt. However, avoiding challenges in the hope that they will go away by themselves is an extremely risky attitude. Many challenges in life such as financial debt or ill health can often become much worse if left (only to create more challenging situation for the future).

Take a moment and reflect upon any situations during the course of your life which at the time felt overwhelming and you avoided them in the hope that things would get better, yet they only became worse. This could be a job, relationship or another area. Although it is true that sometimes we need to go through hardship to realise something about ourselves, here I am talking about the internal anxiety of denial. If you cannot think of any in your own life then choose another person you know of.

The mind won't reject a thought

Although the conscious mind can understand that a joking negative statement is not meant as a negative statement, the subconscious does not have that same ability. If a person tells themselves that they are 'not bad', although they will know they mean 'they are ok' their subconscious will start to react upon the words it hears (bad or unwell).

During the course of the next few days become very aware of the words and the tone of voice which you use to describe yourself and other situations in life. Focus your attention on any feelings which arise as a result of any negative words. Do they create a feeling of power, anger or heaviness?

Habits grow

As mentioned...life can be challenging! There can be many times in life where we feel we want to avoid it all when things become overwhelming. Doing this every now and then can be fine, but as long as action is eventually taken. However, each and every time we choose to ignore a challenge because we have become too anxious we are in fact building a habit pattern. If this habit is practiced on a regular basis it can lead to the mind automatically avoiding challenges all together. This is when masks will begin to compound on top of each other to cope with the increasing avoidance and stress.

Take a moment and look at any avoidance habits which you have allowed to grow in your life. This could be anything from not paying a bill to something as seemingly small as doing the laundry each week. An avoidance pattern is an avoidance pattern and even the smallest things can spread.

Walk a mile in their shoes

Although it is true that there can be many people who project their confusions and anxieties onto other people around them, there is still a huge number of people who are kind, warm, giving and want to work together. However, to achieve this it is important to understand not only our own anxieties but also those of other people. There are many people in the world would love to be whole in their emotions but are struggling, and it is important to be aware of that.

Take a moment and list out all of the people in your life who you may find frustrating and take a step back and then look at the world through their eyes. What are the anxieties which may make them an angry or a rude person? Why do you feel they talk to other people in that way? Although I am not insinuating that you allow poor behaviour or accept abuse, just take a moment and ask yourself what may have happened to make them the way they are. What may they be struggling with?

13

Are You Addicted?

Why the con can be hard to break and what happens if you don't..

Remember this…

ADDICTIONS ARE PAINKILLERS!

Any addiction that a person develops in relation to their mask will be linked to their pain-pleasure cycle. The person is subscribing to the addiction because they feel it alleviates some form of discomfort (or pain). This pain is and can only ever be experienced physical or emotionally.

However, in reality it is not the drug (mask) itself that they are addicted to. What they are really addicted to is the pleasure it creates for them. It is the feeling of pleasure by the apparent removal (or reduction) of the discomfort (or pain) that they are feeling in their lives due to supressed or distracted emotions. This is why people can go from one addiction to the next.

"Every form of addiction is bad, no matter whether the narcotic be alcohol or morphine or idealism."
Carl Jung

Take for example three of my client's experiences in relation to the con…

Person A feels inside that they are not desired or wanted by peers or friends (stage 5 internal paranoia). However, they have a multitude of friends and are a member of several groups. Their mask is that they constantly resort to checking emails or social networking sites. They do this often to reassure themselves that people want to speak to them and are thinking about them.
They do this so often that it starts to affect their work life. One day their manager has a meeting with them and explains that if they keep checking social media during work time they will lose their job. To this person the pain of not being wanted is more horrifying than losing their job and so they keep going online. Needless to say, they eventually lose their job!

Their perceived addiction was going online to check if anybody had contacted them. If they received an email or message, they felt elated and connected. They assume it was the email that caused the feel good factor, but in reality it was 'their perception' of being wanted from receiving the email which then caused an emotional reaction of pleasure.

For this client, the supressed emotion was that they feel they are not wanted or seen as valuable. If they can continually see that people message them, they can consciously convince themselves that people do like them.
Eventually though (as the underlying emotion has not been resolved), the anxiety of not being wanted comes back and they go online again. They receive another message or speak to somebody on instant chat and again they think they feel better.

Using this method to reduce their low self-esteem will only create a pain loop as they are not facing the underlying issue but just masking it. Their 'real addiction' was the pleasure they felt from their own physiology. They themselves created their emotional high by believing that they are wanted… NOT THE EMAIL!

Person B is continually anxious of appearing lazy to their peers because they were always told they were 'idle' from a very young age. Now they are an adult and work 60 – 80 hours per week. They do this to prove to other people that they are a motivated and trustworthy person.

However, they know underneath that working like this will eventually destroy their marriage, but they feel too trapped in anxiety to work less hours. Eventually, two years into their trainee management position their manager says that if they keep working in this manner there will be a big promotion in a year. So, they continue to work in this manner and eventually their marriage falls apart. They get their promotion and pay raise just in time to pay for their divorce.

Their addiction is not the job or the continual reassurance that their manager gives them. Their addiction is the pleasure they feel by being able to reassure themselves that they are not the 'idle' child and are therefore less likely to be rejected.

Person C begins a new relationship and is happy, and the feelings of love are beginning to grow. Yet inside they have always had a deep insecurity that people will leave them. This was formed because they watched their most loved parent go to prison when they were too young to understand why. This created deep abandonment issues.

One evening their new partner decides to socialise with their old school friends. Person C's new partner lets them know that they are going out by themselves as it is a private function.

This causes an emotional backlash and Person C is now sat at home alone. Whilst they sit there their paranoia gets out of hand, creating images that their partner is now talking about them in a derogatory way, having fun without them and having sex with other people. Their mask becomes one of aggression and control (intimidation / fight).
To calm their pain, they ring their partner several times through the night and demand to know where they are and what they are doing. They do this continually through the evening, disrupting the school reunion.

They tell their partner that they want to know where they are because they 'love' them (an often misquoted word). The partner on the night out feels controlled and smothered. When the partner's friends hear about this they define this behaviour as 'controlling', which causes arguments between them all.

In this case, although it would appear that Person C is addicted to control, it is not in fact that which they are addicted to. Their addiction is the feeling of pleasure when they feel reassured themselves that their partner is thinking of them rather than somebody else. Even though there is a heated debate on the phone, Person C feels reassured that they can hear their voice. Sometimes people would rather be in an argument than have no contact at all.

Remember

People are not addicted to their actions, they are addicted to the 'feeling' it gives them. Addictions are simply painkillers!

Why do this?

In relation to the con there will be a list of reason why people become addicted to this way of thinking and acting. In most cases it is not that people are twisted or damaged, it is just that they have not learned how to control their emotions in a harmonious fashion. In this chapter I have created several reasons as to why this can happen. There may be many others that you feel belong in this list, and if you do please add them in. However, here are some of the main reasons.

Reason 1: It is all you have ever known
Reason 2: Lack of psychological knowledge
Reason 3: It hurts to let go
Reason 4: Keeping up with the Joneses
Reason 5: The addiction is powerful
Reason 6: It's easy to stay comfortable
Reason 7: Too many others support the addiction

Reason 1: It is all you have ever known

Imagine a person growing up on a private island where everybody is taught that 2 + 2 = 5! They will believe this equation as that is what is taught, but it does not mean it is correct. Now imagine that person then coming to your country and when you ask them what 2 + 2 equals, they say 5. They will do this because it is all they have ever known. This is the same in the story with Joe from an earlier chapter. There are many things in life that we are taught and through trusting other people who teach us we simply accept them. This does not mean that we are wrong in any way; it just means that we didn't know any different.

Given that there are so many social pressures in the world today, we are all just doing our best to survive. Our grandparents more than likely wore masks, which may have led to our parents wearing masks. Again, this does not mean that people are evil or to be blamed, it is just their way of coping with stress.

However, if a person is born into a whole community whom wear a variety of different masks, it is possible to believe that masks are normal. That person then creates a mask, but may be unsure as to why they have done that. Subliminal social influence is very powerful. If 100 people in your community do something a certain way and you are born into that community, you may do the same believing that it is right until you realise different. If this 'way' is never questioned because the majority of people continue to live this way, the mind habituates.

As you start to put the information in this book into practice, it will soon enough become very apparent just how many people actually wear masks.

The first time I really noticed it myself was from a manager at my old workplace who used the 'smug look' when he used trigger intimidation in me by staring at me aggressively. However, the first time I questioned myself as to whether his 'look' was really a mask; I noticed that my anxiety vanished. It vanished for me as I realised that if his aggression was a mask then underneath he must be anxious (as only anxious people attack for no reason).
Once my anxiety vanished I found that I did not react to his 'look' in the same way. The reaction I used to have was to be very accommodating and agreeable to him (through my own anxiety). However, after I realised the loop I stopped running round after him. As an employee I was still respectful, but I wasn't nervous. His reaction to the change in me was quite dramatic; at first he was completely confused and then he just started running round after me!!! The roles completely reversed, and all I did was stop reacting. It doesn't always happen this way, but be aware that games can change quickly.

Reason 2: Lack of psychological knowledge
To start with, how many people do you know that received powerful and strategic emotional or psychological education in their school? If you do actually know people who did, they were the fortunate ones. However, when I say powerful and strategic psychological education, I do not mean the history of Freud's birthday or other useless facts. For psychology to be effective it needs to be practical advice that can be taken away and used in a person's life the way 'they' need it.

Unfortunately in many education systems it is possible to go through 11 years of education in the mainstream world and not once be taught practical life skills. To form a healthy understanding of life it is essential for young minds to learn about areas such as how to communicate with aggressive bullies, how to care for another person, the feelings of love or how to connect with someone in a relationship, and these are just a few examples – there are many more.

Other subjects such as written language and maths are essential, but many children are sat in a classroom to be force-taught about trigonometry, foreign language and history. If a child is in a harmonious environment these can be great subjects to learn, but for the millions of children who feel unhappy or are struggling with their emotions, it is a different story.

Learning information is one thing, but knowing how to actually apply it to everyday life is something completely different. If a person learning this information does not have the self-esteem or confidence to apply it to their lives, the information can in many cases be virtually useless.
This would be similar to giving a person who has a phobia of driving and has never learned HOW to drive a top-of-the-range Ferrari. They will most likely feel poorly prepared and very unsure of their abilities. When they get behind the wheel they find they are too terrified to drive; they go into 'freeze mode' and can't think clearly. A lack of information can lead to devastating effects in later life. We have seen this in various models through this book such as the peer idolisation and self-esteem recovery model.

Reason 3: It hurts to let go
Letting go of an addiction in any area can create pain or discomfort unless replacement measures are put in place. Even then it can still sometimes be a challenge. For many people, the longer they have had the addiction, the harder it can be to let go of. In many ways the habit of the addiction (mask) becomes a part of that person.

How many people who continually check social networking sites, text their partner 20 times a day, contact their staff unnecessarily or feel the need to compulsively buy things would happily go on a detox with no replacement? Not many. Why? Because it would CAUSE PAIN!

In many of my workshops I suggest this as an option for the students to try. Then, after the first day I ask them to share how they are feeling if they chose to do it. Many students explain that their minds were flooded with excuses such as "I have to check the office as they may need me." or "If I don't text my partner they feel upset."

Sometimes people can wrap themselves so tightly in their mask… that their mask then owns them! If they put themselves in the centre of their company for example and have lots of people depending upon them, yes it will be unhealthy to stop as the company would struggle. In many of these cases though, it is simply the person who has subconsciously created a valid 'reason' to keep their mask.

Reason 4: Keeping up with the Joneses

Keeping up with the Joneses is an apt saying at this point. If you have never heard of this phrase it goes as follows.

You live in a house and the Jones family live next door. You have a car but the next day the Jones family buy the upgraded version of the car. You feel that now they 'look' better than you so you buy the upgraded car 'with' better wheels than they have.

The Jones family say they are going to visit 4 countries this year, so you have to visit 5.

Basically the phrase 'keeping up with the Joneses' means that a person does not want to feel inferior to other people who have more or do more than they do. Now we can see that these actions are from a person who is relying on their value from what they have, not who they are.

It is well known that people will try to 'out do' each other in life. If a person naturally wants to achieve something then that is healthy. However, the area that we are talking about here is when a person has a drive to succeed only to prove that they are as good as the other people around them. The underlying driver is that they are anxious that if somebody else is more successful, then they will be more popular.

These areas could be the clothes they wear, the car they drive, the sexual attractiveness of their partner, their physical shape or the money they have; the list could go on for the rest of this book, but hopefully I've been able to get the point across.

Anybody who is 'keeping up with the Joneses' is caught in a loop of trying to ensure that their mask is the most powerful of their peer group.

Their protector self is taking this action to ensure that they are seen as the most valuable (in their eyes). This is not 'only' in relation to their external acquirements either, as remember, a mask can be anything.

For many though, it can become much more complicated than simply keeping up with the Joneses. In life, most people will unknowingly follow the crowd. Celebrities, the rich and famous and mass advertising all have the power to subliminally suggest things that people 'should' follow because so many people tune in to them. To connect and want to grow is a natural human trait and this is where advertising becomes the sugar in the salt! Once a person tunes into what the celebrity or advertising says, if they accept it… they follow.

Many people are reluctant to give up their mask because it is what everybody else is doing. It is seen as 'the norm' and that can be perceived as how life should be lived. Breaking that 'norm' would mean a potential risk of being different, and if being different could potentially risk rejection then their protector self will take over. Although many people post images on social media about 'being unique' or 'don't follow the crowd', in my personal view I have seen many of them living the exact opposite way.

Unless a person wakes up to the con, it is easy to create the belief that states…

Our friends do it, our families do it, (they may assume) celebrities do it…….. So why shouldn't I?

After all, we wouldn't want to separate ourselves from the pack and be different………… would we?

Reason 5: The addiction is powerful

Many people can get caught in the loop of believing that avoiding emotional pain by relying on external acquirements gives the impression of inner peace. This could then give the 'appearance of' an increase in self-esteem. However, this is not the case and is simply denial. This inner pain could have been sat inside the subconscious mind for many years, but through continual avoidance and by becoming addicted to the mask, the pain often grows into something much larger in their mind.

Once the paranoia has multiplied and warped the original experience, it can (for many) seem too much to handle and just be buried again by the protector self. In the mind it will appear to be much bigger than it actually is (as it will be viewed as it was as a child / time distortion). With paranoia, what a person is actually looking at is vastly mutated images on the internal cinema screen rather than actual reality. They see images 'as they were' when they happened, which, if it happened when they were a child, causes them to see a distorted image.
As discussed though, unless consciously controlled (and eventually sub-consciously), a person's stress trigger reaction will appear as real as the actual physical world.

On a very serious note, people do not become alcoholics, drug addicts, criminals, manipulators, workaholics or serial shopaholics (who end up in debt) because they are 'bored'. Nor do people end their lives because they are just 'having a bad day'. For the emotions to reach a stage where a person would rather physically harm themselves than actually face their world, they have compounded a heavy sense of paranoia and stress that has become too much to cope with.

To an onlooker, they may observe the addict to be 'weak' in some way, but this is not the case. By the time a person becomes an addict they will have probably been bombarded from their internal cinema screen for many years and eventually given up the fight. Their thoughts can be awash with images of pain and paranoia and very dark images. This 'illusionary pain' (anxiety) is what they are attempting to escape from.

NB: *it is important to note that drugs and other substances can become physiologically addictive. This is when a person suffers physical pain or extreme hormone trauma if they suddenly stop. Some forms of antidepressants or mood stabilisers come with warnings of stopping suddenly as they are altering a very finely tuned neurological* *system within the brain. It is important to recognise the difference between this and the emotional mask.*

The deeper a person's emotional pain from internal paranoia, the greater their need for a coping mechanism to reduce the suffering. Again, if this is twinned with a lack of knowledge, the person will turn to the only thing that they know that helps to lessen the pain.

The mask is powerful because in many cases it has become such an integral part of somebody's life that to simply 'give it up' creates a pain in itself. The continual loop of 'choose mask = less pain' is the easiest option, and if this has been neurologically bound into a person's physiology (through neurons and hormone release) the mask has become its own entity and is a self-generating addiction.

Remember, ignorance is definitely NOT bliss!

Reason 6: It's easy to stay comfortable

Anybody who has ever started an exercise regime will know that it can feel like the body is not overly comfortable doing exercise until a habit takes over. This is back to the pain-pleasure principle we spoke of earlier. A body which is used to not exercising will feel discomfort when forced to move beyond its current limits. However, once an exercise habit has formed and the feel-good factor hormones are flowing, exercise becomes pleasurable. It is to be noted though that there can be many other factors which can knock this off course.

This in many ways is similar with the mind. Yes, we all have a desire to grow, but like electricity; our mind will do its best to get there in the quickest possible manner, taking the most effective route. This will also happen more powerfully if a person is laden with other things on their mind, such as debt, their mask, daily chores and distractions.

If the habit of the mask is the most practiced habit then that will be the strongest bond. Hence, changing the habit of using the mask in the initial stages will feel challenging.

In life, when a person is under pressure the quickest assumed way to survive is to do what is easy, and so many of us are sold the 'buy now pay later' way!

We have all seen the adverts…

"Lose 10lb of body fat in one week with only 10 minutes of exercise a day!"
"Become debt free by taking this consolidation loan!"

etc….. etc…… etc……

As we all know though, the reality is that there is no quick fix!

You won't lose 10lb of body fat in one week with only 10 minutes of exercise a day (or if you do you will gain it back soon enough) and you won't be simply debt free by taking a consolidation loan!

As we can see, these products and services are those that are offered to those people in the world who are under immense pressure. As we now know, these are the ones who are very open and vulnerable to the con. They are distracted by their emotional pain and easily guided by a supportive con trickster posing as their 'best friend'.

Anxious people will buy through panic! This is why when some people are rejected in a relationship they may go into what is known as a 'rebound' and get into another relationship that same day. They may find themselves 'falling for' a charming character offering to take away the pain of their loss (this is a dark way to look at some relationships, but is the truth in some cases).

Reason 7: Too many others support the addiction
Let us take a slightly paranoid but 'real' view of the world for some parts.

For some people with a mask, an effective way of reducing their anxiety (they believe) is to buy new clothes to change their appearance. Buying a new wardrobe of clothes creates a feel-good factor and gives them a rest from the internal paranoia. It also offers a distraction from the fact that underneath they may perceive themselves to be worth 'less' or not good enough. So, the question can then be asked:

"How many shops and shopkeepers are ready to take hard-earned cash in exchange for that new set of clothes that will seem to make all the pain vanish?"

Or what about if a person is feeling alone and just wants somebody to care for them because they believe nobody wants them? How many other people who also have these needs will say...

"I will be there for you and care for your every need"?
Or again as discussed, what about the employee who wants to impress their peers so they feel accepted? How many managers would offer praise when they realise that their staff work harder and create huge profits?

Again, this is in no way to insinuate that everybody does this for dark and manipulative reasons (buying clothes or praise may just be from creative expression). Also as mentioned, in my own opinion the great majority of people who do meet others' needs to mask their own insecurities have no idea they are doing it.

In this world there can be a great many people who will support another's addiction. Though the other side of the coin is that in many cases it is not just one way; it often comes from both sides. What is meant by this is that it is both sides supporting each other's addiction, which is known as a co-dependent relationship.

Co-dependent relationships can be extremely draining on both parties' self-esteem. The more they attempt to help each other, the more they become caught in the con. Yet the more they help each other, the more the alleged pain reduces. As we saw earlier, this is very common in relationships where both people get together because they are lonely rather than because they want a fulfilling connection of growth.

A look at co-dependence in the mask

Let's look at the three situations earlier.

In the case of the shopkeeper of the clothes shop in the above example (if they wear a mask), they may feel that they are more valuable to others in society through the more clothes they sell. However, they may feel that the more clothes they sell, the more they avoid their anxiety. So they want to sell more clothes and look for customers who are more eager to buy, which means they are looking for 'easier target' customers. If the easier target customers are those who will buy through their mask then this will be the shopkeeper's focus (co-dependent con).

This is why some clothing manufactures can offer the 'same material' as a cheaper brand, put a well-known fashion label on it and triple the price. People will sometimes buy the 'brand' before the item of clothing. A while ago I was in a shop in the UK and saw a simple cotton t-shirt for £380 which looked quite bland, but it had the label.

In the second example above we saw the person playing the "I will be there for you" game with a person who had recently gone through a relationship breakup. This person may also feel alone and need somebody to be there for them. Which is the easiest person for them to attract if they are suffering from low self-worth? The one who feels vulnerable and in need of connection through pain, which again leads to a co-dependent con.

For the third example we see the manager who lavishes praise on their employee who chooses to work 80 hours in a week for approval. The manager may feel that their words are now important and that they are respected more, whereas it may have been that before they didn't feel other people valued their words or saw them as un-important (co-dependent con).

In all three above situations, the person using the con is in fact attempting to solve their own pain by reducing another person's pain. But if it's done from their mask, in reducing the other person's pain it also keeps that person trapped in their mask too. As discussed, a person trapped in their mask will continue to thrive from the con trickster, so the shopkeeper wants to sell more clothes, the new relationship will be more intense and the manager will give more praise. Remember the sugar and salt!

As it is very plain to see now, using the words con and con trickster can take on a whole new meaning and is not as sinister as it may have first sounded. In many cases the reality for people doing the above actions is simply that they are just trying to get by in life. They are trying to get their emotional needs met. Yet whether they are aware of what they are doing or not, if they are doing it from the mask driver, the co-dependency con is still being played out. Ignorance is not bliss!

Again - and I will repeat myself here - this does NOT mean that any of these people are evil twisted manipulators. They are just people getting on with their lives and in most cases are completely unaware of what is going on. My purpose in this book is to make people aware of the underlying co-dependence when a mask is involved so that people can live a more connected and fulfilling life. Simultaneously it is also to be noted that society does carry with it very troubled people who will overstep the social boundaries. These people can be extremely violent both physically and emotionally. The reason for this is that their pain is so intense that their coping mechanism is to cause harm, and they do not want to negotiate. Therefore, these people will need to be given a wide berth for your own safety.

Separating the sugar and salt

As I've said, in no way is this book to insinuate that all of the people in the world are driven by the motivation of anxiety and reaching for a mask. We must always keep in mind the sugar and salt story. We need to be aware that one thing can appear as another and it is essential to know which is which in order to have a complete and fulfilling life.

The real message which is to be conveyed is that we do not have to suffer from low self-esteem anymore if we do not want to. We do not have to suffer from a sense of guilt if we choose to say no to something. This could be from a manager asking us to stay late or a partner giving us 'that look' if we do not visit the in-laws.

When you learn how to control a mask, you can control the con attached to it. You can stop the con and the addiction to it by altering the perception of life and releasing Pandora's Box memories, however there is much to learn in this area. When you gain this control, the outside world (or the physical world) will continue as normal. For the mask world, shops will continue to offer 'sale ends today' products, weight loss products with images of scrawny beach bodies will still pack the shelves and other people will continue trying to emotionally control and guilt trip co-workers. Life for everybody else wearing their mask will be the same, but the one difference is…

"You won't 'need' a mask to hide the pain as you won't be reacting to the pain!"

You will no longer be able to be guilt-tripped, manipulated or conned. In the story of the 'sugar and salt' from the introduction, it was the salt that gave power and energy, but the sugar that took it away and made life more difficult. As both were mixed together for so long, who would know the difference and how would it be separated?

The sugar is the con

The salt is your freedom of choice

Remember, if the pain is too great, the protector self will seek the quickest way to end the pain. If that is from buying a £40,000 car or praise from the manager, then the cheque is signed or the hours at work will add up and the con begins.

Another con is that the sugar tastes so nice doesn't it? So very very nice!

But remember, you can only be conned or manipulated in those areas of your life where your self-esteem is vulnerable. Understand your insecurities and the mask and the con will be no more.

Q: What if I don't want to give up the addiction? What will I lose?

A: Your freedom of choice

A refusal to give up the addiction to external acquirements or emotional control driven from low self-esteem will take away **your freedom of choice!**

From the outset, the phrase 'freedom of choice' may not sound too serious, but take a moment to really think about it.

1. Your Pandora's Box mind is supressing an emotion which it feels is too much for you to cope with.

2. While it is supressed it will create distorted images upon your internal cinema screen.

3. Your protector self will begin to react to these distorted images to protect you (fight, flight and freeze).

4. The internal stress will grow due to the confusion.

5. Your protector self will aim to conceal your stress by the use of a mask.

6. Whilst the pain remains supressed the mask and suppression will take priority.

7. Any conscious attempt (positive self talk) to change this will cause your protector self to fight your conscious choice seeing it as a threat.

8. Eventually your conscious mind will be overpowered and the mask will be back in control.

Not convinced?

What about…

The workaholic who says they will change and makes a choice to work less, only to be back to their overworked state after 3 weeks?

The compulsive 'dieter' who loses weight only to gain it back again year after year?

The drug addict who promises their children that they will never touch it again? Then end up using again

The millions of people who set a 'New Year's Resolution' only to quit by February?

The person with social anxiety who 'visualises and meditates' about having high levels of confidence but within a month feels like they have failed because they haven't changed?

The sex addict who still chooses to accept sexual offers even though they may contract an STI?

The millions of people who aim to give up smoking with will power but weeks or even days later start smoking again?
The person who really wants to be in a relationship but keeps choosing the 'wrong' person?

As we can see, the list will be endless!

In essence, if the protector self feels self-conscious around other people (anxiety of rejection), it will create a mask that aims to create a feeling of security for the person without them even realising it. This is because the protector self is doing its best to stabilise the world it sees and the more it controls other people (through the mask), the more secure it feels.
The person may not consciously want to do these actions but they feel subconsciously compelled to (the confusion of irrational behaviour). This is because, as with any addiction, there is always the anxiety that one day the external acquirement (mask which hides a perceived low self-worth) will disappear and then the very thing that they are reluctant to face will be laid bare for the entire world to see.

Let's look at these on a deeper level.

Your freedom of choice

"I **have** to check my emails 100 times a day or I will have to listen to the anxiety that I am not valued."

"I **have** to work 70 hours a week or people will think I am lazy."

"I **have** to spend all of my money on weight loss products because I am anxious of rejection because of my shape."

"I **have** to buy the latest phone (even though I don't have the money) just so I fit in to my group of friends."

"I **have** to run my own business so people see me as a leader."
"I **have** to have sex with many people just so I feel wanted."

"I **have** to listen to every friend pour their heart out or they may think I'm ignorant."

"I **have** to please my partner or they may leave me."

"I **have** to stay in this job (even though I hate it) because I will let the team down if I leave."

The list goes on....
When a person is caught in the addiction, the one distinguishing factor they will display (as previously mentioned) is that they can't give up what they are addicted to without feeling some form of pain (withdrawal). It is the pleasure of avoiding the pain they do not want to feel that they are addicted to rather than the action and coping mask itself.

The loss of 'freedom of choice' happens because while the mask addiction remains, a person will choose the only thing they know that stops the pain, i.e. the mask - therefore leading to a loss of choice or options.

The mask will control everything you do if you do not learn how to control it!

- It will control the amount of money you earn!
- It will control the people you spend time with!
- It will control your addictions!
- It will control your coping mechanisms!
- It will control your emotions each minute of the day!
- It will control...YOUR LIFE!

As you can see there is a great deal to lose in life by staying dependant on the mask. However, not only does it keep us in a weak state, but it literally robs us of the true joys of life. Joys such as that of truly being free to choose the life we want and also the ability to truly connect with the ones we care for most.

Many people with low self-esteem are convinced beyond a shadow of a doubt that they would never control those they love the most in order to stay secure. If they do think this they are right... because 'they' don't! Remember, it is the protector self that will take control when it is overwhelmed with stress.

If we look at the mind, in reality the person will only be able to consciously control their conscious thought, which only equates to around 5% of their abilities. A person's protector self has access to everything they think, say and do. It has access to all perceived memories and all the subconscious abilities and functions 24 hours a day. This may not be the nicest thing to hear but it is the truth.

Every time a person has hurt someone close to them and did not intend to, it will have been their protector self hijacking their actions into fight or flight mode (controlling behaviour is a mannerism of a person in fight or flight mode) (this is not to be used as an excuse though!).

The ideal world!

True unconditional love is to be there for another person and support them in their life without controlling them in any way to support your mask. This is the ideal aim, but it's not as easy to get there as it sounds. In this state though, you will feel naturally wanted and valuable and therefore have no need to control other people for reassurance. In order to achieve such a level of awareness any supressed pain must be resolved, which can then end the need for a mask.

However, life is a most definitely work in progress for us all and we need to accept that and start from where we are. Life is not about placing high expectations on ourselves or others as that is simply another mask.

In life we can hear many 'self acclaimed' gurus claim that they are in a state of complete connectedness and never judge, but then their actions may contradict this. Please be aware that the term 'spirituality' can be quite a hiding place for these claims as the field can be vague. Ideally we are all working together and doing our best to live a happy and abundant life, but challenges will come and slow us down - this is 'just' life!

Life is about working together and seeing past the masks that people wear. However, if the other person's mask is too controlling then you will have to choose whether to remain in contact or not. True connection is about supporting each other in times of weakness and in times of confusion. In reality many relationships are the strongest and most abundant because two or more people are working together to let go of their inner insecurities (masks). To do this they have to work with another person at their own level, whatever that level is. When a person meets another person of their level in a non-judgemental fashion it can help them feel connected within who they are (though this is different than one person 'always' supporting the other).

Without us all being there for each other, the human societal structure would collapse in minutes. Being there for each other does not mean we have to be perfect (as perfection is impossible), but just to do our best to accept each other's weakness and insecurities and dig in deep to help each other. That is, as long as both people want to become free!

As mentioned though, some relationships are formed where one or both partners refuse to look within or to support their partner or friends. This may be because they feel they are not capable emotionally or simply refuse to let go of their mask. If this happens then they will both remain co-dependent and are doomed to stay in the addiction control cycle until they decide to change. Unfortunately though, the longer a person avoids the change, the harder it will become as the mind is forming new thoughts and beliefs each minute of the day!

True magic happens when people work together!

Chapter summary

Addictions are painkillers

There is no shame in feeling overwhelmed in life! When situations become too challenging it is only natural to want to have some respite and a little breathing space by the use of distractions. The problems will arise when these distractions become a dependency. These dependencies can then allow us to distract ourselves from the core challenge so often that the mind will become weaker in regards to dealing with future challenges. Therefore, addictions are simply painkillers!

Take a moment and look through all the current areas of your life and ask yourself if you have become dependent on anything that gives a quick fix from an underlying pain. This could be the odd drink of alcohol after a hard day at work, going on social media rather than actually socialising, or feeling the need to entertain friends to gain their approval. If you find that you do have any of these, then look underneath at what pain this may be covering up or something you feel you may not be able to face. Again, be cautious with this area as it can often be quite sensitive.

The anxiety of withdrawal

When the mind has become addicted to a certain situation or 'avoidance drug' to avoid a deeper issue, your protector self may also have a belief that you are too fragile to face the suppressed reality without it (habit pattern belief). This can then lead to a secondary challenge, which is the anxiety of removing the addiction itself. If the mind assumes that coming off the addiction can be a trauma then it will naturally fight back to keep the mind as safe as possible by staying on the addiction. Although this is actually making the person's emotional mind weaker by not facing reality, the protector self in its confusion is still trying to help. The key is to realise what the underlying pain is and then work out a strategy of facing it in a comfortable manner.

Take a moment and look through any addictions that you may have and then ask yourself how you would feel if it was suddenly no longer there. What would the deeper anxiety be?

From my view it can be risky to suddenly stop an addiction as it can send the mind into a panic. The mind may feel that it is being forced to face a suppressed emotion that it does not feel ready for or has not been prepared for. Taking this action can often do more harm than good. Yes, it is important to face the inner trauma, but only in a strategic way.

The self generating addiction

Addictions can become extremely complicated in a very short space of time! Any time a person subscribes to an addiction long term (which is there to cover an underlying pain), they are also accepting the belief that they are not capable of facing the reality which the addiction is covering up. This could be boredom, stress, rejection or any other perceived pain. As the addiction becomes a habit, so will the belief that they are weaker than their pain and so the addiction becomes self-generating.

Take a moment and observe anything you feel that you have come to depend upon in life as you can avoid a certain discomfort and really look within to see if the addiction has actually made you feel any more anxious or weaker as the time has passed. For example, if somebody has supported you too often, do you now feel you can't do it by yourself? Or has the odd drink of alcohol that soothes the senses after a hard day's work become the 'only' thing that can make you feel better?

The ultimate cost

When a person subscribes to any form of addiction they also deny the gift of reality! An addiction can also be likened to saying no to the present moment or living in 'the now'. As we have seen many times through this book, living in the past or future (which is also not being present) will bring with it an endless loop of unhappiness, leading ultimately to living in a perception of reality rather than reality itself (though it is also important to use your imagination to move forward towards your goals or outcomes).

Take a moment and reflect upon what you are actually losing out on if you are subscribing to any form of addiction. For example, long periods of time on social media may be costing the gift of sharing real time with friends. Or continually talking about other people who have wronged you in the past may be costing you the enjoyment of moving on and connecting to new things in life.

The ideal world

Each and every person will face their challenges along the road in life and one of the most important things we can do is to truly understand that. Although this is not to insinuate that we have to be best friends with everybody we meet, it can make life a lot easier if we can learn to understand other people through their eyes. In the ideal world people would understand each other and work together to support each other through challenges without judgement or demand. Taking this approach when other people may be rude or aggressive can be a challenge in itself. The urge to lash out or attack back may be the first thing that comes to mind, however this will only keep you stuck in the past. It is also very important to note that the more secure you feel, the easier it will be to see life this way.

Take a moment and reflect upon how you normally react to rude or challenging people. This may be a controlling parent, a rude co-worker or a guilt-tripping friend. If you find that you normally attack back, then try asking yourself how it would feel to take a step back and look at 'why' they are acting this way. What is it they feel so insecure about? Then, see if you can reach within yourself and give them the support they need.

It is important to value your own needs whilst doing this. This exercise does NOT mean letting another person walk all over you, nor does it mean you sit there for hours whilst they talk on repeat. All it means is to see 'reality' (their insecurities being projected) rather than your internal cinema screen reality (they are attacking you and so it must be personal). Remember that people will only attack when they feel insecure about the situation.

14

Create a Cocoon and Build Your Strength

Personally I feel that sometimes in the world of personal development there is too much emphasis on 'taking action to confront fear' and going out and 'facing your demons' without taking the time to prepare. However, we could see the negative implications of this when we spoke about the person driving the brand new car who had not had any driving lessons. Action without preparation can be dangerous!

To ensure the most effective solution to any anxiety you may be facing I have created a progressive strategy to guide you. As I have mentioned all along, this is not the only way and is just suggestions based on what I have used on my own learnings. Bear in mind that your greatest skill and strength will come from your own creative abilities to adapt these suggestions to your own life. This chapter is about creating a protective bubble around you so you can start to feel safe; I call this bubble 'the cocoon' (as in that of a butterfly).

Whilst facing up to stresses and challenges it is essential that you create for yourself a protective space in which you can have time to think and asses the world (a healthy mask, in some ways). This will allow your protector self to relax and stress reaction to lessen.

The following chapter will cover the 8 stages which I work through with my one-to-one clients. These 8 stages can be likened to breaking the cocoon and flying free. Do not be tempted to skip this chapter and move to the next if you are eager as this will cause you to lose power. When you do not allow yourself space to think and grow before trying to fly, it will be exactly the same as this story….

The butterfly tale

There once was a little boy who found a fascinating caterpillar. He carefully picked it up and took it home and showed his mum. He asked his mum if he could keep it, and she said that he could as long as he took good care of it.

The little boy got a jar for the caterpillar and gave him plants and a stick to climb on.

One day the caterpillar climbed up the stick and just sat there and started to change. The boy became upset and ran to his mother who sat him down and explained that this was normal and that the caterpillar was creating a cocoon. She told him that the caterpillar was going to go through a change in the cocoon and become a butterfly with beautiful wings.

The little boy was very excited about the change for the caterpillar and watched it every day, waiting for the butterfly to emerge. One day, to the little boy's immense joy, a small hole appeared in the cocoon and the butterfly started to fight its way out.
As the butterfly was struggling the little boy started to worry as although it was pushing and pushing, it didn't seem to be making much progress and he was afraid that it would starve to death.

The boy was so concerned and wanted to help as he loved his new friend with all his heart. So, out of his love for the little creature, he ran to get some scissors. With very careful hands he snipped the cocoon to make the hole bigger and the butterfly quickly emerged from the cocoon!

However, as the butterfly came out the boy was confused. It had a very swollen body and small, shrivelled wings. He continued to watch patiently expecting the butterfly to spring into life in full bloom…he wanted the wings to dry out and expand to support the swollen body and its body to shrink so it could fly free. Unfortunately, neither happened!

The butterfly spent the rest of its life crawling around with a swollen body and shrivelled wings. It was never able to fly…

The little boy was very upset and went to speak to his mum. His mum, also confused, took the little boy to a local vet to find out what had happened. The vet sat the little boy down and carefully explained that the butterfly needed to struggle to break the cocoon by itself. When the butterfly struggles to push its way through the tiny opening of the cocoon, it pushes the fluid out of its body and into its wings. Without the struggle, the butterfly would never be able to fly. Unfortunately, it was the boy's haste and good intentions that stopped the butterfly from being able to grow strong and to fly free.
It is in the struggle that you gain your strength!

Where are you right now?
Any decision made to end the game of the mask and con is entirely yours to make. If you have made it this far into the book you can now place yourself into one of three categories.

Category one:
You are completely comfortable in your own skin and living your life abundantly. Yes, you have challenges but you face them head on as a challenge and grow from them. You were already aware of the mask and

con and they haven't really affected your progress in life today or in a long time.

In this reality you will have a deep connection to keeping focused on where you are heading in life and make steady steps to get there. You do not become anxious of losing external acquirements, but you know that if you do you can rebuild them. Although you enjoy material wealth, your self-esteem and self-worth does not rely on anything external. You do not worry about the future and you are completely comfortable with your past. You have no anxiety when it comes to rejection.

Category two:

You feel that this book is of use to other people, but not you. You are even telling yourself as you read these words that you belong in category one, but in reality you know that you are in denial. You know deep down that parts of your life are vulnerable to the con. You feel anxious about your past and your future. You also feel quite alone or lonely at times, but have found powerful masks to keep yourself safe.

Although you may realise that you are caught in the loop, you do not really want to admit it to yourself, as admitting it means potential pain that you will have to work through. At this moment the pain may feel too overwhelming to work through. You make the decision that it is easier to live behind the mask and that ignorance is bliss. Through the anxiety you feel you choose to keep the addiction.

However if you are in this category, this statement is not to insinuate ANY guilt to you and as mentioned it is essential that you work at your own level. If you feel uncomfortable in any way about facing a mask then it is YOUR choice and not anybody else's. Yes, there are options open, but it is YOUR choice and what you choose is ok!

To look at this category in more detail we can further define two areas.

Category two: Area 1 – Post Traumatic Stress

At the start of this book I mentioned owning your experience. This means to do what feels right for you and not what other people attempt to push you into! If you find yourself in category two where facing a mask may feel far too much to handle then it is essential that you own that.

Personally I have suffered from post-traumatic stress in my own past and felt vulnerable and unable to move forward. In this state pushing too hard can actually cause more harm than good. Sometimes well-meaning people can suggest that you 'jump into the fear blindly', but as we now see this can sometimes send the protector self into full lockdown. Extreme care should be taken if you feel you are in a state of post-trauma (or PTS or PTSD) and it may be worth looking into professional support rather than going it alone.

Category two: Area 2 - Denial

Regardless of whether you are in a state of post-traumatic stress or not, it may still feel very hard to face the mask or there may be so many things in your life wrapped within it. As mentioned, some people may have built their entire life around a mask and therefore just 'letting it go' may do more harm than good.

In situations like this, facing the mask may feel like an overwhelming task and that it is easier to put to one side. If this is how you feel, then again it is your choice and your right to do so. There are many people in the world who are aware that they are in the con, but as mentioned… it's just too easy for them to use their masks to get through daily life.

If this reflects you and you feel unsure of which way to go with it, I would suggest a piece of paper and a pen. Writing out your thoughts can be extremely reflective and helpful.

Alternatively, you could discuss it through with a person that you can trust and rely on to give you an honest opinion and not one which they are personally invested in. Again though, I will say that it is your life and you have the right to choose what you feel is best for you!

Category three:

You have had an underlying feeling for some time that something is not right. You now realise that some parts of your life can be manipulated with the con and maybe that your mask is quite powerful. You may not be too sure how deep the mask goes or what it is controlling in your life, but you are ready to look within. Although you know you are in the con, you and accept it and are ready to change, learn and grow.

You realise that it may feel uncomfortable to work through, but you are prepared to go through what steps need to be taken. You are focused and prepared to invest time in yourself so you can be free to make the decisions you choose. You also realise that letting go of the mask will give more connection to your friends and loved ones. You have an adventurous heart and refuse to be manipulated any longer.

"Our lives improve only when we take chances - and the first and most difficult risk we can take is to be honest with ourselves."
Walter Anderson

Depending upon the decision that you make in regards to moving forwards will determine how you perceive the steps covered in this chapter. It will also determine the actions you take in the coming weeks, months and years. Also, how you perceive the steps affects how much benefit you will gain from them.

Planning your exit – preparing the cocoon

For a plan of action to be effective it must be adequately prepared for. Not only does this mean strategically, but also emotionally. It is true that there is a place for hard-core motivation and really going for it with all guns blazing, but structure and strategy are essential to the success of any journey. One of the most important areas to consider in regards to strategy is how your protector self will react during the process. The less your protector self feels that you are moving towards pain, the less it will react and take control of your actions. As the often quoted phrase goes, failing to plan is planning to fail.

"Being busy does not always mean real work. The object of all work is production or accomplishment and to either of these ends there must be forethought, system, planning, intelligence, and honest purpose, as well as perspiration. Seeming to do is not doing."
Thomas A. Edison

It is important to remember though that regardless of how intelligent, creative or skilled you are in life, these capabilities may be drastically reduced when working through your mask.

The reason for this is that you are not just 'learning new information' cognitively, but you are in fact also questioning your protector self's reality. If this is not worked through strategically it can make change feel quite uncomfortable. Therefore, it is essential that you take each step is taken carefully and reflectively and in your own time.

Working through emotional challenges is a reality that is more unique than any other learning you will face. Your protector self knows everything about you and your mind and because of this (and its caution of change), it will try to keep emotions hidden if it is unsure of what you are doing. Hence, if you unknowingly trigger your protector self in a stress reaction it will naturally attempt to slow your progress down, believing that to be the best option for your safety.

Write it out!

As mentioned earlier in this book, I would highly recommend keeping some form of a written journal. If the information is extremely sensitive or at risk of causing a disagreement if found by other people, then hide it or use a password-protected file hidden within several files or a private online journal. Be sure to make as many notes as possible! Many clients I work with can sometimes find that they 'forget' or 'can't find time' to make notes, but in reality this will be coming from one (or both) of two reasons:

Reason one: They are not convinced of the benefits to their progress about making notes.

Reason two: Their protector self has used a protection mechanism to screen out the learnings. This 'screening' is intended to reduce tampering with what the protector self feels is the safest belief structure in relation to the outside world.

Any reluctance to make notes on findings related to emotional beliefs could delay growth and therefore keep you trapped in your mask indefinitely. Sometimes when an emotional realisation breaks through from the subconscious to the conscious, it can create a powerful realisation and the answer that you need to see is sat right there in front of you. However, if this answer is not written down as soon as possible, the realisation can quickly be swallowed back up by the protector self trying to protect you from making an overly drastic change. Writing it down means that it can be there as a continual reminder of the answer.

The level of access to your memory whilst you are unlocking the mask will directly reflect how secure your protector self feels in the moment.

"I've a grand memory for forgetting."
Robert Louis Stevenson

To make the process as effective as possible I have divided it into 6 steps of progressive advancement. The 6 steps aim to support you with planning a structure for your own success. These are a similar to the structure I used on my own journey and with clients. Each step will also be sub-divided into further steps. This can also help make the understanding and learning of your future achievement flow smoothly.

The steps are as follows…

Step 1: Begin with the end in mind

Step 2: Create a healthy mask (the cocoon)

Step 3: Separating from your old mask

Step 4: Cut the addiction and see the reality of your old mask

Step 5: Reconnect to your true self

Step 6: Escape the cocoon

NB: *Any steps within this book and chapter are only suggestions. Any actions taken upon any of these steps are your choice and you must be prepared to accept full responsibility for the results of your actions. There are situations that people may be facing in life which are very delicate and sometimes may involve serious situations including debt, addiction to harmful drugs/alcohol, violence or crime.*
If you are currently in a potentially harmful or dangerous situation, please take extra care and maybe contact a professional consultant in that particular area before making changes.

Step 1: Begin with the end in mind

If you don't know where you're going, how will you know when you get there?
As we have already covered in earlier chapters, effective planning is by far one of the most overlooked areas in life by people who want to reach their aims. Ask any bank manager or business advisor just how many people attend meetings with a poorly-prepared business plan and still expect to get a loan. Effective planning is essential!

Step one is about taking time to look within and asking yourself what it is that you really want from all of this. After all, this is your life, and as they say… you only get one!

Here are some suggested steps.

1.1: Write down what you want

This may sound straightforward but is again one of the most overlooked steps. When a person is continually hijacked by their protector self and trapped in the con it is very easy to become more focused on the con rather than the escape route. Writing down the future that you want to create, even if it seems unachievable, will set the wheels in motion.

When I was in the depths of my own struggle and started writing a desired future, I will be honest… I felt like I was lying to myself! Who was 'I' to deserve this kind of life? Other people deserve happiness but

not me. However, a strange thing happens when you write your dreams out on paper… it starts to make things happen in your mind!
It feels like a backup drive on a computer. If these thoughts are just in your mind they are at the mercy of every other thought you have and against your protector self, but on paper it has a different energy.

NB: *If you are writing things out, please be careful as other people who may disagree or not be happy with what you write may have a different perspective. Remember, creating a cocoon is about keeping yourself protected!*

Now although writing things out can set the wheels in motion, it is not enough to make it an emotional connection just yet. Written goals are commands from the conscious mind rather than the subconscious, so in essence this is just the thought rather than the experience, yet it's a good start and every journey begins with the first step. There will always be an urge to go back to 'the norm' when you start. This is because the protector self will be trying to re-stabilise the change the conscious mind is trying to make. So, stay focused and be dedicated!
Some suggested written goals are…

- *Where you want to be in a year or one hour from now*
- *How you want to feel relating to confidence and self-esteem*
- *How you want to feel relating to others*
- *The lifestyle you want to lead*

Exercise 1.1 – Practical application
Take a piece of paper or use a computer/laptop and write down 5, 10 or 20+ things that you would want in an ideal lifestyle!
Remain open whilst doing this as it may feel unachievable, but keep writing!

1.2: Commit to yourself
This is a decision of the heart and one that is not to be made lightly. In my own opinion, this is the biggest and most important step in everything that you can do.

Once you make a decision to reach the life that you want, it involves the deletion of all other options of retreat. It is a commitment to achieve that life no matter what! Commitment it is an attitude!
The thought of doing this may (for some) feel like the heaviest decision to make. I was one of those who found it hard, so if doing this feels scary, you're not alone. Just take each day one step at a time.

Committing to yourself is not saying that you will achieve all your aims in a week or that you will suddenly become invincible, but it is to make a decision to FIND A WAY AND KEEP GOING!

There is a difference between talking and walking. Millions of people all over the world make goals each and every day. They will put them in nice folders and even write them in all different colours. They make endless tasks, sit in their office and create to-do lists, and even sit in the bar or cafe telling everyone what they are going to do and how amazing their life will be when their goals have been achieved. Yet for many of these people these plans usually end up as nothing more than empty dreams that never reach fruition. The reason why they never materialise is because the person has never committed to themselves! Writing down a goal or a dream is one thing, but committing yourself to achieving it is something completely different!
Committing to yourself to achieve your goal and future is a decision of the heart!

Exercise 1.2 – Practical application
Sit quietly by yourself and reflectively look within. Notice how you feel about committing to yourself. Do you feel nervous, anxious, or is your mind awash with a flood of reasons for why you can't do it? Or do you feel a deep spirit of adventure and confidence to take action?

This exercise can take some practice to achieve. The aim here is to say to yourself (not others just yet) that you are going to commit to doing this, no matter how scared you feel and no matter how many doubts appear. Go deep within your own mind and commit to finding a way!

Step 2: Create a healthy mask (the cocoon)

Whilst you are going through a change, just like the caterpillar you will need to keep yourself safe. Each person's life is very different and it is your responsibility to look at your life reflectively and take precautions to keep yourself as secure as possible at all times.
It can be very useful to revisit the chapter on preparing for your journey and review it with your new mindset having read the rest of the information.

This step is about using all of your current situations to your advantage, namely… the mask! Although it may sound like a contradiction to use the mask to keep you safe, it is not. Remember, your protector self has created your mask to keep you safe, so if you now use the mask in a constructive manner, you can trick your protector self into believing that you are still completely safe, which in all reality you will be if done correctly.

2.1 Transform your mask

In this step we are going to create a cocoon from your mask, thereby keeping any hidden insecurities safe from the immediate future. Depending upon the type of mask you are currently using, a little extra creative strategy may be required to change an unhealthy mask into a healthy one.

In the cocoon step, the mask is an essential part of the path to freedom, for it is the mask that allows us to feel safe and protected. Once we feel safe we can then look out into the world and see potential threats from a distance. So imagine that the mask is now the hero you have always wanted by your side, which in fact from one point of view, it is! The mask keeps you safe from prying eyes and manipulators.

How I changed my unhealthy mask into a healthy one! (From Paul Ryder)

Through my years of being bullied I cannot begin to explain how angry I felt underneath, but through the shame in myself I suppressed it. As we all now know though, supressing it does not make it go away!

Although I did my best to keep it hidden I found that my mask became one of anger. I used to believe that if I could just intimidate everybody to leave me alone then I would be safe. So I used to shout a lot and be in a bad mood.

Although people avoided me, I wasn't getting anywhere in life. This left me feeling very alone and very lonely. So I looked within to see how I could use my current mask to my advantage.

My mask was very expressive and one of control, and I have always had a very keen interest in exercise and fitness. Although I had no experience of working in the fitness industry I decided to progress to a career as a personal fitness trainer.

It took time, but soon enough I found myself in a position where I could stand in front of a group of people and shout as loud as I could and push people as hard as they could go (whilst being respectful to their health), and they loved it! Gym members came up to me afterwards and thanked me for my support. Finally I felt like I could start to reintegrate into society.

This is an example of transforming an unhealthy mask into a healthy and useful mask.

Exercise 2.1

List all of your current masks that you can think of and also how they make you feel. List them all, even the ones that you may feel very uncomfortable about.

Next, take a look at any options you have where you can use them in a healthy way and to your advantage. Ideally, if you can transform any masks you wear so other people will benefit too then you will often find that you have more energy to support the change you choose to make!

No mask?

To some it may feel that they do not have a mask and as if they are laid bare with no defences (steps 4 & 5, personality shutdown and internal paranoia). If this is the current situation it may be advisable to create some kind of mask that increases the feeling of value. This could be voluntary work, training in a new career or a new hobby. Personally I would say that it is unadvisable to start a romantic relationship or to begin something which is high pressure as a mask. In a volatile environment this situation could become too erratic and pressurised and have the reverse effect on the emotional well-being.

Exercise 2.2: Look at all the areas in your life in which you can use your new mask to your advantage

How could you help other people with this mask?

Will this new mask protect you in the areas in which you feel vulnerable?

Do you feel in control of the mask or does the mask feel in control of you?

Exercise 2.2: Look at how other people relate to your mask

Do other people feel comfortable around this new mask?

Do other people want to be around or distance themselves from the new mask?

Note on sex appeal

It is very important to note that very physically attractive/sexy people may sometimes use their looks as a powerful mask. However, this is possibly a risky mask as the human race has a deep and natural connection to the sex drive. Anybody with a very high sex appeal may in fact cause unwanted attention and feel even more pressured. Some of my clients have actually chosen to dress down (but still smart) or look less glamorous as their mask as it creates less unwanted attention. Plus, they noticed that other insecure people did not feel as intimidated by their looks. However, this is only as suggestion and one which clients have chosen to do and was entirely their choice. The reverse of this could also be equally effective if in a specific environment such as changing body shape, looks, dress style and other options of appearance to enhance the looks.

Note on health

Drugs and alcohol are also classed as a mask, but it is highly recommended to find an alternative in this case as these can obviously cause physical and psychological damage as well as increasing paranoia. Seek medical and psychological support before changing addictions of this nature as sudden changes with drugs and alcohol may have serious side effects.

Step 3: Separating from your old mask

A mask can be extremely beneficial as we looked at in step 2. In challenging times it is essential that we can keep ourselves protected. However, to move forward we need to be able to own the mask rather than having 'it' own us.

A choice to make a separation from an old mask that we have become comfortable with may seem an arduous task and for many people there can be a feeling of withdrawal. However, by using strategy it can be relatively easy or easier. There is no doubt that it will still require effort, but strategy can lessen the emotional drain.

3.1: See your mask as a separate part of you

The mask is in many respects a part of you. Although life may feel more secure with it there by your side, it is still a mask and therefore created from a feeling of insecurity. People who have lived beneath their insecurity mask for many years can find it difficult to see the separation as it feels difficult to define the person from the mask and the mask from the person (as in the story of the sugar and salt).

Indeed, the mask is directly linked to your anxiety and therefore your pain. Every time you are afraid to…give something up, take on a new challenge, not be the centre of attention (or be the centre of attention) or need to own something of material value to impress other people, you are being controlled by your mask.

Exercise 3.1

1. List all of the things that your old mask commands you to do; buy things, impress people, etc.
2. Look within and notice the difference between what you want and what your mask tells you to do.

3. Practice becoming aware of this and notice the difference between your feelings and the subconscious reactions of anxiety, and realise that there are 'two' minds at play, not just one.

3.2: Write a letter to your mask

Many years ago a young lady who suffered for many years from bulimia (an eating condition) decided to face her anxiety of not feeling good enough. Through amazing dedication and support from her family she came to terms with the issue and wanted to move on. She chose to see the bulimia as a mask and decided to start supporting other girls who face the same crippling situation.

Whilst she was doing her best to support others (a healthy mask), she decided to say goodbye to her current unhealthy mask by writing 'it' a letter.

The letter started…

Dear Bulimia,

We have had many challenges in life and I know that you came into my life to help me in your own way. Although it has been very hard for me to see you this way, I now realise that you have helped me in the following ways…

It was a very heartfelt letter and caused many a tear, not only for her but also for those reading it. She finished the letter by saying that she is grateful for Bulimia's support but now it is time that she moved on with her life. She will never forget the journey and will promise to love herself the best she can. Again though this was only after a great deal of self-reflection and support.

Another amazing reflection of coming to terms with a mask is the film 'Drop Dead Fred' with the highly talented Rik Mayall.

Exercise 3.2: Say farewell

Once you have a new and healthy mask in place that you feel secure with, take some time to really look at the old and less healthy mask that you have used, such as anger, bullying, bravado and others. Then ask yourself whether you feel prepared to come to terms with accepting that the mask is not you and if you can separate. Although this may sound easy, for many people it is not and can be immensely emotional.

When you feel ready and committed in your heart, take a piece of paper and a pen and write a letter to your old mask. Explain how you realise it has supported you by trying to keep you safe all these years. Explain that you can now keep yourself safe by using other options (if you feel you can). Let your protector self know that you will do your best to love yourself and keep yourself safe so that it doesn't need to take over again and that you will do your best no matter how hard things get.
Ensure that you have time and space to do this. Don't quickly scribble it down on a lunch break; give it the time it requires!

Step 4: Cut the addiction and see the reality of your old mask

Remember that your mind is governed by two experiences, which are pain and pleasure. As we have already discussed, addiction is created by the mask feeling pleasurable and therefore something which the mind feels drawn to. The aim of what we have done so far is to create a new and healthier mask that you can use not only to keep you safe, but also to help yourself progress. Again, as mentioned, if your new mask can help other people then there will usually be more of a pleasure response as people will be drawn to you or feel more supported in your company and this will therefore lower your protector self's reactions (unless other limiting belief hijack the mind).

4.1: Create a pain association to your old mask

As the mask is a coping mechanism it is the best your protector self could provide at the time the trauma. However, if your present-day mindset realises that this mask is still running from an old belief that you are in some way inadequate or worth 'less', then it will be causing loss to you.

Ideally your new mask will become so pleasurable that you can just use that one and let the old mask go. However, it is not always that simple. If you find that you are struggling to let the old mask go then the aim is to create an association of pain toward your unhealthy mask.

This pain may be anger or frustration or others, but usually the best emotions are the fight emotions of the fight or flight reaction or simply just the pure logic of realising its loss to you.

Using your 'fight' towards the old mask can give you motivation and energy. Although anger or frustration are classed as negative emotions, personally I do not see it that way as it has the benefit of high energy! Yes, it is true that energy from frustration is not the best energy in the emotional spectrum, but it is more powerful than apathy. When the higher emotions such as joy and inner peace feel too far away you need to use what is closest to you in a constructive way. If you do choose to use anger then do so with caution, and focus any anger into constructive energy to move yourself forward in a healthy way.

Exercise 4.2: List any losses that the old mask is causing you

Losses you may suffer include…

- Time
- Freedom
- Love
- Peace of mind
- Energy
- Friendship

- Money
- Happiness

Look at the time you are losing out on by trying to achieve tasks to cope with feelings of insecurity, time that you could otherwise spend with friends or relaxing with a hobby. Be aware though that sometimes as one mask is reduced another may take its place; needless to say, the protector self is very powerful.

Look at the loss of real connection with other people which is happening, because while there is anxiety or a distraction (focusing on protecting the low self-esteem) we cannot really 'be there' in the moment with our loved ones.

"WHAT IS YOUR GREATEST PAIN JAKE?"
Jake – "Humiliation and loss!"
Avi – "How radical are you prepared to be?"
Avi – "The more power you think you have in Gold's world, the less power you have in the real world. You are still in prison Jake, in fact you never left, it's the pain of turning you against you!"
Quotes from the movie 'Revolver'
('Gold' is referring to Mr Gold, a hidden character from the movie; Mr Gold's world may be viewed by some as what we class as the mask and the con in this book.)

Step 5: Reconnect to your true self and choose your mask as an option

This is a very important step, if not the most important step! Reconnecting to your true self is about coming to terms with who you really are, accepting any mistakes you feel you have ever made and letting go of any guilt. However, this may require a great deal of delicate work.

Author note

I am fully aware that the above statement is something that's easier said than done. As I mentioned at the start of this book, I have had my own challenges and I know how it feels to be disconnected from the inner self. At the time I felt anger, guilt and even hate towards myself. In this state I deemed myself as pathetic and utterly worthless for being scared and because I used to allow others to walk all over me and bully me, I saw myself as second rate and worthless.

Looking within to reconnect was something that was the furthest thing from mind. At the time all I wanted to do was to be as far away from 'myself' as possible.

However, even though I was using my new and healthier mask I still found lots of supressed emotions underneath. After the anger exhausted me, I realised the impossibility of ever escaping from the inner self, which I had so many negative emotions toward. Although living in my mask was an escape… it felt empty.

The main mask (after I had constructively used my anger) was physical fitness. Doing my best to be a highly-skilled personal trainer and exercising as often as possible consumed my life. For me, I had to be the best at everything I did; there was no room for error and failure was not acceptable! Many other people in my life saw this as an admirable quality, but behind closed doors it eventually drained everything I had. I eventually had a nervous breakdown that 'woke me up'.

After looking with and when I finally reconnected to my true self (the 'I' self), I saw that the mistakes I felt I had made were not mistakes, but the best that I could do at the time. As millions of people do to themselves, I too have said so many hateful things to myself over the years, punishing myself for not being able to live up the unobtainable high expectations of others who projected their insecurities on to me (which I then expected from myself).

In all honesty, to reconnect and to find inner peace is a beautiful thing, and to love the self is beyond the comprehension of words. By this I don't mean a portrayal that we turn into some happy clapper, walking around, singing hymns and hugging everybody who walks past. Nor do I mean that we would be acting as if we are on a continual ingestion of hallucinogenic drugs. To truly love the self is a very grounding and connecting experience that brings inner peace. It is an ability to see the world as it truly is and to know that each person is equal. The mask that I once created has now ceased to be a mask that owns and controls me and transformed into a creative expression of my personality that can help other people from my heart - how else do you think this book was created?

5.1: Realise that there are times when using your mask is a healthy option

It would be so nice if we could simply remove the mask and live in the ideal world; however that reality is not always possible. As we have seen, millions of other people are also dealing with their own insecurities and wear masks. Some of the masks other people wear will not be a direct threat to us while some will.

Seeing reality for what it is means accepting that other people can sometimes be aggressive or manipulative through their insecurities, and if you want to lead a healthy life it is essential to protect your boundaries. This is where a mask can become immensely useful, however this time you will be consciously choosing to use the mask rather than your protector self forcing you to use the one it thinks is best.

Another way of looking at this is a method of creating different personality traits that you can choose to use for different situations in life. This is in reality something that we all do anyway, but here we are just bringing that part of your personality to your conscious awareness.

Exercise 5.1: List all the situations in life where it can be helpful to choose to wear a mask

An example here would be if you are at work and you know that you have a manager who is bullying or manipulating you and at the moment you are unsure of what to do.

Whilst you work on a solution of how best to manoeuvre round this challenge, your mask could be one of composure and appearing as if the situation is not affecting you. However, this is beneficial as long as you are working on a solution.

The reality of this situation could be that due to the abuse you are seething in anger. Here you would have every right to feel disrespected (though anger is an anxiety reaction unless in physical danger) as in reality you are being taken advantage of. However, showing anger or presenting a lack of control may cause further challenges. This is where the mask may give you breathing space whilst you figure out a solution.

5.2: Forgive yourself

This section for some will take a great deal of focus and very delicate inner conversation. When it comes to forgiving the self we have to take into account that there could be many masks compounded upon each other and a great deal of self-resentment. Personally I used to find it immensely irritating when I would read the self-help books and go on courses only to hear the speaker say,

"Just forgive yourself; c'mon you did your best. Let it all go and live your life."

Years ago I recall tearing a book into shreds when I read such a phrase. If you ever hear somebody say that, in my opinion they have no idea what they are talking about!

To forgive yourself means to accept who you are and all of the decisions you made during the path of your life. It is easy to blame yourself for making mistakes, to get angry at and even hate yourself for choosing an action that may have ended up in you getting rejected if your mind became confused in the moment.

We all make choices that we wish we could have took back, but to blame yourself for making a decision cuts you off from who you are. However, for many people forgiving the self can be one of the hardest things that they can ever face. Every now and then I have seen some clients go into a blind rage even discussing this area, let alone working through it.

During all my years working as a coach, I have never seen any client I have ever worked with come to an emotional reconnection without first forgiving themselves. Forgiving themselves for their apparent mistakes, self-resentment, what they feel they 'should have done', how they should have been perfect, or stronger, or whatever high expectation they placed on themselves. Forgiveness is the reconnection between the two minds within. Remember, the mind moves away from pain, so if you refuse to forgive yourself, you are in fact still punishing yourself. If you do not like yourself and blame yourself for apparent wrongdoings then your protector self will keep supressing that part of you, assuming it will cause you pain.

Refusing to forgive yourself is like holding a hot piece of metal and refusing to let go, then blaming your hand for the pain. If you feel pain, it is your refusal to forgive yourself that is causing the pain! Again though, I will say that this is a very sensitive area and sometimes upon hearing this, people can say, "See, I can't even forgive myself, I'm such a failure." However, when people feel this reaction it is the mask doing its best to protect them. Though it is essential to note that self forgiveness is often tied in with suppressed memories and self expectations of guilt and shame. So it is important to work through those whilst working on self forgiveness and acceptance.

Exercise 5.2: If you feel ok doing so, list the things that you blame yourself for and realise that you were struggling with your own life and weren't able to do any better.

NB: *Before you do this please take as many precautions as you can. If you feel that this is too much of a challenge and looking at this will cause you a great deal of pain then maybe seek some further support such as a professional therapist or somebody whom you can trust who is capable of supporting you.*

Some examples here could be:

"I blame myself for not standing up for myself at school"
"I blame myself for being a failure"
"I blame myself for always making mistakes"

One question I always ask my clients when working through this is…

If you had a child (or your own child now) who did the same thing that you did when you were younger, do you feel that they should punish themselves the way you are punishing yourself? If not, why do you feel you deserve this type of punishment?

5.3: See the 'inner you' as a small child

In reality our true self that was rejected before the mask was formed will probably be stuck at the age of a child inside our subconscious mind. We usually form the separation when we are too young to realise how to cope with trauma.

How many people reject the perceived 'weaker part' because they were not able to cope in the social world? As children we were **not** supposed to be fighters or machines or socially perfect. We were not able to be everything adults wanted us to be. This happened because WE WERE CHILDREN - innocent little people trying to make it in the world, and we didn't have a clue of how to get by!

As children with this lack of knowledge and therefore inability to act, it is possible that certain unknowing adults or peers may have expected us to be like they were and punished us if we were not. However, in reality it was impossible for us to be what they wanted us to be at that time because we were still learning. It is in this confusion and trauma that we could reject ourselves for not being 'good enough', and thus the mask begins.

If you do feel a rift of disconnection, remember that you were only a child trying your best in a world that may have expected you to be something or someone that you couldn't be at that time - you did your best!

Exercise 5.3: Connect to the younger you

Have a look to see if you can find any photos of yourself as a younger child. If you have some, really look at yourself, really look into your eyes. When you do this then ask yourself, do you honestly really feel in your heart that that part of you deserves to be criticised and pushed to 'be the best'? If the 'you' as a child was 'your' child, would you push them so hard?

Once you connect to that part of you, take time to feel them in your heart. Connect to that playful side of you and spend some time to let them speak. When I was doing this for myself I felt quite uncomfortable as I was trying to be the 'hot shot' personal trainer and doing all this 'being a kid' stuff was weird, or so I thought at the time. Now though, I do this on a regular basis now and it feels very grounding! Every now and then some people will try and criticize me for it. They may try to insinuate that I'm being childish. However, I simply explain that if they cannot do this exercise themselves then it is coming from a deep suppression within their own emotions. True connection is the ability to connect to 'all' of who we are.

5.4: See the good parts of you

It can be easy to assume for some people that they do not have any good points (or not enough good points), but in reality we all have them. No matter how bad things seem or how unimportant a person can feel, there is always something that makes each individual valuable and always something to connect to.

Exercise 5.4: List your good traits…

What hobbies do you like?

What nice things have you ever done for people?

Do you have any pets that you care for?

Deep down inside you, what change would you like to give the world if you could?

Make a list of as many things as you can, remembering that when the mind is feeling low self-esteem (and especially when in step 4 - personality shutdown) it can be difficult to see the good parts of who you are.

The fact that you are reading this book means that you want to change for the better. This shows you have a desire to grow and also have dedication, compassion and intelligence. Look deeper than the surface; you will be surprised at what you may find.

Look for the good parts of you and list them all!

Go easy on yourself!

As mentioned (and something that I will refer to continually), it is really important that if you want to move forward and reach the state of mind where you are free to be your true self and find inner peace and confidence, that you take each of these steps slowly and steadily.

A good friend of mine once said…
'Grass doesn't grow quicker if you pull on it!"

And it is the same with this!
This is back to my original point in regards to some of the quick-fix personal development which I have unfortunately encountered on my own journey. It is possible to find many a book or read in the classified ads that claim it is possible to solve all your problems in minutes… just book a quick session and all your dreams come true! However, I sincerely hope that I have done a good enough job for you to convince you that this attitude is simply a mask for the author or therapist!

A true author or therapist will carefully explain to you that there are no quick fixes and that you will have to work in a steady, disciplined fashion to move forward. The first time I met and worked with somebody who really supported me and told me the reality of it all, I didn't really want to hear it, because I wanted it 'now'! However, he just looked at me and told me straight… THERE ARE NO QUICK FIXES!

Use strategy! The 8 stages of personal development

In the next chapter I will cover the 8 stages with you. These are the ones which I work through with my clients in the one-to-one coaching sessions. The first step starts at gaining focus where you are right now and each step progressively feeds into the next.
Again, patience and discipline must be used in these 8 stages. Each stage must be completed before moving on to the next in session. Just like the butterfly you will need to draw strength from what you learn in step 1 to

then progress to step 2. Then you will gain strength from step 2 to progress to step 3 and so on.

Step 6: Escape the cocoon

This is the final step of this chapter and the real test to discover whether you are prepared to let go of the mask that is controlling parts of your world. When the mask is released and you are able to see both the true self and the social self, you will be free to make choices in your life without anxiety of low self-esteem pulling you under or controlling your decisions (which also releases you from the con).

"Named must your fear be before banish it you can."
Yoda (Star Wars)

6.1: See reality

When a person is in a dream and being chased by a big scary monster, the urge to run away is natural. Though in reality the monster is not there, and it is just a dream, a pattern of thoughts on the inner cinema screen which makes your mind think that it is real. This misperception of reality causes anxiety and further increases a desire to avoid life.

Your anxiety of not being good enough or not worth others' attention is just the same as a dream. It is an image inside your mind trapped in time from years ago. In reality it is true that others in the world today may still treat you the way you are scared they will and they may even abuse you, but it does not mean that you are not good enough. It just means they are taking advantage of a perceived weakness in you so they can feel more secure by controlling another person. If you are in an environment where you feel constant pressure from others, you will just be aligning to your perceived law of expectation (see earlier chapter). But reality there is not just one environment; there are many environments all over the world and many options within them. If you are being abused or manipulated at the moment, ideally remove yourself or change the energy as soon as possible in the safest manner as possible.

Reality is forever changing and there are connected people and disconnected people everywhere. The more disconnected people you spend time around, the weaker your self-esteem will become, because disconnected people want to keep other people in a low state of energy so they can feel more secure by having control. Essentially you are conned into thinking you are inadequate so they can have power in their world.

6.3: Be disciplined when the withdrawal hits

Withdrawal is something that everybody who chooses to separate from their mask will go through and in some cases it may not feel nice. You may have been living with the addiction to your mask for many years and now letting go of your security blanket to look at that which you do not want to look at anyway may cause a reaction. Not only that, but you are relearning how to feel by becoming your true self and using a completely different mindset - a mindset of self trust! Such a change is not always as easy as it sounds and it will be sometimes much easier to subscribe to the old ways of the mask as they are so easy. Yes, they are easy, but you are still a prisoner of your insecurities and therefore unable to freely think for yourself.

'Freedom is never voluntarily given by the oppressor; it must be demanded by the oppressed."
Martin Luther King, Jr.

If your mask is so powerful that it can have people eating out of your hand for being a leader (or feeling sorry for you), it may seem as though it is giving you great reward, but if you feel unable to separate from the mask then in reality you are not free, you are in a prison. Choosing not to always be the leader or choosing not to be the victim to gain attention and choosing to be an equal in the social group may at first feel daunting and possibly overwhelming. It would be so much easier just to go back to the old 'leader or victim self', claiming it is just 'who you are', but if it is done just to feel secure, it is just another ploy to hide behind the mask.

Be strong and be disciplined! The addiction of the mask can often be powerful when you want to change.

"Remember, a Jedi's strength flows from the Force. But beware. Anger, fear, aggression. The dark side are they"
Yoda (Star Wars)

To close this chapter; a poem of inspiration.

When things go wrong, as they sometimes will,
When the road you're trudging seems all uphill,
When the funds are low and the debts are high,
And you want to smile, but you have to sigh,
When care is pressing you down a bit-
Rest if you must, but don't you quit.

Life is queer with its twists and turns,
As every one of us sometimes learns,
And many a fellow turns about
When he might have won had he stuck it out.
Don't give up though the pace seems slow -
You may succeed with another blow.

Often the goal is nearer than
It seems to a faint and faltering man;
Often the struggler has given up
When he might have captured the victor's cup;
And he learned too late when the night came down,
How close he was to the golden crown.

Success is failure turned inside out -
The silver tint in the clouds of doubt,
And you never can tell how close you are,
It might be near when it seems afar;
So stick to the fight when you're hardest hit -
It's when things seem worst that you must not quit.

Unknown

15

Break the Cocoon

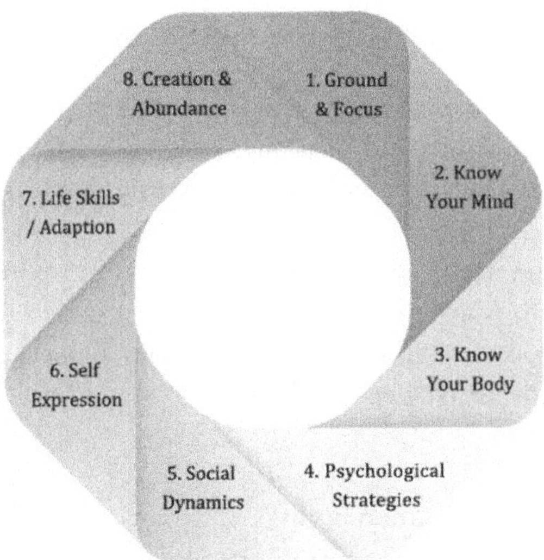

Moving forward in life from where you are now to where you want to be relies entirely on how much planning you do and what actions you take. However, sometimes even making a start can feel overwhelming as there is simply so much to look at. When I first started on my own journey I remember becoming completely confused with the overwhelming amount of conflicting views from many of the trainers that I spoke to!

"It is all about mindfulness!"
"No… it is about facing fears first!"
"No… you should reach your goals and live in abundance first!"
"No… you need to sort your diet out first!"

The list goes on and on and on………………….

So who is right? Where do we start? Which is the best option? Which way do we turn?

Well, if you are feeling in any way confused about making the first step, let me save you the trouble of the near insanity I went through trying to find my way out of the extremely deceptive smoke-filled room of Pandora's Box!

Whereas is the last chapter we looked at steps to understand and gain power over a mask that may be taking control, there is still much more to consider. During this chapter I will be covering the 8 stages of personal development.

After spending many a year bouncing back and forth in complete confusion as to which 'therapy' or 'coaching model' to follow (and thus spending a considerable amount of time and money), I stopped and looked at the bigger picture.

The analogy of the human body

The human body is a true work of art! The lungs allow oxygen into the blood, the heart pumps the blood around, the muscles use the oxygen, and these are only 3 functions of the millions of processes that happen each and every minute of the day.

The point I wish to make is that all the parts of the body work in harmony with each other. The body is a team and each part supports the other. It is only when one part stops doing its job (or is unable to) that the rest of the body struggles to function adequately or in form.

It is with this analogy that I aim to show you the 'bigger picture' of the field of personal development. The key to it all is not to focus on just one area, but to understand how each area connects with the other. For example, how mindfulness can connect with nutrition, how connecting to a mentor can support physical ability, and how allowing tears of sadness to cleanse the subconscious can help create an abundance of material wealth.

NB: *The great news to be aware of in today's world is that so many more coaches and trainers are now working on this 'holistic' view in regards to helping people.*

The confusion which many people face when they start their journey is that there too much emphasis on claiming that you can reach your dreams if you 'just' follow NLP, or 'just' follow the Carl Jung methodology of the archetypes, or 'just' follow… (fill in the blank). Yet when we only follow one aspect of development we weaken the entire structure. Just following one therapy for example would be like a gymnast 'only' strengthening their legs or a yoga trainer 'only' stretching their arms. To reach your true state of self-connection and abundance you must embrace 'all areas' of personal development.

"You must be shapeless, formless, like water. When you pour water in a cup, it becomes the cup. When you pour water in a bottle, it becomes the bottle. When you pour water in a teapot, it becomes the teapot. Water can drip and it can crash. Become like water my friend."
Bruce Lee

The 8 stages of personal development

The 8 stages are my own interpretation of creating a progressive flow of energy and strategy to embrace all forms of personal development. From following this process myself I found that it allowed me true flexibility in all areas of self expression and also an ability to discover where I was at any particular time.

Life will always offer challenges, that is just life, but when you can flow with those challenges you can learn to surf the waves rather than feel overwhelmed by them.

The 8 stages of personal development is the same structure I cover in my one-to-one coaching sessions and it allows powerful results. When working with the emotions one of the most essential things to be able to track and measure is where a client is on their journey.

Through this chapter I will describe the purpose of each of the 8 stages and then cover some further information and suggested steps. Although it is not possible to cover all of the information of each of the steps in this book (as there is too much information), further books will cover each stage in more depth. This chapter is also just an overview of steps you can take in the future rather than a DIY guide. No book in the world can ever give you every step to take as there are too many variables.

The 8 consecutive stages are…

Stage 1: Ground & Focus
Stage 2: Know Your Mind
Stage 3: Know Your Body
Stage 4: Psychological Strategies
Stage 5: Social Dynamics
Stage 6: Self Expression
Stage 7: Life Skills / Adaptation
Stage 8: Creation & Abundance

Please refer to the diagram below…

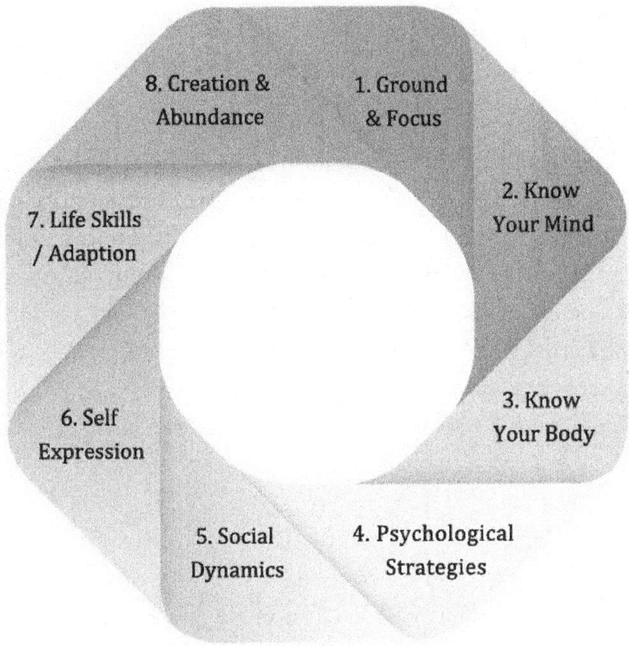

© The 8 Stages of Personal Devlopment - Paul Ryder - 2012

To give a comprehensive overview, each stage will be divided into the following sub-sections.

1. **A description of the stage**
   Here we will cover what the stage actually entails and the information covered. The benefits of this are that it can then allow the conscious mind to begin to build a mind map of that stage.
   This can be likened to drawing a map of a town and listing all the shops and services that can be used by a person (what they offer).

2. **How the stage integrates**
   If full understanding is to be enabled it is important to firstly understand how it connects with the rest of the stages. This will

allow the conscious mind to create a structure and therefore enable the ability of logic.
This can be likened to understanding how all the shops and services listed on the map can work together to help the community.

3. **The benefits of this stage**
Simply learning information without knowing why you are learning it or what relevance it has in your life can sometimes be a waste of your precious energy. If you are to learn something it is essential that you can relate it to something you are working towards. The purpose of this point is so you can begin to see the practical application of this stage.
This can be likened to knowing what you can purchase from each shop in the town and how each product can help you move forward.

4. **Exercises**
In this part I will be covering a selection of two exercises from the entire toolkit which I use in the stage. Practicing these and applying them if applicable to your current stage can enhance your development. These will be techniques and exercises which I have used myself and clients with successful application. As mentioned though, any decision to use these exercises is your choice and your responsibility. Bear in mind that I have also exercised caution on this and some of the exercises I do in one-to-one sessions I have omitted as they require considerable preparation beforehand. Also, some of the stages may not be applicable if you are not currently resonating at that stage in your life at this moment and can be included as you progress.
This can be likened to using the products of each shop in harmony to move forward which you have acquired from the shop on the mapped-out town.

So let's begin!

Stage 1: Ground and focus

1. A description of the stage

The ground and focus stage is about bringing the attention back to present-tense reality rather than the reality of the internal cinema screen. It is essential to note that although the protector self could be seen as the bad guy in all of this by hijacking the mind continually, it is actually doing its best to care for you. Through the years of either social conditioning or poor education the mind has been trained to use this style of self-reflection and therefore the protector self is only doing what it knows best.

The ground and focus stage then is not about making any direct changes to the information in the subconscious mind, but simply to allow the protector self to relax and start to understand that it does not have to work so hard all the time. In my workshops I will describe this as the state change. It is not to try to tell the protector self to change (as that will never work), but simply to offer another point of view which is more positively inclined and to see how it feels.

2. How this stage integrates

As mentioned, if changes are made which are too much for the protector self to cope with based upon the information it views upon the internal cinema screen, it will cause a stress reaction that slows progression. This stage therefore integrates like water into sand. It is essential at this stage that the protector self feels secure in what is happening and that any exercises are not in direct confliction with its information. Thus, this stage is integrating with the protector self at 'its' level, thus allowing rapport.

3. The benefits of this stage

When life throws the mind a challenge that it cannot cope with it will naturally react in an expression of pain. The purpose of this is the protector self attempting to either remove the threat or remove itself from the threat. As we have seen, this is called the fight or flight reaction.

However, as we have also seen, many of the reactions a person can face are anxiety based (a perceived threat). When the mind is reacting in state of anxiety it is actually self-generating its own stress and therefore in some ways could be seen as attacking itself.

Stage 1 (ground and focus) is about bringing the focus back to the conscious mind and being present to allow the mind to see reality rather than what it thinks is reality. As discussed this is not always the easiest task as the protector self may be continually attempting to hijack the conscious mind with what it feels is reality.

An essential aim to learn at this stage is the ability to gain power over the illusion which the subconscious mind is attempting to claim is reality. This is where many people can receive misguided information with claims that if we are mindful all the time then all will be well. As we have seen though, the mind will keep being hijacked and the loop continues.
Although 'just' continually practicing mindfulness will not always create long-lasting inner peace, it can give you breathing space to notice the deception of the protector self which creates the anxiety from the internal cinema screen.

4. Exercises

Exercise 1.1: See reality

When a person is in a dream and being chased by a big scary monster, the urge to run away is natural. In reality though the monster is not there; it is just a dream, a pattern of thought on the inner cinema screen making your mind think it is real.

Your anxiety of (for example) not being good enough or not worth others' attention is just the same as a dream. It is an image inside your mind trapped in time from years ago. In reality it is true that other people may be disrespectful to you and they may even abuse you, but it does not mean you are not good enough. It just means they are taking advantage of a perceived weakness in you so they can feel more secure by controlling another person.

Practical application

1. Sit quietly and listen to the inner dialogue within your mind – such as how it may tell you that you should avoid things, do better, stop letting people down or the hundreds of other internal cinema screen 'realities' posing as the truth.

2. Once you have listened to them all, make a list of them and write them out on paper.

3. Then, go through each one and ask yourself whether they are true.

Many clients I have worked with, when they get the 'I am not good enough' voice, will say "yes, it is true", however that is just their belief and beliefs are not facts!
Until something can be proven it is not a fact, and just because somebody tells you that you are not good enough, does not mean they are correct! Again, simply admitting this may not make any dramatic changes, but the aim is just to be aware of the truth and the illusion.

Exercise 1.2: Become present

It is an impossibility to focus your attention on your physical body and your internal cinema screen at the same time. To focus on the physical body requires that you are seeing reality for what it right now; this requires left brain dominance (logic). However, to create anxiety requires imagination and therefore is right brain dominance (creative).
Practicing being physically present therefore means that you have to detract the attention away from the internal cinema screen and thus stop anxiety.

Practical application

1. Allow yourself time where you will not be disturbed. Turn off the phone and other electrical equipment.

2. Sit or stand and take all of your attention to your breath. Breathe in through your nose and out through your mouth. Do this 5 times, slow and steady.
3. Then take all of your attention to your feet, really focus on how they feel.
4. Then take all of your attention to your legs and again really notice how they feel.
5. Do this for all of the parts of your body.
6. As you focus on your body you will find it impossible to focus on your anxiety. They may flicker back and forth, but one will cancel the other out.

This will require continual practice as your protector self may aim to distract you back to your internal cinema screen. If this happens recall the exercise 1.1 and take your attention back to the body part you were just focused on.

Stage 2: Know your mind

1. A description of the stage

Stage 2 covers in full detail about how the actual mind functions, such as:

- The conscious and subconscious
- Belief structures
- Values
- Understanding the range of emotions
- How the mind relates and associates
- The language of the different parts of the mind
- Creative ability
- Visualisation
- The mask and coping mechanisms
- And many other areas

Stage 2 is about learning to understand how your mind sees the world and understanding its tremendous power. As mentioned, many people are expected to function adequately in all the areas of their life, yet they may never have been given a user guide.
Trying to gain control of your mind without sufficient education is like waking up inside a car driving at 100mph and not knowing how to drive.

There is a great deal of information to absorb in this stage so it is essential that stage 1 is practiced until competent. Once stage 2 has been absorbed, the creative mind can begin to understand why the composure was lost in the first place. With this new information the creative mind can now start to restructure any confusion. This can begin to create a longer-lasting composure for the internal cinema screen, thereby slowing the reactions of the protector self.
Although I cover how the mind puts the world together in this stage, we do not start to change the information within Pandora's Box. The reason that we just observe rather than change the information is because there is much more to consider than just knowing how the mind works. It is in this area where an untrained therapist or coach can cause considerable damage if done erratically. For example, using high levels of motivation with a form of hypnosis in addition to creative NLP scripts can cause the mind to become confused and open up Pandora's Box, believing the environment to be safe when it is not.

Take one step at a time

An example of when things can go wrong with poor quality trainers would be a situation I witnessed myself live in a weekend workshop. It started with a man who was married to a lady and they had two children. However, he found himself caught up in the hype of the workshop driven by the overzealous trainer.
The workshop leader kept saying that… you can do anything and do what you want! This is extremely irresponsible to say to a group of 50 people after knowing them for 1 hour as anybody in that group could be volatile or unstable.

After two days of the hyped-up carnage, the married man then suddenly announced that he was a gay man in denial and that he would go and phone his wife immediately to let her know that he wanted a divorce! To which the group leader…… applauded him (as he walked from the room)!

Nobody heard the end result of this or the effect it had on his life, wife or children. A few of us kept in touch from the course, but nobody heard from him, not even the organisers. A worrying sign was that the trainers were quite urgently trying to get hold of him but couldn't. We can only hope it all worked out for him.

It is for reasons such as this and many other cases that I keep repeating myself to exercise caution when allowing another person to access your emotional programming, whether that be friend, partner, co-worker or therapist. The mind is a very highly-tuned precision instrument and works by using thousands of equations a second. Just because the conscious mind cannot understand its drivers does not mean it is malfunctioning! Things can turn dark very quickly if slow, steady steps are not taken.

2. How the stage integrates

Once a person can ground their energy and become aware of the illusion their internal cinema screen is creating, their stress levels will begin to reduce. This happens because the mind will become present-tense focused rather than reacting from a pain-filled imagined future.

Cognitive abilities will be limited when the mind is in a high state of anxiety due to the more animal instinct part of the brain being triggered. Until the mind can distinguish between actual reality and perceived reality it is extremely difficult to understand new information. This happens as the protector self will continually be trying to take control. This stage is about showing 'why' the mind will loop.

3. The benefits of this stage

There have been many people who have quoted the phrase;

"We can feel anxiety about that which we do not understand."

The reason for this is simply that if we do not understand something then we may not know how to defend ourselves if it becomes a threat. If we are not aware of how to control the situation this can trigger the protector self. This is where the anxiety of irrational beliefs comes from. They just seem to appear and take control when they want, leaving us at their mercy. However, as with the information in this book we can start to understand 'why' things are happening and then take back control.
The benefit of stage 2 then is to understand how the mind works so that we can control its reactions and create stability during challenging times that occur in our daily lives.

4. Exercises

Exercise 2.1: Name your emotions

When a stress reaction happens it can sometimes feel like everything is coming at you all at once. When this happens it can sometimes create major confusion. However, if the focus is allowed to dwell on the internal cinema screen it will dominate your mind and will move too quickly for you to consciously rationalise and or understand.

Naming each emotion as you are feeling it will force your mind to become logical and therefore present. Being present will force the internal cinema screen to reduce.

Practical application

1. When the feeling of stress hits your body and causes confusion, stop what you are doing and remain still (if you have the option).
2. Take all of your attention to your physical body.
3. Once you are centred, take your attention to listening to your mind chatter.

4. As you hear it, begin to name all of the emotions which you can feel; I feel angry, I feel confused, I feel hate, etc.
5. Keep your focus on naming each emotion as they arise.
6. Eventually you will start to notice the anxiety lessen.

The aim of this is not to connect to the emotion - it is just to observe! If you connect you will be in reaction mode and the grip of the protector self, but if you observe, then in time you will become physically and emotionally present.

Exercise 2.2: Discover the mind

As you have already done by reading this book, it is essential that you make a study of the mind a continual process. By this I do not mean techniques, I mean the mind itself! Techniques are often about controlling the mind, not always about understanding it.

Understanding how it works could perhaps mean creating your own storyboard of the protector self or how the mind puts the world together. Other topics which can be of great benefit are to understand how the creative part of the mind functions by reading amazing authors such as Tony Buzan or Edward De Bono.

Practical application

1. Make a list of what you actually want to discover about the mind and why.
2. Then go online (or to your library) and make a list of books, website or blogs etc. which refer to the topic you want to learn about.
3. Make yourself a checklist and a rough time frame and progressively work through it.
4. You could possibly ask a friend to help support you or get a study partner.

Stage 3: Know your body

1. A description of the stage

Through the 15 years of working in the personal fitness industry I noticed a very common trait that would cause so many members of the health clubs to fall short of their goals or aims. Many people would come to lose weight and become healthier, which is fantastic as they are taking action to improve their world. However, for many people their health goals were to make themselves 'feel more valuable by looking better', which as we now know is a mask. As we can also see, the underlying stress reactions will create hijacking and thereby bring erratic results. Hence, some people have very erratic health regimes and others can be obsessively strict.

This stage is about looking at all areas of your physical health and growing your awareness to ensure your energy is at an optimal level as you progress.

The main areas that will be covered in this stage are:

- Sleeping patterns
- Nutritional plans
- Breathing and breath work
- Flexibility and joint mobilisation
- Strength and stamina
- Learning about the parts of the body and brain
- The immune system
- Stress levels

2. How the stage integrates

Once the mind has been grounded (stage 1) and has the ability to have more control through understanding (stage 2), it is important to align the physical energy to increase emotional stamina and vitality. Once physical energy has been aligned to a high potential the above exercises will become easier (however this stage can also be started earlier in part).

Many people at one point or another have felt the heavy energy of apathy creeping in through exhausted adrenal glands. Here it is important to use stages 1 and 2 to give reason as to why we need to work the body. Any attempt to align the physical world whilst there is continual hijacking or no understanding of the emotions can make physical actions or focus extremely difficult.

3. The benefits of this stage

With the physical body being a synergistic component, everything functions in relation to each other. Knowing how one part of the body works in harmony with another begins to allow for optimal performance and optimal health.

For example, understanding how eating certain poor-quality foods can confuse the body into thinking it is still hungry even though it is full can help with weight regulation. Understanding how to reduce body fat can then help preserve the energy systems and reduce stress levels (both emotional and physical). Also, learning how to reduce stress levels can help reduce the body's craving for a very powerful antidepressant, for example in the form of sugar.

NB: *It is only my opinion that sugar is an antidepressant. The reason I stated this is the fact that I have personally used it in my own past through depression. Also, I have found that many other people feel drawn to it and become addicted to sugar as they feel 'numbed out' on it.*

4. Exercises

When making changes to the physical life it can sometimes require a great deal of dedication and persistence. Neural patterns may be set in a habit and the physical body itself may be in poor shape, requiring a great deal of effort before the desired results are seen.

The exercises in this section will therefore be an overview that you may have already heard of. Rather than these being stated as one off techniques though, these will need to be viewed as a continual way of life.

Exercise 3.1: Taking up physical exercise

Physical exercise has a great many benefits, but as the saying goes… everything in moderation! There are many types of exercise, such as anaerobic for strength and power, and aerobic which can increase stamina. There are other areas too, such as flexibility and co-ordination. It is recommended to train for your health rather than for aesthetic reasons only, as again this reflects as mask. For example, choosing to lose weight is great for energy and many other health benefits and if done correctly will bring optimum health, whereas losing weight just to look a certain way may create a temptation to taking extreme supplements or starvation, thereby causing damage to the body.

Practical application

1. Take an honest review of your current health and list any health concerns you may have, then make a list of what you would like to achieve.
2. If you do not have any health concerns, pick a list of aims you would like to achieve and why, such as toning up, a 5k run, building muscle etc.
3. Enquire with a trainer or perform your own research as to the steps you would need to take in order to attain these goals or aims.

The main aim with physical health is the question of why and to check whether your aim is a mask or not. Many people I have seen in the gym have trained for 'the look' even though they are injured as they are that desperate to create the mask.

Although it is always a great feeling when a person attains their ideal shape and feels desirable and/or sexy, it is still advised to train for health first and appearance second. There is nothing wrong with wanting to achieve the ideal shape or extreme fitness for example, but only as long as your foundations are in balance.

Exercise 3.2: Regulating sleep

Just the same as exercise, sleep is a huge area and much too complex to cover in this chapter, so I will simply cover the highlights. So many areas of daily life can disrupt sleep, and although millions of people do survive on less than adequate sleep, eventually it will catch up! Unfortunately though, most sleep disruptions result in a gradual numbing of the body and mind. People who feel drowsy in their daily life may be experiencing what is known as 'sleep debt', which is when the body is trying to slow itself down through lack of healthy sleep.

Practical application
In this section I will give you some suggested tips to try to support healthy sleep.

1. Try going to bed before 11pm if possible (ideally 10pm) and awake at 6am or 7am.
2. Write out all of your worries before going to sleep.
3. Test eating patterns e.g. not eating sugar too late (as it spikes insulin which can disrupt sleep).
4. Never go to sleep on an argument with your partner or friends if possible.
5. If you have children, make sure they go to sleep feeling loved and connected as this can support their sleep, which in turn supports your sleep.

Stage 4: Psychological strategies

1. A description of the stage

Stage 4 is a two-part process about creating a blueprint of the self-identity and about gaining further control.

The first stage covers how to understand the belief structures, personality traits, ego defence mechanisms and the full emotional scale of the identity. This is the complete self-reflection and internal programming. Here we will cover all of the masks and coping mechanisms whilst simultaneously observing the cause and effect path. As we have seen, every action and reaction in the human mind is an effect of a cause. At this stage though we will only be looking at the effect, the smoke from the fire if you will.

The second part of this stage is to learn a vast array of skills and techniques of gaining control over the mind. This will not be limited to any one particular style of therapy, but to include as many as required to ensure the mind has the essential toolkit, allowing versatility and adaptation to challenges as they arise. This stage can cover techniques that could be classed in the field of NLP, transactional analysis, CBT, life coaching, social influence, leadership, hypnosis, creative thinking and any other area that would be useful to allow for the client to grow. In my own personal belief, if we limit knowledge to only one style of therapy or 'way' it can limit progression and therefore it can limit the best option of growth.

2. How the stage integrates

As we have seen in this book so far, looking at the masks and limiting beliefs could be an extremely sensitive area for many people. If their protector self has had a great deal of power over the years then looking at this area without stages 1, 2 and 3 can be extremely challenging.
It is at this stage where I will use the reference of the 'New Year's resolution' syndrome. This is to describe the multitude of goals that are set and started and a few weeks later the protector self shuts the person's energy back down again, thereby stopping the fruition of the goal.
To look at self-reflection and options of moving forward without securing the foundations first will usually be a futile effort.

3. The benefits of this stage

Many clients I have worked with have mentioned how their life has felt in the past like it is really struggling or they keep making the same errors and do not know why. Now, as this stage is split into two areas I will describe it as follows.

Stage 4 – Part 1:
Looking at the belief systems can bring a great power of control over the options available. Not knowing how the beliefs are creating results can be likened to walking round in a dark room and continually bumping into objects. If we cannot see what is in front of us we will continue to make the same errors no matter how often positive thinking is performed.
However, once we understand how the beliefs are creating the result we can then change them to what we desire.

Stage 4 – Part 2:
Changing beliefs does not happen by simple affirmations and positive thinking, as we now see via the protector self. For change to take place it is essential to understand how the beliefs are functioning and also why they are there (with the inclusion of stage 5). As the mind is a logical processing unit it therefore operates under structure. Once the mind understands how to gain control it can then begin to practice the techniques to become more efficient. Although this stage it can work at a deep level, it is still not the very deepest level.

4. Exercises

As stage 4 is one of the larger stages the list of exercises is quite numerous and will be adapted to each individual client's needs and requirements. Here I will be covering one exercise from each of the two parts.

Exercise 4.1: List any masks you may have created
Although we have already covered this in this book, it is still a very essential exercise to perform. It can be a very challenging task to look at any masks as they are obviously covering up a deeper issue. Here again I stress being aware that the deeper issues can be extremely sensitive and if you are unsure of opening up Pandora's Box by doing this exercise then please look at the inclusion of professional support.

Exercise 4.2: Seek professional help

Unfortunately some areas of society still view visiting a trained professional in the psychological field as a form of weakness. Yet many in society do not see it strange to learn English or maths, which is simply another form of education. Professionals in the psychology field are in many ways educators of the mind and can support a person to reconnect with their truc sclf and lct go of suppressed memories which cling to the past. Sometimes, for some people it can almost be an impossibility to connect to their true selves without the support of a trained professional due to the protector self having too much control.

Again though, please note caution! In the field of psychology just because a therapist has a 'qualification' (which the industry is very difficult to regulate) does not necessarily mean they have an ability to understand the mind and/or your emotions. Although the therapist may have had extensive training and 'know' the information, this does not mean that they have fully cleansed their masks or possess sufficient people skills. As we have seen, a mask is a perception and can easily be hidden, and as qualifications rely on logical structure the two can conflict.

The main reason this is important to note is that if a therapist has not fully faced their own issues, their protector self may hijack their mind when it sees the same suppressed emotion reflected in their client.

For example, if a therapist has suppressed sexual expression due to an anxiety of rejection, then if a client (who they were working with) wanted to explore sexual expression in themselves, the therapist may find this subliminally distressing or be limited on their own abilities. This situation could result in the client being restricted in their progression or a co-dependent relationship between coach and client. For a therapist trapped in their mask, it is possible for them to displace their insecurities on to the client, keeping both sides trapped. A very powerful mask indeed!

Practical application

When seeking further help please use the following guidelines

1. Observe their reputation, previous testimonials from their clients, social media and any other information. You can even ask people you know who may know them.

2. Go with your gut. Your inner guidance system (the gut) is very powerful. Notice if you feel really connected or uneasy to the therapist. Don't ever be afraid of asking questions; this is your future! If you feel uneasy by yourself, ask a friend to support you or go in with a list of questions written down. A good therapist will be more than happy to go through all your questions as long as they are relevant.
3. Be aware of an 'overly helpful therapist' - this may be a mask. It is good to help but offering too much may be a mask of seeking approval.

4. Be aware of continual references about money. If you are booking a flight then it is quantifiable, you know what you are buying. However, therapy is different and not quantifiable, and it is possible that a therapist may have money concerns which can then be projected onto a client. If a therapist places money before making a difference to a client then my advice is stay clear of them as this is often a mask.

5. Ask about timescales and a structure. It has been known for people to be in therapy for 5, 10 or 20 years, and some their entire lives. If progression is extremely slow then it usually means that either the outside influences (including self-sabotage) are still overpowering their progression or the therapy (therapist) is of poor quality. It can be difficult for a therapist to define timescales until they have had a chance to assess the client, and even after doing so Pandora's Box may still unlock as it chooses. Personally I would also advise caution of any therapist claiming 'a guarantee' after one session! Of all the therapists I have known over the years, I have never seen one who can honour their word of a

'guarantee' in the field of psychology, as there are far too many variables to say such a definite word!

6. Again, go with your gut! You will know when you find the right person. You will feel supported and as if they 'see through your eyes'! Empathy is essential! Be open until you find the right connection for you.

With the above being taken into account, a skilled coach or therapist can literally transform a person's life and make huge changes to their future. Yes, it is the client allowing the process to happen, but the coach/therapist is a catalyst for that change. Please feel free to add your own checklist to what to look for in a therapist, because as mentioned this is YOUR life!

Stage 5: Social dynamics

1. A description of the stage

Like stage 4 there are two parts to this stage. The first is to understand the overall area of social psychology and communication, and the second is to look at the client's personal social world including family, friends and interactions during the entire course of their lives.

Let's give the two parts a deeper look.

Part 1 – Social psychology

As we have seen throughout this book, how people interact with each other can have a profound effect upon another person's belief structures if they are not aware of how the mind and their emotions function. It is in this part where we begin to take a deeper look at how society as a whole begins to interact with each other in the different environments.
When enduring a stress-filled environment it is sometimes easy to feel that any attack or challenge from another is personal and therefore

disconnected. However, as we now know, people will only attack (rather than discuss) if they are in pain and therefore it will not be personal, but simply their protector self doing its best to harmonise their internal stress. Although this is the case, it does not mean that we should allow poor or aggressive behaviour to continue. So this part covers how to be aware of social dynamics and counter measures to take if challenged. The counter measures are there to ideally create a win-win for both sides.

Part 2 – Your own journey

It is here where we will look at the most sensitive area of life. One of the greatest pains that a person may ever face is the confusion of feeling a loss of love or shame / guilt, but not be able to explain why. A child will find disconnection extremely difficult to understand, such as why a parent or family member feels unavailable or any of the other masks a parent, family member or friend may unknowingly wear.

For example, in my own journey, although I could logically understand why my dad was drinking alcohol and therefore emotionally unavailable (his own challenged past), I struggled to face the confusion that I felt towards his emotional availability being erratic.

Stress reactions and trauma are not always created when we are a child. Some traumas can be created in later life or when the mind is intensely vulnerable.

Here we will look at areas such as bullying, unrealistic expectations, projections, family member's masks, the client's role in the family and many other areas. It is to be noted that a great deal of emotion can arise as a result of even breaching this area. Emotions such as anger, sadness, betrayal, hate, loss, guilt, shame and many others may arise and feel as if they are 'appearing from nowhere'. However, as we now know, they are not magically appearing, but rather have been supressed inside Pandora's Box through overwhelming emotional pain.

2. How the stage integrates

Each stage becomes progressively more revealing leading to this sensitive stage. This is the stage that contains the most potent confusion and can leave the mind feeling very confused and disorientated. This is why it is extremely essential that the other stages and the ability to control the emotions are practiced before looking into this area.

To look into this area without being grounded and understanding the mask can sometimes cause a person to experience a huge tidal wave of emotion, which in turn creates an extreme fight or flight reaction. However, reacting in this way will never usually be of any benefit as the reaction is driven by confused emotion. Saying or doing an action whilst not seeing clearly can cause much more damage than may have already been there in the first place.

3. The benefits of this stage

To give a personal reflection of this stage would be when I suffered from continual anger through my perception of how the bullies used to treat me over the years. The anger and hate of their insults, punches and destroying/stealing my property ate away at me like acid.
However, once I understood how the system was working and how my actions interacting with the masks created the reality which I faced (stage 2 of the self esteem recovery model), I noticed that my anger dissipated dramatically. In no way do I feel that what they did was acceptable, as what they did was still disrespectful. Understanding what people have done does not mean allowing people to treat you poorly; it just means you understand why they did it.

The main benefits you can expect from this stage are to understand how certain other people may be unknowingly manipulating your environment through their own masks and then how to gain control and breathing space. Also, this will cover how to protect yourself from their actions and reactions by creating a harmony or avoidance strategy. Remember that some people are willing to let go of their masks once they understand that they have them, although this will be directly related to how secure they feel. Everybody has the ability, but taking action on the change is a different story.

4. Exercises

Exercise 5.1: Be aware of your social circle

It is said that you become a reflection of the five main people you spend the most time with. This is a fascinating quote and something which is much more complex than it may appear. If we take a close look at the phrase 'who you spend your time with' it does not necessarily state that it is physical time. Remember, the emotions and reactions we feel are usually driven from our perception. Therefore, the people who we spend the most time with are the people who we **think** about the most rather than actually spend time with physically.

For example, take the two following scenarios:

1. A person who is experiencing bullying at work and is thinking about the situation not only while at work, but also in their home time.

2. A person who is in a new relationship and feeling connections of love. They think about their new partner all through the day even whilst at work.

Practical application

1. Make a list of all of the people in your life whom you think about the most (this can include alive or deceased).
2. Look at each person and place them on a scale of 1 – 10 regarding how much you think about them, whether or not you are with them.

3. Then write down three or four emotions you most associate with them.

4. Ask yourself how thinking about this person really makes you feel… positive or negative.

Awareness is the first stage to change. Upon doing this exercise, many clients are shocked as to how often they actually think about a person whom they do not particularly like or want in their life.

Exercise 5.2: Be aware of Pandora's Box projections

Each and every day millions of people find themselves drawn to thinking about another person whom they may not like or do not want to be around, yet they still think of them.

Remember the protector self is only concerned with one thing… to protect you! If it is holding a memory or an associated memory to a person who is perceived as a threat or a potential threat then it will keep that person in the forefront of the mind as an early warning system.

This is why (if this happens to you) simply keeping yourself busy or using distraction only works temporarily, as the potential threat is the greatest emotion to your protector self.

Practical application

1. List all of the people who you may not want to think about, but find yourself drawn to thinking about them on a too-frequent basis.

2. Go through each person and list all the reasons why you may feel hurt or angry with them.
3. Look at the situation through your protector self's eyes and ask yourself what it may be trying to keep your attention on this person for. For example, Is it that you want an apology or do you want them to need and respect you?

4. Make a list of the ideal outcome for each of these people and how it would affect your life if you had this. Remember you may not get your desired result from them, this is just for your own awareness.

Although other people can bring challenges there are also good people everywhere! This is regardless of the con or the insecurities that they may be trapped in! People do kind things and are caring and giving every day all over the world. It is so easy for a person to believe that 'everybody will let them down' or 'nobody is there for them'. In some cases, yes that's true, but not for the whole world, and it is through believing in these good and heartfelt people that we have a beacon of light when the lights go out.

Stage 6: Self-expression

1. A description of the stage

Stage 6 is about creating a direct connection with Pandora's Box and expressing the unspoken voice of any challenge or trauma that has been suppressed. This is where the client will connect with 'their' traumatic pain (stage 3 of the self-esteem recovery model) and allow the trapped emotion to be released.

This is by far the most sensitive of all of the stages as the client is literally reliving the emotional pain in real time and allowing it to be updated through neural plasticity (the brain altering the perception of the memory). The reason this stage can be so emotionally charged is because although the memory may have happened many years ago, it is actually frozen in time and looping. So for example, if the client was 5 years old when a trauma happened, then to revisit that memory can create the exact same feelings when it is released. This is where major confusion can occur as although the conscious mind may know that it happened many years ago, to the subconscious mind it may feel as if it happened 10 seconds ago.

The reason this happens is because of the way the different parts of the physical brain store information. The part of the brain that is thinking the trauma happened 10 seconds ago has stored the memory, but does not have the ability to update the memory and therefore it is stuck in time.

When the trauma memory is expressed it can then be processed by a different part of the brain and updated to today (the conscious mind).

When a client is in the process of re-experiencing the trapped memory they can go through something called 'state recall', which can be quite unnerving for them if not prepped by the therapist.
Personally I have experienced some clients who may spontaneously have a full-blown tantrum as a child would, stamping their feet and screaming. Although this can be only a small percentage, it is how the client chooses to react and therefore very normal. Whereas for other clients, their voice may take on that of a child, where it sounds as if their vocal chords have changed. For many though, it is a re-experiencing of the sadness or trauma that they did not feel loved, wanted or accepted. Once released they can allow the old memory to update and it no longer needs to keep projecting onto today.

An analogy I use is like that of a filing cabinet. If a file is not in line with all the other files it will not sit right in the drawer and therefore cause the other files to be pushed out of line (the mask). When all the other files are not in line, the drawer will not be able to be closed and will keep opening up by itself (trauma recall). It is possible to tape the drawer shut (coping mechanisms), but the secretary will always be trying to re-open the drawer to file it correctly (the higher self).

2. How the stage integrates

If you are going to choose to let a wild stallion out of captivation you had better make sure that you can control it! If you can't, the damage it can cause could be catastrophic. We can see the result of this when people drink alcohol at the stereotypical office party and then 'tell the manager what they think of them', only to regret it the next day.

Allowing the suppressed emotions to express themselves without projecting onto other people in confusion is a very delicate process. For example, a client may have extreme anger towards a parent for their inability to love them the way they needed due to their alcohol, drug abuse or simply a lack of ability. If the previous stages and especially stage 5 was not introduced first, there may be a temptation for the client to take their anger out on that parent. However, the pain is not from the parent but the client's inability to cope when they were young. In stage 6 the client can express their pain in the privacy of the session and hear their words and understand them. This then allows the file to be filed correctly in the cabinet and the drawer can close.

The previous stages are intended to educate the client's mind that their emotional trauma and pain does not actually lay with anybody else, but with their inability to cope due to not having the resources at the time the trauma happened. However, to get to this stage they have to understand that part of them is still blaming another person and to voice that so they can understand and consciously realise that it is not another person who they are really angry with. As we now know, the anger is a mask to protect the wounded child and cover the confusion.

3. The benefits of this stage

While the old belief systems are still trapped in Pandora's Box, the mind will keep reliving the trauma until it is resolved. Whilst the old beliefs are still trapped the protector self will continue to create masks, and while masks are still being created you will never be truly in control of your own life. So, the benefits of this stage are all about freedom! It will give you freedom to take back control of your own life and make your own decisions without being hijacked by anxiety.

The benefits that can be experienced at this stage are

1. Inner peace
2. A dramatic reduction in anxiety
3. An ability to think clearer
4. Extra motivation to take new actions
5. An ability to feel more emotion and connections
6. Higher confidence and self-esteem
7. A loss of desire to use the mask associated to the trauma
8. And many others

It is also to be noted that whilst working through this stage, as one supressed belief is released, a deeper, more painful belief may arise in its place, giving the illusion that the process is reversing. However, as the phrase goes, therapy is like peeling an onion - the more layers you peel, the greater the chance that it may result in tears until you get to the core.
It is when working through this stage that you must ensure the therapist you are working with is confident and has sufficient skill to cope with any type of release, as once the emotion has started to release, if another person's negative reaction triggers your protector self then it may re-suppress, creating further discomfort.

4. Exercises

It is with complete respect to yourself as the reader and the fact that I am unaware of your current emotional state that I will refrain from suggesting any exercises for this stage. The reason for this is that the exercises at this stage are extremely potent and allow the self-expression of trapped emotion. Allowing the emotions to be released can become immensely erratic unless the previous five stages have been completed.

Stage 7: Life skills / Adaptation

1. A description of the stage

Once the supressed emotions have been released the mind will in a way be 'reset' back to its original ability before the trauma happened. Yet the added bonus is that now the mind will also have access to all of the information it has learned over the years in addition to the new ability to resolve conflict. As this will now be an automated habit, it will often function without the requirement of conscious attention.
With the mind now having new skills and abilities to hand, it can create a new source of motivation to move towards aims or outcomes at a much more effective rate.

However, this 'new way' of thinking can bring with it a requirement to learn new skills to adapt to the new lifestyle that you can experience. This is provided that you want to change your life, as it is entirely your choice - if you just want to enjoy the inner peace without changing life itself then that is what is best for you as is your choice.

However, some clients notice that they may want to set up their own business for example. This then may require that they learn new skills such as marketing or networking. Other clients may find that they feel secure enough to start a new relationship, which then may require that they learn about romance, empathy, compromising and other such areas.

This can be quite an enjoyable stage as it allows for untold creativity and true harmonious self expression (rather than self expression in the form of a mask as in stage 6).

Here, when challenges arise the mind will work as a complete unit to negotiate the best option to move forward in the most efficient manner whilst ideally creating a win-win for all people involved.

2. How the stage integrates

As often mentioned, the reason that so many people struggle with their New Year's resolutions or reaching their aims in general is that they are fighting against their supressed beliefs, masks, coping mechanisms and protector self. Once these have been resolved and harmoniously integrated, true growth can happen.

Attempting to learn new skills or reach aims whilst still holding onto the past traumas and negatively-charged emotions will just make their attainment challenging.

That is not to say that new skills cannot be learned whilst there is still protector self activation, but when in that cycle it may be difficult to know which is true drive and which is the mask.

3. The benefits of this stage

A great way to describe the benefits of this stage is to imagine your skills as a toolkit. Each item has a different function and therefore will offer you more options or things you can do. If you have a toolkit with only a hammer and a screwdriver, as long as you 'only' did repairs which required either of these two tools you would be ok; however, if you needed a chisel, spanner or pliers you would struggle to complete the task smoothly.

The benefit that this stage offers is that you will have the ability to gain full access to your skills and learn new ones without the protector self hijacking your learning. With the new range of skills you can become more flexible to the things in life that you choose to perform. These new skills may be to increase your income, start a new relationship (or enhance your current one), learn a new language, change your career, find inner peace, find your purpose or many other things. This stage could be likened to the butterfly finally breaking free from the chrysalis and learning to use its wings for the first time. The butterfly may not be completely sure how to fly at the start, but it has no real restrictions either.

4. Exercises

Exercise 7.1: Revisit your aim and goals

When working through the 8 stages, this list would already have been created in earlier tasks. This allows the mind to create focus and momentum that allows motivation during discussions of challenging areas. Sometimes at this stage though, some clients find that their aims or goals have changed to a healthier aim. This would be if the first aims were in any way driven by a 'sugar disguised as salt' mask.

In this stage, when the mind is clear it will want to focus on attaining things in life for a 'higher purpose' and to create harmony for all concerned. Any form of succeeding to prove others wrong will vanish and a healthier aim will naturally take its place in your mind.

Practical application

1. Revisit the list of aims or goals that were made before the removal of any masks.

2. Notice how you feel towards them now.

3. Look deeper at any mask-based drivers that were creating these aims.

4. Now either make a new list or adapt the current list to match the new views and beliefs that you have acquired.

5. Then take each new or adapted goal and create a separate list of all of the things you will need to gain or learn to attain its success.

Exercise 7.2: Support your current social group

Many clients upon reaching this stage can find that the people they are closest to notice a 'big change' in their attitude to life. Although this is great for the client, it can in some cases be quite challenging for those around them. Anybody in their social circle who has been in a co-dependent mask or relationship can in some cases feel quite confused or disorientated by the change (this may often be done in stages 1 and 2).

As this stage is about creating a win-win for all concerned it is essential to support those closest once the change has happened. Sometimes other people may not want to accept the change and it causes a separation. Ideally though, any unsettling feelings that those closest to the client may feel can be supported to create the best outcome for all (with children, for example).

It is also to be noted that at this stage if one person changes and becomes free, they may suddenly realise that their current environment may not be healthy for them. If they are to remain in the new state changes may be required. Sometimes this brings with it separation (if they choose that), which should be taken into account when starting this journey.

Practical application

1. List all of the main people in your life whom you are concerned about and have their best interests at heart.

2. Take a closer look and ask if there is any co-dependence or joint mask between you both.

3. Assess what they may feel or react with if you are to change your attitude / let go of any masks.

4. If possible maybe talk to them about it and ask if there would be any concerns.

5. Create a plan of what you could do if it does cause challenges for them.

6. Maybe ask a friend or a therapist for another point of view whilst making the plan.

NB: *Caution is advised before speaking to other people in life about change as if there is uncertainty about the change or the journey has not been started yet it can cause confusion for others. Always be respectful to other people when discussing this topic.*

Stage 8: Creation and abundance

1. A description of the stage

This final stage is about embracing life to its fullest!
With all previous stages complete, the mind and body have now been completely prepared to live life to its full potential. So now it only leaves you to walk it and enjoy it!

Creation and abundance is the same cycle as path one of the self-esteem recovery model, which if you recall is:

1. Discovery
2. Face a challenge

3. Realise that you can find a way around the challenge
4. Take the path and learn a new skill
5. Grow and create a new ability, skills or material aim
6. Move on to the next stage of growth (return to discovery)

As human beings we are programmed to move towards pleasure. This is also the attainment of things and growth of who we are. Therefore, stage 8 is what we would naturally do if we never had any trauma in the first place.

In this stage we can truly enjoy the success and joy of life and bask in true wealth!
Wealth is an interesting word as many people relate 'wealth' to 'money', however in my opinion true wealth is not actually money. Money is a thing that allows another person to purchase something that they want and in many ways money doesn't even exist. If you look at an English note it says 'I promise to pay the bearer on demand', so money is simply an 'I OWE YOU'!

True wealth in my opinion is where you can truly enjoy what you want in ways such as…

- Loving connections where you understand and are understood
- Time with family and loved ones
- The freedom to do what you want, how you want, when you want
- An ability to make true contributions to others through your gifts and abilities
- To enjoy optimal health and vitality

In essence, stage 8 is to enjoy freedom both internally and externally!

2. How the stage integrates

Although embracing true abundance is something that everybody would like to do, if the protector self is engaged it can be immensely challenging to stay focused. An analogy I use in the courses I teach is to imagine having sex or making love with your partner, and then you hear somebody throw a rock through the kitchen window. When you are in an intimate moment your environment needs to be safe and secure, however any part of you that is unsure of your security will then trigger your protector self.

In this analogy the description of 'making love' is to be in a true creative flow, which requires openness. The window being smashed could be likened to a challenge, of which you are not sure of its impact (it is in another part of the house, therefore you are not fully aware of how to protect yourself). The anxiety this causes engages your protector self and then you can no longer focus on making love (losing the creative flow).

Yet if for example you knew that you were in a secure room in your house and you had three very powerful bodyguards that you completely trusted to take care of any situation, your ability to stay in an intimate moment would feel more secure. The bodyguards would be a metaphor of your skills and abilities of being able to deal with challenging situations as they arise.

So in essence the previous stages are there to support and create security within the emotions. This will allow energy to flow so when you are in a true creative space, if challenges happen you can deal with them.

3. The benefits of this stage

Being able to truly enjoy life and 'being in the moment' allows the energy and vitality to return to the body, mind and soul (or spirit / essence of the self).

This does not mean that all of a sudden there will be no challenges. There will always be challenges in life as that is life, but in this stage you will be able to work around them and grow.

Imagine being in a state where you can truly be yourself, connecting to others in a loving and harmonious way and to enjoy the life that you truly want.

To describe this stage with words would not do it justice, but this is more of a feeling!

4. **Exercises**

Just as in the self-expression stage, it is not the easiest to write a task to do, as if you have not completed the other stages then there is a possibility that your motivation is driven by other emotions or by masks. However, for a client attaining this stage in session, an example exercise would be to go through their list of goals and aims from stage 7 and then begin to follow their plan of action to discover the results.
Like any action taken there is always a 50-50 chance that they will meet a challenge. If they do, the coaching is there as a support system to bounce ideas around and re-evaluate. After several test actions and as their confidence grows to seeing challenges as an exciting adventure rather than a chore (when the protector self may hijack results), the sessions are spread out further and further until they are only used for extra updates when required.

It is at the stage that the mind will be automated to deal with its own challenges and therefore be self-sufficient. The coaching can always be on stand-by for stage 7 updates if required, but other than that the client can then simply embrace life and enjoy the fruit of their work!

The unorganised organisation of coaching

Although there was been a strong focus on logic when I created the 8 stages which ensures the stages flow in harmony with each other, in session it can be quite different. The reason for this is that the stages need to be adapted and the techniques to pattern match any resistance the client's protector self retaliates with. If this is not achieved then the clients protector self will continually hijack their mind and no progression will be made. Also, progression will struggle if the client is too strongly linked to their mask and refuses to do the required work.
Usually in the first few sessions the client is quite unaware of their protector self's mask of control so it can initially be challenging. Therefore, it is essential that the techniques during the coaching are

intertwined with conscious and subconscious language, in essence talking to the client's conscious and subconscious at the same time.

As the client's protector self starts to become aware that the coaching process is slowly working its way towards the stage of self-expression (or reliving the past trauma), strengthening techniques will need to be included. If these are not their protector self will naturally begin to defend the client by hijacking their mind. This is what happens many times when new goals are set and the protector self feels it will bring trauma (a fear of failure for example).

Due to the client's protector self having access to the client's emotional drive, it can appear to make the client's focus seem to appear to 'jump all over the place' in what could be classed as 'erratic focus'. However, this is not erratic for the protector self and it is working through logic. To effectively coach a client through this it is essential to be able to recognise the pattern and accommodate techniques to match.

16

Conclusion

There we have it - the mask, the con, and the 8 stages fully explained in detail!

I'm sure that if you are like lots of other people, there will be many unanswered questions in relation to what has been covered through the chapters of this book. If that is the way that you are currently feeling, then that is a good thing!

To finish reading a book on psychology and feel like there is nothing more to do or no more questions to ask means that although you may have learned some information, it has not inspired you to reach further. Life and every aspect of it should be embraced and to do that it requires that you observe it from every angle. To reach further and to grow to your full potential is the deepest essence of who you are as a human being.

You may have also found that there were parts of this book which appeared to be confrontational, and in reality that was the aim. Some people may have been wearing a variety of masks for many years and not been aware of them. People who have been wearing any masks for a long time may have also become comfortable with them, and a comfortable person does not change if there is no challenge. So, please accept my apologies if any offence was caused, but my job as a coach is to get you to question your reality and become aware of whom you are. Without this challenge it is easy to go along in life unaware of another life that could be lived. There is a very strong message which needed to be conveyed to you in this book, and tip-toeing around with a reluctant half-hearted voice will neither get the message across to you nor help you to succeed.

Watching life from a distance

Millions of people each and every day feel pain, loss and shame for not living the life that they long to live. They want to be free, but they are weighed heavy with the icy grip of anxiety which slows their breathing like vines wrapping around their lungs. When energy runs low and options appear unavailable life can feel like a struggle. In this state many people will resort to existing rather than living. As we now know this is a coping mechanism and the best option the protector self could create at the time.

The bitter pill

Every time you back down from a new challenge through anxiety, every time you give up when you know that you could have done it if you would have fought a little harder, or every time you stay in a relationship because you are scared to leave (or will not get into a relationship with anyone because you are scared of getting hurt), your self-esteem will take a kick. As we also now know, living like this will make you vulnerable to the con. There may never feel like there is a good time to face your insecurities, and trust me they will often seem much bigger than what they actually are, but if you don't make a start you can never change. However, nothing is irreversible and the mind is extremely versatile!

"Procrastination is the bad habit of putting off until the day after tomorrow what should have been done the day before yesterday."
Napoleon Hill

The driver of your anxiety is the key to all your suffering! The very feeling that you have been trying to avoid all these years is the very place in which you will find the answer as to why you may be holding yourself back in life or why you do not reach up and live the life that you deserve. Your emotional weight is coming from backing down to that electric shock of anxiety you feel when the worry of what 'may go wrong' floods your mind. When you avoid looking at the driver of your anxiety, you are in fact cutting yourself off from the very solution to the riddle which perplexes you! The solution to all of your emotional suffering is right in front of you! The answer is behind your anxiety…the illusion within your mind!

Go into your anxiety and the answer you seek will be waiting. However, that is often the opposite of what we feel like doing!

Metaphor

1. Imagine you are in an empty swimming pool 5 meter in depth and you are attached to a rope. The rope is attached to your waist and also the bottom of the pool. The rope is 2 meters in length.
   The attached rope represents your protector self, which limits your choices or how far it will let you go. It is attached to the bottom of the pool to represent past trauma.

2. Water starts to fill the swimming pool and eventually gets to 2 meters in depth. The water is not above your head yet, but is getting close and the water is still filling.
   The water is the pressures of daily life.

3. Although the rope is stopping you from staying above the water, every time you try and pull the rope from your waist you find that you cannot free the knot.
   The knot that cannot be freed is to represent your protector self that will always stay with you as it is your survival instinct.

4. As you try to pull the rope free from the bottom of the pool you find that you cannot get enough leverage by treading water.
This represents what will happen if you attempt to overpower your suppressed beliefs by using positive thinking, denial or reframes. In essence, this is disagreeing with your protector self.

If the water continues to fill it will eventually go above your head, so what do you do?

Some people say that they will try to splash the water out of the pool, thereby lowering the water level. Trying to lower the water level can be likened to controlling life, which as we now know is a mask. Using this option though can be risky as eventually life can always throw us a challenge that we can't control.

But imagine if emptying the pool was not an option, then what would you do?

What do most people do in this situation? Usually it's one of two options…

1. Try to swim harder to keep their head above water
2. Try even harder to pull at the rope

However, the truth is that you can't overpower the rope! It is a survival mechanism and is stronger than you. To destroy it…will destroy you! To try to swim against it will just be a waste of energy and create a battle within, and to try and break it will cause major internal stress.

So what do you do?

The answer (and the only option left) is not the one most people like to hear.
The answer is…

To swim down to the bottom of the pool to unhook the rope!
This is a metaphor of going within and disconnecting from your old beliefs.

The rope is not bolted on - it is just hooked!
This is a metaphor of your mind being able to update (neuroplasticity).

However, if a person was to fight the rope, it can feel like it is bolted fast as the harder they struggle the more the rope seems to stay stuck. This is when people can feel trapped and lose heart if they have used lots of energy by continually trying to 'stay conscious' (when there are many suppressed memories), reframes or using positive thinking.

Any pain that you feel which is coming from a belief that you are in some way not good enough or that people will reject you if you do not live up to their standards is an illusion (although who 'they' are is yet another illusion). It is an assumption that may feel real, but in reality it is an old projection upon your internal cinema screen. Yes, there are people with greater skill, better looking or more powerful, but skills change, looks are skin deep and power will always be overcome one day.

To accept that you are valuable in who you are is the key to an endless source of self-esteem and confidence. As mentioned though, it is impossible just to state a new belief and then it all miraculously changes in the blink of an eye. This is where I advise extreme caution of those claiming otherwise, especially if money or commitment is concerned.
Opening the doors through the 8 stages of personal development which can allow you to truly connect with people and love them is one of the most wonderful gifts to experience. So is the ability of self connection and creative expression. This is what we were all born to experience!
Where you go from here my friend is entirely your choice…

Option one: You are one of the very rare few who do not wear a mask from anxiety and therefore have nothing you need to let go of. If this is you, you will already be living the life you want, the way you want and anxiety will just be a word in the dictionary.

Option two: You are currently living with a mask and you decide to stick with it. Yes, there may be uncomfortable points, but it's easier to live that way.

Although you may feel that you might not be living to your fullest potential, you are comfortable and happy with what you have, which is a gift in itself. Remember - you are here to live YOUR life and NOT somebody else's expectation of you. Also, remember that you can always start your journey when you feel more prepared!

Option three: You have a mask and want to be free to choose the mask rather than have it decide your destiny. The frustration has built up and you want to live the way you want. You are sick and tired of being sick and tired with the continual drip of anxiety and stress.

The world is waiting for you in all its splendour! So, get ready for an adventure you will always treasure!

Walk your path

It is your life and your choice as to what you do with every minute of every day. The choices you make today will determine the future you have and the life you live tomorrow. Remember, life is far too short to live with grudges. Holding anger towards another person for something they did or did not do for you will only cause you suffering. This can be an extremely sensitive stage though, especially if deep childhood trauma has been experienced. Again though, when working through this area please ensure it is taken carefully and one step at a time as 'unlocking' the past is not as easy as just saying 'I let it go'.

On our journey we can unfortunately meet lost, angry and hateful people, but the good news is that not everybody we meet will be like that. There is a great deal of love in the world from kind people, or even those who are going through their worst nightmare yet find time to put aside their trauma to give kindness to another person.

"We are each of us angels with only one wing, and we can only fly by embracing one another."

Luciano De Crescenzo

Life will bring challenges, of that there is no doubt! We may not like what happens and the challenges could range from a slight bump in the road to a full-blown tragedy. The key to transcending the pain is to stay focused. This does not mean that you need to be a machine that feels no pain and keeps on going no matter what though. During very challenging times (although at certain parts we may not have the opportunity to rest), being honest and admitting that we feel scared, weak or are in need of support is actually showing great strength. We are only human after all.

Also, always be aware that it is not all one sided. Every cloud has a silver lining if you are looking for it. There are always pots of gold along the way during challenging times. One of the greatest gifts could be a friend who is there to offer support, a supportive co-worker who goes out of their way, or an extra strength that you find within yourself that you never realised. Remember the story of Pandora's Box - after all of the sorrow had escaped…'hope' appeared to bring salvation!

People are people and will come from all walks of life as you walk your path. Some people will come into your life for a short time, some a while longer, and some for the rest of your life. Good people are everywhere, but it can sometimes take time and patience to connect to them (but also be aware of those who are out to hurt others).

Keep on pushing

If you want the results to continue now that you have started your journey of self-development it is imperative that a complete study of this kind becomes a part of your life. Throughout my previous career as a personal trainer, I have seen thousands of people start a training plan, exercise regularly and get in shape, feel really good and then **stop** exercising completely!

Then they slowly watch as their weight begins to creep back up to the same as before, leaving them with that horrible feeling of regret and failure. It is the same with your emotional well-being! Discipline is a must; whatever results, awareness and benefits you have gained from reading this book could easily be lost without constant and regular reviewing.

No one person has the answer

Throughout my journey in this field I have personally heard a few authors and therapists claim that 'they' have the key to success and that 'their' way is the only way. Be very cautious of this claim as I believe that nobody has the answer to everything. As I mentioned, everything I covered in this book is only my own perception and therefore is not the only way.

Variety is the key! Study authors of different backgrounds and styles, study information you agree and disagree with, read science, physiology, social psychology, outdoor pursuits and DIY. Read anything and everything in many areas rather than just one.
When I first heard my martial arts teacher tell me to do this I looked at him with confusion, but now I understand. Life is similar to a jigsaw puzzle - each piece is different, but also a part of the whole picture.

As stated before, what you do with your own life is your choice, but you will only get back what you put in. Study as much information as you can, or if you're happy with your life as it is then you don't have to study at all; it's all your choice.

Whatever decision you choose to make my friend, I wish you all the best.

Regards,
Paul Ryder

"In the end, the love you take is equal to the love you make."
A quote from the song 'The End' by the Beatles

Recommended Reading

Here is a select few books, however for other recommendations please visit www.lifeperformancestrategies.co.uk

The 50th Law	Robert Greene
Why Zebras don't get ulcers	Robert M. Sapolsky
Awaken the giant within	Anthony Robbins
Surviving aggressive people	Shawn A Smith
You can heal your life	Louise Hay
How to win friends and influence people	Dale Carnegie
The Body Remembers	Babete Rothschild
Rich dad poor dad	Robert T Kiyosaki
The elephant and the twig	Geoff Thompson

The 7 habits of highly effective people	Stephen R Covey
The millionaire fastlane	MJ Demarco
Feel the fear and do it anyway	Susan Jeffers
Men are from mars, women from Venus	John Grey
Emotional intelligence	Daniel Goleman
Games people play	Eric Berne

Logic will get you from A to B.
Imagination will take you everywhere.
Albert Einstein

CPSIA information can be obtained
at www.ICGtesting.com
Printed in the USA
FSOW04n1304080316
17792FS

9 780956 933553